RECREATION
FOR TODAY'S SOCIETY

"Life Drawing" class at the Westchester, New York, Art Workshop, a facility of the County of Westchester Department of Parks, Recreation, and Conservation. Photo courtesy of the County of Westchester Department of Parks, Recreation, and Conservation.

RECREATION FOR TODAY'S SOCIETY

CHARLES A. BUCHER

Professor of Education, New York University

RICHARD D. BUCHER

Instructor in Sociology, Rock Valley College

Graduate Student, College of Arts and Sciences
New York University

PRENTICE-HALL, INC., Englewood Cliffs, New Jersey

Library of Congress Cataloging in Publication Data

Bucher, Charles Augustus, date
  Recreation for today's society.

    1. Recreation – United States. 2. Leisure – United
States. I. Bucher, Richard D., date   joint author.
II. Title.
GV53.B76   790'.0973   73-22177
ISBN 0-13-768721-4

To Jeff and Jackie Grantz

© 1974 by
PRENTICE-HALL, INC.
Englewood Cliffs, New Jersey

Printed in the United States of America

10 9 8 7 6 5 4 3 2 1

PRENTICE-HALL INTERNATIONAL, INC., London
PRENTICE-HALL OF AUSTRALIA, PTY. LTD., Sydney
PRENTICE-HALL OF CANADA, LTD., Toronto
PRENTICE-HALL OF INDIA PRIVATE LIMITED, New Delhi
PRENTICE-HALL OF JAPAN, INC., Tokyo

CONTENTS

v

PREFACE

The need to awaken Americans to the value of spending their leisure hours in desirable recreation is increasingly recognized as an important goal for the future of this country. Whether or not our citizens spend their free time in constructive or nonconstructive ways will determine in large measure what happens to this nation in the years ahead. Therefore, professionally trained leadership is imperative in order to interpret, organize, and administer organized programs in a variety of settings, since they will only be as strong and effective as the recreators leading them. Once a field of endeavor guided by persons with very little training and few qualifications, recreation has now developed into a profession in which select qualities and college and graduate work play an important part in determining who its leaders will be.

This book was written in order to provide such information for a better understanding of the field of recreation, as the philosophy that guides it toward worthy goals, services that it renders, settings where it is conducted, principles by which its programs are organized and administered, social factors that affect its role in society, and its relationship to such current national and world problems as ecology and the environment.

This book is designed not as a lengthy treatise that delves deeply into all areas of recreation, but instead, one that treats carefully selected topics in detail and other subjects in a way that provides an overview of the field of recreation in general, showing how it has developed over the years, its potential for the present and the future, and the opportunities it provides for the person seeking a challenging vocation. In order to determine what topics should be discussed in this text, a national survey was first conducted to identify those areas of greatest interest and importance to present and future recreators. This survey resulted in the selection of the subjects discussed in this book.

This publication can be used very effectively as a text for introductory courses in recreation in four-year colleges and universities, and should also have great appeal to the growing number of two-year colleges in which recreation courses are being offered on an increasingly larger scale. Of course, not to be overlooked are the contributions and understanding it can provide for the recreation leaders in the field, the many dedicated volunteers who are helping with recreation programs across the country, lay personnel interested in recreation, and the public in general.

Particular thanks are due to Myra E. Madnick for her great help in the writing of this manuscript. She spent many, many hours helping the authors in the preparation and organization of the material. Also, to such organizations as the National Recreation and Park Association and other state and local recreation and/or park departments, are due many thanks for their cooperation and help.

Charles A. Bucher
Richard D. Bucher

part I
nature and scope
of recreation

Teen Repertory Theater Production of "Oliver," Recreation Division, Parks and Recreation Department, Hempstead, New York. Photo courtesy of the Town of Hempstead Parks and Recreation Department.

1

RECREATION: A PROFESSION
FOR A CHANGING AMERICA

America's way of life is changing rapidly. Young people are determined to eliminate war as a means of solving international problems. Women are asserting their rights in the American way of life. Environmentalists are more than ever determined to stop the chemical, noise, and waste pollution of the environment. Cities are struggling against rising crime rates, poverty, poor housing, inadequate public transportation and the many other problems that are unique to the large cities. Blacks are mobilizing their resources in order to have a greater voice in the political life of this country.

As a result of America's changing way of life, young people are seeking meaningful careers that will challenge them, use their abilities, and contribute significantly to their fellow men. They want to become involved in activities that have meaning and importance in their lives. Having seen the horrors of war, the stress of materialism, and the misery of poverty, they feel that something must be done, and they want to be involved.

Many high school graduates who are now in college will want to explore the field of recreation as a rewarding career. America's changing way of life and many of the problems it faces can be helped through recreation, which can help to re-create America into the type of nation that young people envision.

This first chapter provides the student with a brief orientation to recreation by answering such questions as: What is recreation? Where do we have organized recreation? Why do we need organized recreation? Who is involved in organized recreation? What is the present status of organized recreation? Why should today's college student be interested in recreation? and How can this text help the student to better understand recreation?

WHAT IS RECREATION?

One method of defining a term is to identify its key concepts. These concepts, in turn, will provide the reader with a better understanding of what is meant when the term *recreation* is used in this text. These key concepts are:

Recreation is concerned with many types of activities. Here among the wild sea oats along South Carolina's coast, a couple look for giant sea turtles and sea shells. Photo courtesy of the South Carolina Department of Parks, Recreation, and Tourism.

1. *Recreation is concerned with various types of activities in which human beings engage during their leisure hours.* What a person does when one is not working, studying, or making a livelihood is, in its broadest sense, recreation. The activities pursued during one's free time might be photography, gardening, or a multitude of other hobbies or interests for which there is not time for participation during working hours. These, then, are recreation activities.

2. *Recreation is concerned with activities that human beings find pleasurable and satisfying.* The reason human beings engage in recreational activities such as boating is that when they participate they receive immediate satisfactions, pleasure, and happiness. It is not necessary to wait in order to have these rewards — they occur as a direct result of participation.

3. *Recreation is concerned with activities in which human beings engage voluntarily.* They participate in recreational activities because they

decide on their own that it is something they want to do; it is their own decision. They are not required to do it because someone else has ordered or requested that they do so. Instead, the activity has been freely chosen without any coercion by someone else.

4. *Recreation is concerned with various types of activities in which the activity itself is the reward.* The person chooses to participate in an activity, whether it is going on a hike or working on an arts-and-crafts project, because of the benefits and satisfaction gained from actual participation in the activity. She does not participate because of profit, or any other reward she might derive from the activity. Satisfaction derived from involvement in the activity is its own reward and is the joy of participation in a recreational program.

In order to clarify these concepts further and to prevent any misunderstanding of what we mean by the term *recreation,* some points of common misunderstanding are discussed here:

1. *Recreation is not the same as work.* Some persons have claimed that work can be so satisfying and absorbing that it becomes a form of recreation. Thomas Edison is often cited as an individual who was so consumed by what he was doing and enjoyed it so much that to him it was a form of recreation. Although this belief is held by some people, the term *recreation,* in this text, refers to activities that are engaged in during hours other than work. The basis for this is that, generally interpreted, work is compulsory, involves money, and the reward is often oriented to the future rather than to the present.

2. *Recreation is not earned.* An idea that prevailed years ago was that the person who worked hard was entitled periodically to some recreation. In other words, recreation was something that provided benefits only after many hours of labor had been accomplished. It was a reward and offered an opportunity for the worker to relax after long hours of work. This text, although recognizing that recreation provides a change of pace and has many benefits for the person who works long hours, nevertheless, maintains there are many other benefits that accrue to the participant. These dividends may be physical, psychological, social, or spiritual. For example, a benefit could be learning a new sport skill or increasing one's knowledge of photography.

3. *Recreation activities should not be antisocial in nature.* If it is accepted that recreation activities are those engaged in during a person's leisure hours, it must also be accepted that some of these activities, gambling for example, are not socially acceptable. In the broadest and most general interpretation, a recreational activity, i.e., one that a person engages in during one's free time, could be socially or not socially acceptable. However, the authors hasten to add that recreation education, to be described in the next section of this text, is concerned with socially acceptable and constructive recreation activities. In this section, however, the main concern is to define the general term, *recreation.*

4. *Recreation is not idleness. Idleness* is a much-confused term; it is often defined as inactivity or engaging in wasteful or useless activities. However, just because a person appears to be doing nothing is not

conclusive proof in itself of being idle. That person may be just meditating about something, such as the best way to tie trout flies. In the general interpretation of the term *recreation,* a person can sit around, engaging in any activity, be it wasteful or worthwhile. However, recreation from an educational point of view involves seeing that free time is spent usefully and constructively.

WHAT IS RECREATION EDUCATION?

When the word *education* is added to the word *recreation* it takes on a new meaning: *recreation education* refers to an experience that is aimed at the enrichment of life. This, in turn, implies wise selection of activities in which one participates during one's leisure hours. The education that professional leaders in recreation are encouraging is one that is constructive and enhances an individual's life. Recreation leaders are concerned with providing programs that are in the best interests of the individual and of society; their expertise, understanding of human beings, and recognition of human needs, help them to achieve such goals.

Recreation education is concerned with the re-creative — that is, activities that will bring about a renewal of the spirit and the body. Not a time-filler or idleness, it is concerned with activities that possess potentialities for the enrichment of life since they satisfy basic human needs. Representing an outlet for one's physical, emotional, mental, and creative powers, it is concerned with attitudes and behavioral changes that relate to human fulfillment and the betterment of society. It is opposed to activities that are harmful to a person or to society, physically, socially, or in any other way. Furthermore, it is not concerned with survival activities. For example, "recreation" as defined in this text does not include eating and sleeping, which are essential to survival.

THE RELATION OF RECREATION TO LEISURE

Leisure and *recreation* are not synonymous. *Leisure* refers to a time element, i.e., the time an individual is not working, the time that can be spent as one pleases, one's free time, the time that is left over after formal duties and the necessities of life have been cared for, the time beyond existence and sub- sistence time.

Whereas *leisure* refers to free time itself, *recreation* refers to the activities in which one engages during this time. *Recreation education,* furthermore, implies that these activities are worthwhile and constructive in nature.

The words *leisure* and *recreation* have had many different interpretations down through the years. For example, the Greeks looked upon leisure as a time to improve oneself and an opportunity for self-fulfillment, whereas many people today see it as a time to do nothing at all, such as sunbathing or just sleeping. In this text, however, leisure is regarded as all the free time a person has after the work is done and the subsistence needs, as eating and sleeping, are cared for.

THE RELATION OF RECREATION TO PLAY

Plato defined *play* as "that which is neither utility nor truth nor likeness, nor yet, in its effects, is harmful, can best be judged by the criterion of charm that is in it and the pleasure it affords. Such pleasure, entailing as it does not appreciable good or ill, is play."

Play, like *playful,* implies full, happy, joyous fun and natural expression. Therefore, play involves activities that yield these results. When the cultural anthropologist uses the term *play,* he usually refers to a pattern of recreational activities engaged in by a culture or a society. Whereas the sociologist thinks of play primarily as adult activities, the psychologist thinks of it as a form of childhood behavior.

The popular context in which the term *play* is used refers to the activities of children. Recreation activities, on the other hand, are activities for both adults and children. *Play,* when used in reference to children, has implications for growth. Organic systems of the body, for example, develop and grow best when there is ample physical activity. The expression "play is a child's work" has been frequently used to interpret this concept. Recreation, on the other hand, represents those activities that cannot be achieved while working. In this text, recreation includes play.

THE RELATION OF RECREATION TO ADULT EDUCATION

Recreation and adult education are quite similar in many respects. Their goals, for example, are similar. To attend an adult education class in painting that is offered by the local school system or to engage in painting as a recreational activity is an example of similar goals, organization, and method. Therefore, in order to distinguish between the two, the following will serve as a guide. When the activity is oriented toward vocational goals, it is usually called "adult education"; however, if the activity relates to the development of skills, understandings, and satisfactions that are primarily for use during leisure hours, it is called "recreation."

THE RELATION OF RECREATION TO GROUP WORK

Professionals and agencies involved in group work frequently use recreational activities to bring about behavioral changes in the people they serve. On the other hand, persons working in recreation may organize their activities on a group basis, depending on the requirements of the activity in question. In this context, recreation uses group work as a method.

THE RELATION OF RECREATION TO PHYSICAL EDUCATION

Recreation and physical education have several points in common. The field of recreation uses many physical education activities in its programs, such as all types of individual and team sports. In addition, there are physical fitness clubs and other activities that involve physical skill and physical well-being. At the same time, many other recreational activities, such as drama, arts and crafts, photography, and music, comprise recreation programs.

A person trained in physical education has an important contribution to make to recreation. In some programs, physical educators teach many of the sports and related activities. In other programs, the physical educator is hired to conduct the summer and vacation recreation programs in a community. The trend, however, is to have persons trained in recreation responsible for recreation programs. Such preparation produces a professional that has expertise in such important areas as group work, various types of recreational activities, the structure and organization of the community, and leadership qualities essential to organizing a sound recreation program.

THE RELATION OF RECREATION TO PARK DEVELOPMENT

Recreation requires many kinds of properties and facilities for its programs to function effectively. The parks of this country represent a large resource for recreation. Parks are of all types and are administered at different levels of government and also by nongovernmental agencies. The park, as understood today, can be a land or water area designed for park purposes, which in turn can be used for purposes of recreation. Parks probably make up the largest single setting in the United States today for recreation supported by public funds. They house and incorporate playgrounds, picnic sites, band shells, amphitheaters, museums, camps, beaches, swimming pools, and many other resources.

The parks of the country represent a large resource for recreation. The grand opening of Lakeview Park in Hempstead, New York. Photo courtesy of the Town of Hempstead Parks and Recreation Department, Recreation Division.

THE RELATION OF RECREATION TO CAMPING

Camp sites of various descriptions are located from coast to coast and represent settings for many recreational activities. Camping is a very wholesome and rewarding form of recreation. Camps also exist as commercial ventures and some camps are sponsored by voluntary and semipublic agencies. Camps as recreation settings will be discussed in greater detail in Chapter 3.

WHERE DO WE HAVE ORGANIZED RECREATION?

Questions that may come to the mind of the student not oriented in recreation may include "Where do we have organized recreation programs?" and "Who sponsors these programs?" To answer such questions concisely and clearly is difficult since there are so many different types of recreation institutions, agencies, and governmental units that sponsor recreation programs. This book classifies organized recreation programs into four categories that the authors believe incorporate most recreation programs existing today. This section will briefly outline these four types of recreation programs. A more detailed discussion of each of the four categories will be found in Chapter Two under "Settings for Recreation Programs."

Camps represent an important setting for many recreational activities. Mountain Lakes Camp, North Salem, New York. Photo courtesy of the County of Westchester Department of Parks, Recreation and Conservation.

Governmental Agencies and Institutions
That Sponsor Recreation Programs

Recreation programs sponsored by the government are found on local, county, state, and federal levels. The cost of conducting such programs is largely provided for through taxation. Examples of such programs might be the municipal recreation program that runs the city swimming pools, the state park with its trees and golf courses, and the national wildlife refuge that protects birds and other animals.

Group-work Agencies That Devote Themselves
to Youth Service

Recreation programs sponsored by semipublic group-work agencies are largely supported through philanthropic contributions. Their costs are not covered through public taxation as is the case of government sponsorship. Their programs have as goals the social and moral betterment of their membership. To accomplish these objectives they use professional staff members. Examples of the types of organizations that fit into this category include the Young Men's Christian Association, The Girl Scouts, Boys' Clubs of America, and 4-H Clubs.

Organizations or Groups of Individuals
Whose Membership Share a Common Interest or Belief
and Voluntarily Participate in the Recreation Program Provided

Groups of people having special interests (such as being employed by Eastman Kodak in Rochester, New York, belonging to the Methodist Church in Kansas City, Missouri, or being confined as a patient in a Veterans Administration Hospital in San Francisco, California) are all provided with recreation programs. These programs can be international in scope, such as the Rotary International; national in existence, such as a political party; or local in nature, such as the local garden club.

Commercial Interests Aimed at the Profit Motive

A materialistic society is very much aware of the opportunities to provide various types of attractive recreational pursuits in which people can become involved during their leisure hours. Such pursuits range everywhere from the movie that is being publicized at the local theater, or the circus or professional basketball game appearing in the city arena, to the pinball machine and penny arcade at the beach. Some of these commercially sponsored recreational endeavors are constructive and render a valuable contribution to the community. On the other hand, some have questionable value and in many cases may be detrimental to the public interest.

WHY DO WE NEED ORGANIZED RECREATION?

Organized recreation programs that are constructive and are planned and carried out with the welfare of human beings in mind are an important part of any society and culture. Some of the reasons why such programs are needed include:

1. *To help people have individual fulfillment.* Each individual should want to achieve such goals as growing and developing physically, mentally, socially, and spiritually. Some of these goals are achieved through the formal process of growing up, such as those provided by schooling, family, church training, and one's vocation. However, other aspects of self-fulfillment, depending on the individual, need attention in ways that are not provided for through more formal means. Therefore, recreational activities and programs, if carefully selected in light of a person's individual needs, offer an opportunity to make up for personal shortcomings and thus help an individual to achieve a satisfactory

self-image. For example, a person who has a sedentary occupation and doesn't have an opportunity to engage in healthful physical activity may use recreation to make up this missing element in her life. A person who doesn't have the opportunity for mental stimulation on the job may find the opportunity to satisfy this need by joining a reading club. Recreation programs, therefore, offer an avenue for total self-development.

2. *To provide for the increased leisure available to millions of Americans.* In 1800, the average workweek for Americans was eighty-four hours and in 1950 it was forty hours. The standard workweek is expected to decrease from approximately thirty-nine hours to thirty-six hours by 1976 and to thirty-two hours by the year 2000. Much of this additional leisure will be devoted to recreation. It follows that what a person does with one's free time will determine to a large extent what kind of a person one will be. With the expansion and popularity of commercial rec- reational pursuits of doubtful value, such as gambling on the horses, it is important to provide attractive programs in recreation that will help people reach self-fulfillment. Programs are needed that provide recre- ational activities geared to the needs and interests of all the American people as well as an educational program that will guide them wisely in the selection of these activities.

3. *In light of the changing home life in America.* Years ago the family represented a closely knit unit. The members of the family group relied mainly on their own resources for recreation. Old family pictures show the young and old alike going as a group to church, singing songs in the evening, playing cards, and going for a sleigh ride. Today, rock concerts, movie houses, resort centers, and other interests, together with rapid transportation and greater family income, pull the family members in all directions. In addition, one out of every two marriages ends in a divorce court, and about 300,000 children are involved in these divorces. Each year, one out of eight children are not living with both parents. There has been a fifty percent increase in births outside of marriage in the last decade. Recreational programs, particularly those that stress family recreation, whether family camps or ski weekends, contribute much to family solidarity. In addition, other programs that provide activities for each age-group are important.

4. *In light of urbanization and the concentration of population in cities.* Seven out of ten Americans live on two percent of the land and fifty percent of our people live within fifty miles of the East and West Coasts. Strip cities are forecast for the areas from California to Washington and from Florida to Maine. This means more and more of the nation's population will be living in cities and urban areas. Such dense population centers, with close living conditions and much of the land being used for buildings, highways, and other facilities, increase the need for recreation programs to serve these great population masses.

5. *In light of the industrialization and mechanization of this nation.* Industrialization and mechanization make many contributions to human progress. They produce more material goods, provide fast transportation, and result in a high standard of living. On the other hand, however, they can produce an apathetic, lazy, physically soft, and materialistic society. Well-organized recreation programs can help to counter such products of industrialization and mechanization by getting people involved in stimulating physical, mental, and social activities.

Dense population centers in the nation increase the need for recreation programs to serve these great population masses. South Carolina's Blue Ridge Mountains along the new Cherokee Foothills Scenic Highway offers a respite away from the crowded cities. Photo courtesy of South Carolina Department of Parks, Recreation, and Tourism.

6. *In light of the high crime rate.* Crime is on the upswing, with automobile thefts, burglaries, robberies, aggravated assaults, rapes, and murders steadily increasing. Although crime is a very complex sociological problem and although there are many reasons for a person becoming a criminal, nevertheless, recreation programs do offer a way in which human beings, particularly youths, can spend leisure time more constructively rather than destructively. The old saying of Dr. Jay B. Nash, "that the boy who is stealing bananas should be stealing second base," has a real meaning for students of recreation. When recreational activities are provided that appeal to young people and in which they can experience a feeling of belonging, these activities may prove a deterrent factor to crime.

7. *In light of the unemployment in this country.* Although the goal of this country is to have full employment, this is a difficult goal to achieve. Some degree of unemployment will always exist and as such presents a challenge to recreation. Presently, unemployment ranges between three and seven percent (usually around five percent) of the total population. Unemployed persons want something to do. In the absence of work, it is important that they spend at least some of their free time in desirable recreation. The values derived from such endeavors will not be in the form of a paycheck, but of enjoyment, self-satisfaction, achievement, and other benefits that cannot be overlooked.

8. *In light of the great growth of commercial recreation.* The great number of hours that are spent each day watching television shows of questionable value, the increase in the amount of money spent in gambling, the large number of people who regularly spend hours drinking in bars, and other questionable pursuits to which Americans are attracted, have implications for organized recreation. Quality recreation programs sponsored by municipalities, schools, youth-serving agencies, and other agencies need to be planned and organized so that to Americans, young and old alike, they are as attractive as, or more attractive than, the commercialized forms of recreation.

WHO IS INVOLVED IN ORGANIZED RECREATION?

With the existence of many organized recreation programs in this country, the question follows, Who participates in them?

It has already been indicated there are many organizations involved in these recreation programs, including governmental, private, voluntary, and commercial agencies. These organizations are located in urban and rural settings; some are large and some are small; some offer many recreation activities while others specialize in only a few or sometimes only one activity. Some of the persons involved in organized recreation include:

1. *The consumer of recreation services – the most important person involved.* Nearly every person in the country is a consumer of recreation in some form or other. The young as well as the old, the well and the sick, the unskilled and the skilled, the rich and the poor, the handicapped and the "normal" person are some of the consumers. Consumers, however, represent a conglomerate of human characteristics – some have a sound set of values, others have values that are questionable. Some are interested in recreation as an escape, whereas others participate in order to make reality happier and more productive.

    It is hoped that organized recreation services designed to fill individual needs of all citizens may eventually be extended so that each person in this country, wherever one lives and whatever one's physical, mental, or social characteristics, may have the opportunity to participate in a recreation program that will benefit every one.

2. *Professional recreators.* The field of recreation has become an area of endeavor that requires leadership qualities of trained specialists. These specialists pursue a college program and receive their degrees, which reflect the development of competencies that are needed to carry out their duties effectively. These recreators serve in many different capacities, involving such functions as planning, supervising, teaching, group leadership, organizing, counseling, researching, and conducting special events. Furthermore, they serve in such positions as superintendents of recreation, directors of playgrounds and community centers, supervisors of special activities, group leaders, leaders of recreation in hospitals and industry, and college teachers.

3. *Voluntary workers.* Recreation programs and professional recreators depend to a large degree on voluntary workers to provide the necessary activities and programs that interest their participants. These voluntary workers may be specialists in certain activities in the recreation program, such as in arts and crafts, music or drama, or they may be volunteers who help in the clerical, administrative, or organizational aspects of the program, such as volunteering to prepare posters for special events, or helping the professional organize a group of persons for a particular activity. Volunteers may be unskilled persons, paraprofessionals, or technicians, depending on their professional background and experience and their degree of understanding and contribution. Volunteers play a very valuable role in community recreation programs.

PRESENT AND FUTURE STATUS
OF ORGANIZED RECREATION

Organized recreation must immediately prepare itself for greater person-to-person communication. In past years recreation programs have not been meeting the needs of the majority of American people. In Chapter 6, you will read about the desperate need for organized recreation programs in our large urban areas. The people who live in the inner city have been sorely neglected by recreation programming.

The future of organized recreation depends on confrontation with many economic and social problems of American society. Some of the necessary trends in organized recreation include:

1. *Planning for increased leisure time, population expansion, and urban recreation.* Leisure time is increasing and organized recreation programs can help fill this time in a beneficial manner. At the same time, population increases, especially in urban areas, warrant immediate attention to the need for satisfying recreational pursuits. These topics will be discussed further in Chapters 6 and 7.

2. *Community involvement as essential to success of organized recreation programs.* There is a current trend toward community involvement in all aspects of urban life. Members of a community are thoroughly familiar with the needs of the population; involvement provides jobs and, more importantly, a real interest in the program being instituted. This will also be discussed further in Chapter 6.

3. *A broader base of recreation activities that includes cultural and creative programming.* Recreation programs of the present and future should include creative as well as game-playing activities. Some recreation programs include dance programs, art exhibits, puppet shows, and "rap" sessions.

4. *A redefinition of what a recreation leader is and does.* The new recreation worker is not a game director who wears sneakers and referees activities. He is an administrator, a counselor, and a creative individual who understands and attempts to meet the needs of the community.

WHY SHOULD A COLLEGE STUDENT
BE INTERESTED IN RECREATION?

The college student of the 1970s should rightfully ask such questions as: Why should I be interested in recreation? What can recreation do for me? Why should I take a course in recreation? and What can recreation do for me personally or professionally? The college student should be interested in recreation for the following reasons:

1. *Because of the contribution recreation can make to personal health, happiness, and welfare.* The college student will want to provide for meaningful recreation in his or her own life. During free hours, he or she will want to enjoy and do exciting things, engage in interesting activities, and have fun, at the same time wanting to use the leisure hours in a manner that will enhance personal health, happiness, and welfare as well. In fact, with proper planning and understanding both sets of goals may be accomplished at the same time. If the student relies entirely on his college studies and curricular activities to further his personal and professional growth and development, he will find that his progress will not be as rapid as if he combines meaningful recreational experiences with his curricular goals. The aim of the student should be to follow a balanced program in which the curricular and recreational activities combine to form an integrated pattern of personal and professional growth. Recreational activities, whether physical (such as playing golf) or intellectual (such as belonging to a book club), should complement and supplement his daily routine so that he achieves well-rounded growth. The wise use of leisure can be an asset to one's personality, stimulate mental and emotional life, provide an opportunity to acquire many new and useful skills, and contribute to total fitness.

2. *Because of the career possibilities recreation offers.* In a rapidly changing society, the college student is interested in entering a field of endeavor that is expanding, offers challenges, represents a social contribution, and is a profession of the future. Recreation is one of these professions and, as such, deserves consideration by the college student seeking a career that fits his or her abilities, needs, and interests. The college years represent a time to evaluate one's strong points, skills, and desires, and make plans for the future. Recreation may be a profession to which a young person can wisely devote life's energies.

3. *To determine what support to give to organized recreation.* As a thoughtful and participating citizen in a democratic society the college student should determine what support, financial and otherwise, community recreation programs should receive. Are taxes that are spent for recreation well invested? Is the community recreation program organized and administered in the most effective way possible? Do the activities that are offered serve the entire population? Is the time spent as a volunteer worthwhile in its contribution to people? Such questions can be answered in an intelligent and meaningful manner if a college student has had some background and understanding concerning

recreation and consequently knows what it is and the goals it is supposed to accomplish. The essence of democracy is that citizens should make informed decisions regarding various aspects of their government and public life. A course in recreation will help in making educated decisions about this field of endeavor.

THE PURPOSE OF THIS TEXT

This text is designed to provide the college student who is interested in exploring recreation as a career, as well as the person who is interested in knowing more about this field of endeavor, with fundamental knowledge concerning the field of recreation. It is designed to show what recreation is, the objectives of the profession, the contributions it can make to enriched living, the types of programs that are offered, how these programs are organized and financed, and who provides the leadership. It also attempts to show the relationship of recreation to current societal developments such as ecology, the environment, and cultural change.

QUESTIONS AND EXERCISES

1. Define the term *recreation*. How does this definition compare with the definitions of *recreation* that most of your college classmates have?
2. What is the difference between *recreation* and *recreation education?* Which is more valuable to society and why?
3. List what you consider to be the advantages and the disadvantages of pursuing a career in recreation.
4. Survey a recreation program and then evaluate it in terms of its worth to the community of which it is a part.
5. Write a 250 word essay on the topic, "Recreation is Not Idleness."
6. Interpret what you feel is the real meaning behind Plato's definition of *play*. What are the implications of this definition for recreation?
7. Identify the following terms: *physical education, group work, adult education, recreation,* and *park development.*
8. To what degree is the government at local, state, and national levels involved in organized recreation?
9. What contributions can organized recreation make to inner city youth? Select a city and be specific in your answers.
10. What are some of the major changes taking place in society that have implications for present and future recreation programs?

SELECTED REFERENCES

Butler, George D., *Introduction to Community Recreation.* New York: McGraw-Hill Book Company, 1967.

Carlson, R., T. Deppe, and J. MacLean, *Recreation in American Life.* Belmont, Calif.: Wadsworth Publishing Company, 1972.

de Grazia, Sebastian, *Of Time, Work and Leisure.* New York: Twentieth-Century Fund, 1962.

Dulles, Foster R., *A History of Recreation: America Learns to Play.* New York: Appleton-Century-Crofts, 1965.

Jernigan, Sara S., and C. Lynn Vendien, *Playtime: A World Recreation Handbook.* New York: McGraw-Hill Book Company, 1972.

Kleindienst, Viola, and Arthur Weston, *Intramural and Recreation Programs for Schools and Colleges.* New York: Appleton-Century-Crofts, 1964.

Kraus, Richard, *Recreation and Leisure in Modern Society.* New York: Appleton-Century-Crofts, 1971.

Meyer, Harold D., Charles Brightbill, and H. Douglas Sessoms, *Community Recreation, A Guide to Its Organization.* Englewood Cliffs, N.J.: Prentice-Hall, Inc., 1969.

Shivers, Jay, *Principles and Practices of Recreational Service.* New York: The Macmillan Company, 1967.

Smith, Julian W., *Outdoor Education* (rev. ed.). Washington, D.C.: American Association for Health, Physical Education and Recreation, 1970.

Staffo, Donald F., "A Community Recreation Program," *Journal of Health, Physical Education and Recreation,* Vol. 44 (May, 1973).

Staley, Edwin, *Leisure and the Quality of Life.* Washington, D.C.: American Association for Health, Physical Education and Recreation, 1972.

Stevens, Ardis, *Fun is Therapeutic: A Recreation Book to Help Therapeutic Recreation Leaders by People Who are Leading Recreation.* Springfield, Ill.: Charles C. Thomas, Publisher, 1972.

Swan, Malcolm D., ed., *Tips and Tricks in Outdoor Education.* Danville, Ill.: Interstate Printers and Publishers, 1970.

Waggoner, Bernice E., "Motivation in Physical Education and Recreation for Emotionally Handicapped Children," *Journal of Health, Physical Education and Recreation,* Vol. 44 (March, 1973).

2

SETTINGS

FOR RECREATION PROGRAMS

Recreation programs may exist in many different settings. The home, the school, the playground, the park, and the community swimming pool are just a few of the places where one can find an ongoing recreation program that would interest every age group.

The home is probably the most overlooked recreation setting. Think for a moment about all of the recreational activities that occur in and around the home. They may include outdoor games such as stickball or badminton, indoor games such as table tennis or billiards, arts-and-crafts activities, hobbies, entertaining friends, or recreation that is relaxing in nature. Of course, there are many recreational activities that one cannot accomplish in or around his home. For these activities a person must seek other recreation settings. In this chapter, a number of these other settings will be discussed so that you may learn about their existence and possibly avail yourself of the many recreational facilities they have to offer.

In Chapter 1, the four general categories of recreational settings were given. They are repeated here as they will be the basis for our discussion of recreation settings.

1. Government agencies and institutions.
2. Group-work agencies that are semipublic or voluntary and do not have exclusive membership
3. Private organizations or groups of individuals whose membership joins voluntarily and through a common interest sponsors recreation programs.
4. Commercial interests aimed at the profit motive.

All of these institutions provide a number of different types of settings for recreation programs. Each general category will be discussed separately and in greater detail in the following sections of this chapter.

GOVERNMENT AGENCIES AND INSTITUTIONS

Recreation programs are conducted by all levels of the federal, state, and local governments. The settings for some of these programs include the national parks on the federal level, the state parks and museums on the state level, and the community playground programs on the local level. An overview of the recreation settings offered by these different levels of government is given in the following discussion.

Federal Agencies and Recreational Settings

There are approximately fifty federal agencies that provide recreational settings directly to the public or in cooperation with state or local government. Of course, only a few of these agencies that are primarily concerned with recreation will be mentioned here.

1. *Federal Extension Service.* This service is the educational agency of United States Department of Agriculture. It carries on specific programs that relate to recreation in small communities and rural areas. It also acts as an advisor to the states on all outdoor recreation programs. It is probably best known for its cosponsorship of the 4-H clubs, which have over three million members in nearly 100,000 4-H clubs. Members of 4-H clubs ("4-H" stands for head, heart, health, and hands) are boys and girls between the ages of 10 and 21 who come chiefly from farms and rural areas. They carry on a wide range of projects that include farming, raising livestock for show, soil conservation, homemaking, and community service. The 4-H camp is another recreational setting that serves rural youth.

2. *National Park Service.* This service is under the Department of the Interior and was designated to administer the national parks – one of the major recreational settings in the United States. There are over twenty-nine million acres of land set aside for recreational activities. Included in this acreage are thirty-three national parks and numerous monuments and historic sites that comprise 272 areas under the jurisdiction of the National Park Service. National parks offer a variety of settings for camping, picnicking, biking, hiking, mountain climbing, and numerous other activities.

3. *Forest Service.* This service is under the Department of Agriculture and administers over 186 million acres of National Forest land. There are recreation settings for fishing, camping, boating, exploring, and skiing. Many organizations lease land from the Forest Service to establish their own camping facilities. About nine million acres of Forest Service land is

preserved as wilderness. This land, kept in its natural state, can be entered only by foot, horseback, or by canoe. Many persons enjoy the wilderness setting as a source of recreational activity.

4. *Bureau of Land Management.* This Bureau under the Department of the Interior administers over 450 million acres of federally owned public land that has not been set aside under the National Park Service or the Forest Service. This land is mainly located in Alaska, where the federal government owns approximately 300 million acres. The remainder of this land is divided among eleven western states. Sections of this land have been leased or sold for recreational facilities, including camping sites and museums, and some small tracts of land have been sold to individuals for private recreation purposes.

5. *Fish and Wildlife Service.* This service is under the Department of the Interior and administers over twenty-eight million acres divided into 300 national wildlife refuges and ranges. About five million of these acres are on land controlled by the Bureau of Land Management. These refuges provide ample settings for hunting, fishing, nature study, hiking, boating, camping, and enjoyment of wilderness areas.

6. *Other Federal Agencies.* There are many other federal agencies that provide recreation settings, although this may not be their major administrative purpose. Some of these agencies are briefly mentioned below:

   a. *Bureau of Indian Affairs* (Department of the Interior). Administers about fifty-eight million acres which include all of the Indian reservations. Provides settings for tourism, hiking, swimming, as well as appreciation of Indian crafts and history.

   b. *Corps of Engineers* (Department of the Army). Administers about eight million acres of land and water including 350 water areas and thousands of miles of shoreline. Provides recreation settings for camping, boating, picnicking, and other water recreation at reservoir sites.

   c. *Department of Health, Education, and Welfare* (U.S. Office of Education). Its many services include emphasis on school settings for recreation, conferences on children and youth, maintenance of sanitary conditions of parks and camping areas, and programs that control water pollution.

   d. *Tennessee Valley Authority.* Authority was established to control the Tennessee River for electric power and navigation purposes. Its reservoirs are popular recreation settings providing fishing, camping, and swimming facilities.

   e. *Bureau of Reclamation.* As part of the Department of the Interior this bureau works closely with other federal agencies in the administration of recreation sites at reservoir areas.

In addition to these agencies, the federal government sponsors the President's Council on Physical Fitness and Sports, The White House Conference on Children and Youth, and the President's Council on Aging. All of these committees are essential in the planning of recreation settings for these special groups. There are also special agencies that provide recreation settings for the armed forces, veterans, and civilian government employees. These groups will be discussed in detail in Chapter 3, which deals with recreation services.

The *Bureau of Outdoor Recreation* coordinates the outdoor recreation activities of most of the federal agencies and works with the states in developing state and local recreation services. Its purpose is to clarify the responsibilities of the federal government in relation to present and future recreation needs.

State Agencies and Recreational Settings

The states control parks, forests, and other recreational settings in excess of 39,000,000 acres. There are approximately 1,800 state parks that cover more than five million acres of land. Some of the settings for recreation offered at state facilities include trails, picnic grounds, camping areas, boating and swimming areas, and numerous hotels, lodges, and museums.

Some of the state departments primarily concerned with providing settings for recreation are discussed here:

1. *Outdoor Recreation Services.* This state agency works with the federal government in planning and administering outdoor recreation programs. In some states there may be a separate agency, while in others this responsibility is taken over by the state recreation commission of the state park administration.

2. *State Park Department.* The state parks provide recreational areas and protection for sites of natural beauty. Some state parks are the home of important historic sites. Some of the settings provided by the state parks include swimming pools, beaches, camping grounds, boating areas, zoos, amphitheaters, hiking trails, and organized field trips. Parks that are of historic interest may offer museums, outdoor displays, monuments, and burial grounds. All states differ in the administration of their parks and the facilities offered to their visitors.

3. *State Forest Department.* There are over twenty million acres of state forests excluding forest areas in the state parks. Much of the state forest land was reserved for the production of lumber and for watershed protection. The recreation settings provided by the state forests primarily include hunting and fishing areas, camping areas, and some sites for vacation homes. Other activities such as boating, swimming, and skiing may also be found.

4. *State Department of Fish and Game.* This agency must protect the fish and game in their natural habitats. It enforces game and fishing laws and regulates commercial fishing and hunting. It also provides recreation settings for fishing, hunting, and trapping.

5. *State Agriculture Extension Service.* This agency provides recreation settings in the form of 4-H clubs, camp programs, community programs for singing, dancing, drama, arts and crafts, and nature study.

In addition to these agencies, states provide recreational settings through state hospitals, institutions for the mentally retarded and handicapped, day-care centers, nursing homes, penal institutions, children's homes, and drug control centers. The recreation services offered in many of these settings will be

STATE PARK AND RECREATION AREAS AND ACREAGE

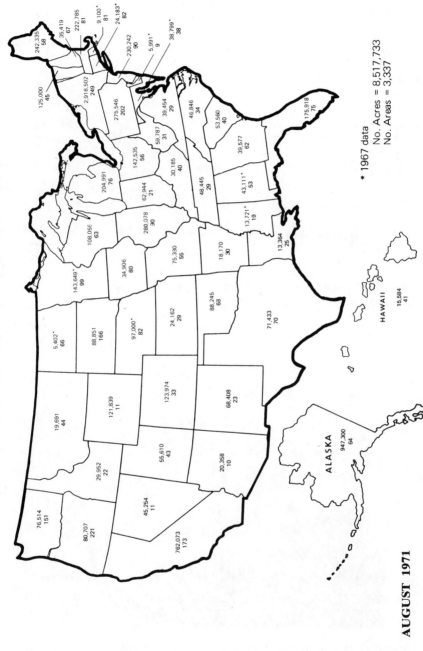

* 1967 data

No. Acres = 8,517,733
No. Areas = 3,337

AUGUST 1971

Parks and Recreation, August, 1971. Reprinted by permission of the National Recreation and Park Association.

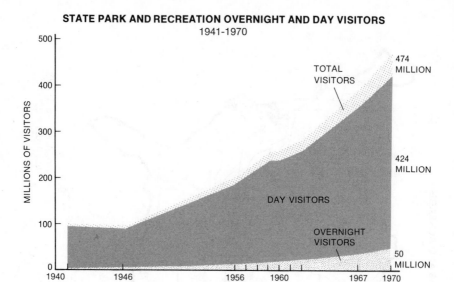

STATE PARK AND RECREATION OVERNIGHT AND DAY VISITORS
1941-1970

Parks and Recreation, August, 1971. Reprinted by permission of the National Recreation and Park Association.

South Carolina's Grand Strand offers sixty miles of clean, wide beach. Photo courtesy of South Carolina Department of Parks, Recreation and Tourism.

discussed in the next chapter. The state conducts commissions on youth and the aged as well as other special groups. Recreation settings are an important factor in the development of any program for these groups.

Local Government and Recreational Settings

Local governments include county, city, community, and neighborhood representation. Schools are also included here as they often act independently in establishing recreation settings. For any recreation program to operate successfully, it is necessary that all levels of government, from federal to local, interact with each other in the planning, funding, and supervision of recreation settings.

The levels of local government and their contribution to recreation settings will be briefly discussed here.

1. *County settings.* In recent years, counties have been playing a greater role in recreation programs. Most counties have parks that have more recreational facilities than their national and state counterparts. These parks may be small by comparison but are developed to include picnic grounds, tennis courts, beaches, baseball diamonds, swimming pools, golf courses, and playgrounds. Many counties operate on a year-round basis with full-time employees for recreation programs.

2. *City settings.* The larger cities often have city planning agencies that work closely with recreation administrators in planning for recreation settings and future growth. Cities have numerous parks for historical and recreational purposes. These parks house game, swimming, boating, and hiking facilities as well as zoos, museums, and exhibits of special interest. The so-called "vest-pocket parks" are a fairly new addition to city recreation. These parks, established in our larger cities, are very small areas that offer a relaxing atmosphere in the center of a bustling city. In many large cities, small areas of the city are designated as "communities." These communities often sponsor recreation settings of their own such as swimming pools, playgrounds, day-care centers, and drug-control centers. In today's society, community involvement of this sort is essential to cope with the typical urban problems of poverty, poor housing, and unemployment. This will be discussed further in Chapter 6, "Sociological Problems Facing Recreation Today."

3. *Community settings.* Communities in this sense include boroughs, townships, and villages that usually have independent administrations. Neighborhoods or districts make up these communities. In recent years, communities have become more and more active in sponsoring recreation settings. There are highly developed community parks that offer facilities for game-playing, picnicking, arts-and-crafts programs, skating, skiing, horseback riding, tennis, and many other activities. In addition, communities sponsor drama, choral groups, orchestras, athletic meets, and community-wide celebrations offering recreational activities. Many communities have swimming pool complexes that offer swimming lessons and lifesaving courses. Community centers are separate buildings with a full-time staff that offer meeting places for all age groups as well as athletic activities, hobby centers, and dramatic and choral events.

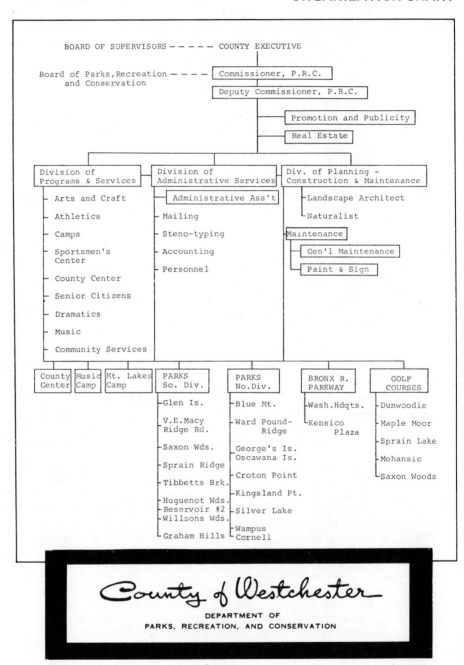

```
BOARD OF SUPERVISORS – – – – – COUNTY EXECUTIVE

Board of Parks, Recreation – – – –  Commissioner, P.R.C.
    and Conservation
                                     Deputy Commissioner, P.R.C.

                                           Promotion and Publicity
                                           Real Estate

Division of              Division of               Div. of Planning -
Programs & Services      Administrative Services    Construction & Maintenance

  ⌐ Arts and Craft         Administrative Ass't       ⌐Landscape Architect
  ⌐ Athletics              ⌐ Mailing                  └Naturalist
  ⌐ Camps                  ⌐ Steno-typing            Maintenance
  ⌐ Sportsmen's            ⌐ Accounting                ⌐ Gen'l Maintenance
    Center                 ⌐ Personnel                 └ Paint & Sign
  ⌐ County Center
  ⌐ Senior Citizens
  ⌐ Dramatics
  ⌐ Music
  ⌐ Community Services
```

County Center	Music Camp	Mt. Lakes Camp	PARKS So. Div.	PARKS No. Div.	BRONX R. PARKWAY	GOLF COURSES
			Glen Is.	Blue Mt.	Wash.Hdqts.	Dunwoodie
			V.E.Macy Ridge Rd.	Ward Pound-Ridge	Kensico Plaza	Maple Moor
			Saxon Wds.	George's Is. Oscawana Is.		Sprain Lake
			Sprain Ridge	Croton Point		Mohansic
			Tibbetts Brk.	Kingsland Pt.		Saxon Woods
			Huguenot Wds. Reservoir #2 Willsons Wds.	Silver Lake		
			Graham Hills	Wampus Cornell		

County of Westchester

DEPARTMENT OF
PARKS, RECREATION, AND CONSERVATION

Courtesy of the County of Westchester Department of Parks, Recreation, and Conservation.

Impromptu jazz session al fresco at the Westchester Music and Arts Camp, a six-week sleepaway camp for teenagers interested in music, drama, dance, and art. The camp, located at Croton Point, is a facility of the County of Westchester, New York, Department of Parks, Recreation, and Conservation. Photo courtesy of the County of Westchester Department of Parks, Recreation, and Conservation.

Police Department personnel use city recreation facilities to stay in good physical condition. Community Center, Recreation Department, North Little Rock, Arkansas. Photo courtesy of the North Little Rock Recreation Department.

Some communities also have zoos, museums, and places for art and handiwork exhibits.

A new concept in family fitness has been rapidly spreading from community to community across the United States. This concept, which began in San Diego, California, is a family recreation program that occurs on certain weekday evenings in the city's nine recreation centers. Families come together to participate in musical exercises, games, instruction in certain sports, and discussions on health and recreation. These programs help to keep families together and to improve physical fitness.

4. *School settings.* The schools are a major source of recreation settings. Some of these settings include park areas, playgrounds, swimming pools, tennis courts, gymnasiums, and track and field areas. For so many years school facilities went unused after school hours. Recent trends are keeping schools open after school hours, during evenings, weekends, and summers, so that these recreation settings can be used to their full advantage. Many schools are used widely for adult education classes in every subject imaginable from real estate to the occult. It is essential for community groups to work closely with school boards to provide the best possible recreation programs.

Schools represent settings for recreation programs. Girls' all-city archery at Marshall High in Los Angeles. Photo courtesy of the Los Angeles City Schools, Youth Services Section.

Local governments also provide recreation settings in the form of libraries, museums, botanical gardens, auditoriums for concerts and lectures, movies, bookshops in all subject areas, dramatic and musical productions, and many other special programs.

GROUP-WORK AGENCIES – SEMIPUBLIC OR VOLUNTARY

Group-work agencies supplement the work done by the government and schools in creating recreation programs. Usually supported by local taxes, voluntary contributions, and funds raised by Community Chest or United Fund campaigns, these agencies include the YMCA, YWCA, boys clubs, settlement houses, Boy and Girl Scouts, nondenominational community centers, drug-control centers, and various other organizations. The membership of these semipublic agencies is seldom exclusive, although some programs of the agency may be restricted to members. A few of the better-known agencies will be mentioned here.

Boy Scouts of America

There are over six million members of this group in the United States today. About one-quarter of this membership is adult leaders. The Boy Scouts offer Cub Scout groups for boys eight to ten years of age, Boy Scout groups for boys eleven to thirteen, and Explorer Scout groups for boys fourteen to seventeen.

The Cub Scouts offer recreation settings in many fields, including music, photography, dramatics, construction work, cooking, and sports. The Boy Scouts offer similar settings that include camping, canoeing, wilderness exploration, and team and individual sports. Explorer Scouts may join air and sea groups and participate in recreation programs for the special interests of their membership.

Girl Scouts of America

Membership in the Girl Scouts, which exceeds three million girls and young women, is divided into four age groups: the Brownie Scouts (seven to eight years), Junior Girl Scouts (nine to eleven years), Cadette Girl Scouts (twelve to fourteen years), and Senior Scouts (fifteen to seventeen years). The recreation settings provided by the Brownies emphasize games, parties, hiking, camping, homemaking, and arts-and-crafts activities. Junior and Cadette scouting stresses recreation settings in four major areas: home, out-of-doors, arts, and citizenship. Senior Scouts emphasize special interests of their members. Some activities may include boating, flying, camping, exploring, and community service.

Boys Clubs of America

Urban boys between the ages of eight and twenty are the primary concern of Boys Clubs. These boys are usually disadvantaged and come from poverty-line homes, inadequate families, and poor neighborhoods. There are more than 800 such clubs with a membership of over 800,000 boys. Boys Clubs usually have their own buildings in inner-city areas. These buildings usually provide recreation settings for gym activities, swimming, indoor games, and arts and crafts. In addition, there are library rooms, study areas, auditoriums and frequently provisions are made for outdoor activities, such as track and field events and outdoor games.

Girls Clubs of America

Girls Clubs, like Boys Clubs, are mainly concerned with girls ages six to eighteen from urban, impoverished areas. These clubs usually have their own centrally located building that provides recreation settings in the form of swimming pools, arts-and-crafts rooms, kitchen areas, sewing rooms, study and music areas, and game rooms. Health, good grooming, theater and dance, and community service are stressed. The clubs also sponsor camping trips and summer camps.

Camp Fire Girls

The Camp Fire Girls are divided by age groupings into Blue Birds (seven to eight), Camp Fire Girls (nine to eleven), Junior Hi Camp Fire Girls (twelve to fourteen), and Horizon Clubs (fifteen to seventeen). Recreational activities stressed include camping, arts and crafts, swimming, dramatics, nature study, and ecology and conservation projects.

Youth Service Organizations

These organizations include the YMCA, YWCA, YMHA, and Jewish Community Centers. They are primarily dedicated to serving youth and have highly developed settings for recreation activities. The range of activities includes nursery schools, swimming and swimming lessons, track and field events, lectures, drama, continuing education, and a wide variety of activities to enhance leisure time. Y's are usually located in their own buildings and may sponsor clubs for different ages and special interest groups. Y's usually sponsor summer day-camps, and groups of Y's working together may sponsor state-wide sleep-away camps. Although they have the words "Christian" and "Hebrew" in their titles, the Y's are open to all people regardless of faith.

Settlements

These agencies are primarily social welfare institutions and are frequently located in low-income neighborhoods. They offer programs for people of all ages and stress social reform through counseling, group work, and recreation. Recreation settings include swimming pools, ball fields, camps, playgrounds, game rooms, meeting halls, gymnasiums, craft areas, and hobby clubs. In addition, settlements offer libraries, cultural activities, nursery schools, and day-care centers.

PRIVATE AGENCIES AND RECREATION SETTINGS

A private agency is formed by a group of people having similar interests and generally restricts activities to members of the group. Private agencies include churches, synagogues, fraternal organizations, industrial groups, labor unions, country clubs, and athletic clubs. These groups are usually funded by their membership or sponsoring corporation and not by taxes, public contributions, or monies from the Community Chest or United Fund. A few of these agencies will be discussed here.

Churches and Synagogues

Of course, the prime concern of these agencies is religious guidance, but they do offer a wide variety of recreation settings for their membership. Groups are usually formed according to age and sex, and they conduct meetings, provide cultural, artistic, and athletic activites. There are also national organizations for young people such as Catholic Youth Organization (CYO) and the United Synagogue Youth (USY). Some churches and synagogues have well-equipped gyms in addition to club rooms, libraries, kitchens, and auditoriums.

Industrial Recreation

Many corporations have recreation programs administered by a full-time director and staff members. Recreation programs are important to many employees, and they help to make their time on the job more productive as well as to alleviate high rates of absenteeism and job boredom. Recreation settings may include golf courses, swimming pools, gymnasiums, game rooms, libraries, ball fields, and tennis courts. The number of facilities depends on the size of the company and the amount of land they have for recreational purposes.

Many corporations sponsor athletic leagues that compete after hours in such sports as baseball, bowling, and football. There are also clubs that are formed with hobby interests in mind such as photography, sewing, or gourmet cooking. In addition, many industries sponsor travel clubs in which vacation trips are planned on charter flights. Another well-known activity of industry is the sponsoring of company picnics, outings, and parties. Often, these are held annually or to celebrate special company events.

Athletic Clubs

These clubs, which are usually formed by members having a common interest in a particular recreational activity, may run the gamut of dance groups, golf clubs, ski clubs, hiking and mountain-climbing clubs, swimming and tennis clubs. Athletic clubs usually have a local membership but some groups participate in national organizations that help to publicize the activity and sponsor meetings and competition.

Other Types of Clubs

In addition to athletic clubs, there are other types of recreation clubs that are formed by local groups sharing a common interest. These include drama, choral, and orchestral groups, art clubs, stamp clubs, chess clubs, travel groups, camera clubs, bird-watching clubs, and a host of others. Some of them have national organizations that keep membership records, publish newsletters, and sponsor national meetings.

Other clubs that sponsor recreational activities are women's clubs, men's clubs, lodges, fraternal organizations, nationality groups, unions, the grange, fire, police, and hospital auxiliary groups, and service organizations.

Private agencies of all types provide the widest choice of recreation settings for their membership. When one considers the number of church, industrial, athletic, and local organizations that sponsor activities, the possibilities for recreation settings become endless.

COMMERCIAL INTERESTS AND RECREATION SETTINGS

Commercial recreation can be defined quite simply as recreation for a profit. In recent years, the recreation business has made several billions of dollars for its owners. Much of this type of recreation is for the spectator and therefore it is of a passive nature, such as professional baseball, football, and ice hockey games, motion pictures, and television. However, some commercial recreation does totally involve the participant, as in skating rinks, bowling alleys, billiard halls, and golf courses. Summer and day camps are often commercial recreation ventures. Some commercial interests will be briefly discussed here.

Amusements and Entertainment

Amusements may be in the form of amusement parks, carnivals, circuses, rodeos, and animal shows. These settings are almost entirely for the spectator. One of the best known and most successful business ventures of this type is Disneyland, now located in Orlando, Florida and Anaheim, California. Both parks have imaginative amusement areas combined with parks, playgrounds, swimming areas, hotels, and restaurants. The parks encompass many different recreation settings that add to the complete enjoyment of one's visit.

Other forms of entertainment also fall into this category of recreation settings. Theatres, night clubs, and motion pictures are very popular recreation settings. Radio, records, television, and musical instruments also provide recreational activities that people spend millions of dollars on each year. Television is one of the most important leisure-time activities for people of every age. However, excessive televiewing is often criticized as it takes time away from recreation activities that provide physical exercise.

Sports and athletics represent one type of recreation activities. Professional sports, in particular, have great appeal to today's youth. Ice Hockey Clinic with New York Rangers. Recreation Division, Department of Parks and Recreation, Hempstead, New York. Photo courtesy of the Town of Hempstead Parks and Recreation Department.

Athletics and Sports

Professional sporting events have grown enormously in recent years. Football, baseball, basketball, golf, tennis, and bowling are only some of the sports that have been very profitable to the professional players. There are also racing events of every type, including horse, dog, motorcycle, car, and bicycle races. Commercial interests have also invested in bowling alleys, billiard parlors, ice skating and roller-skating rinks, as well as bathing beaches, swimming pools, tennis courts, and golf courses. In many cases, community and voluntary agencies have not been able to keep up with the demand or raise the funds for such recreation settings. Because of the need, commercial enterprises took over and developed much needed recreation facilities.

Travel

The largest single recreation expenditure of Americans is travel at home and abroad. Many persons travel with well-organized tour groups that provide charter transportation, hotels, and tours. Traveling may include weekends at resort hotels, visits to different cities, a week at a dude ranch, as well as camping trips. Many persons use recreation vehicles in the form of trailers, campers, dune buggies, snowmobiles, bicycles, motorcycles, boats of all types, and small planes. Vacation recreation is one of the largest business undertakings in the United States.

A fairly new form of travel recreation has come about in recent years with the advent of planned recreation communities. Some of these communities offer year-round homes or vacation homes in the form of apartments, condominiums, and private houses. They are usually located in areas that are conducive to particular sports such as skiing or swimming. The community is planned to offer year-round recreation settings that may include tennis courts, swimming pools, boating areas, golf courses, ice-skating ponds, snowmobiling areas, and ski areas. Many of these communities provide every possible source of recreation setting for the home owner.

It is hoped that this chapter has given one an overview of some of the settings available for recreation. The recreation services offered by these and other settings will be discussed in the following chapter.

QUESTIONS AND EXERCISES

1. Discuss four federal agencies that contribute to recreation settings.
2. What are the principles and contributions of 4-H Clubs to recreation?
3. Discuss four state agencies involved in providing recreation settings.

4. Discuss some urban recreation settings. Do you have any suggestions for improving urban recreation settings?

5. Is there an adult education program in your community? If so, learn how it is administered by interviewing persons connected with the program. Evaluate the program on the basis of courses offered, attendance, and meaningfulness to the entire community.

6. Discuss contributions of group-work agencies in creating recreation settings. Choose one group-work agency and find out about job opportunities for recreation specialists.

7. What is a settlement and how does it contribute to community welfare? If one does exist in your community, write a brief study on its programs, administration, and job opportunities for recreation personnel.

8. Discuss two private agencies that contribute to recreation settings. Choose a specific private agency in your community to report on concerning recreation programs.

9. Are there any organized industrial recreation programs in or around your community? If so, choose one and write a brief analysis that includes activities offered, administration, and recreation personnel employed.

10. Discuss some specific commercial interests and how they affect recreational settings. What responsibilities should commercial interest have toward the public in relation to recreation?

SELECTED REFERENCES

American Association for Health, Physical Education and Recreation, *A Guide for Programs in Recreation and Physical Education for the Mentally Retarded.* Washington, D.C.: The Association, 1968.

Dunn, Diana R. (ed.), *NRPA Recreation and Park Perspective Collection.* College Park, Md.: McGrath Publishing Company, 1971.

Dunn, Diana R., "White House Conference on Children," *Parks and Recreation,* Vol. VI (March, 1971).

Ford, H. T., "The Recreation Director Syndrome," *Journal of Health, Physical Education and Recreation,* Vol. 44 (May, 1973).

Frye, Virginia, and Martha Peters, *Therapeutic Recreation: Its Theory, Philosophy, and Practice.* Harrisburg, Penn.: Stackpole Books, 1972.

Gold, Seymour M., *Urban Recreation Planning.* Philadelphia: Lea & Febiger, 1973.

Hjelte, George, and Jay S. Shivers, *Public Administration of Recreation Services.* Philadelphia: Lea & Febiger, 1972.

Hormachea, Marion N. and Carroll R. (eds.), *Recreation in Modern Society.* Boston: Holbrook Press, Inc., 1972.

Jensen, Clayne R., and Clark T. Thorstenson, *Issues in Outdoor Recreation.* Minneapolis: Burgess Publishing Company, 1972.

Kraus, Richard, and Joseph E. Curtis, *Creative Administration in Recreation and Parks.* St. Louis: The C. V. Mosby Co., 1973.

"Leisure: A New Dawn in America," *Parks and Recreation,* Vol. VI (August, 1971), entire issue.

Rathbone, Josephine L., and Carol Lucas, *Recreation in Total Rehabilitation.* Springfield, Ill.: Charles C. Thomas, Publisher, 1970.

Tillman, Kenneth G., "Recreational Activities Reinforce Learning Experiences for the Disadvantaged Student," *Journal of Health, Physical Education and Recreation,* Vol. 43 (February, 1972).

Weiner, Myron E., "A Systems Approach to Municipal Recreation," *Municipal Yearbook,* Vol. 38 (International City Management Association, 1971).

Willgoose, Carl E., "Recreation – Obligation of the Schools," *The Instructor.* Vol. LXXV (May, 1966).

3

SERVICES RENDERED

BY RECREATION

The last chapter discussed the many possible settings where recreation may take place. This chapter will concern itself with the wide variety of recreation services offered by these settings. For the purposes of this book, a service may be defined as assistance or benefit that is afforded a person or group of people. A recreation service is looked upon as a benefit to those people who are recipients of the service.

Recreational services benefit many people of all age groups. There are organized recreational services for the youth, senior citizens, members of religious or ethnic groups, community members, and persons who live in large cities. Recreation services also benefit special groups that may include hospital patients, nursing-home patients, and the blind, handicapped, mentally retarded, and emotionally disturbed. Good recreation services can have a profound effect on the well-being of all of these special groups.

There are seven major areas of recreational services. Though these services will be discussed separately, they are often interdependent and benefit many of the same people. For example, a person may avail himself of a senior-citizen recreation program and also benefit from a therapeutic service. One service may be sponsored by the community and the other by the local hospital. Frequently, different services make use of the same settings. A YMCA pool may be used by members of that Y as well as in a community-sponsored swim program. As you can see, recreation services and settings are interdependent. Some of the major services offered in most areas of the country include:

1. community
2. religious

3. youth
4. therapeutic
5. industrial
6. cultural
7. services for the Armed Forces

Each of these services will be discussed in detail to better acquaint one with the services available and the job opportunities in the field of recreation that are made possible by the variety of services offered.

COMMUNITY RECREATION SERVICES

There are many agencies within the community that provide recreational services. Many communities have a recreation department or a recreation and parks department. These groups work closely with the schools and voluntary agencies to provide a variety of free or inexpensive recreational services. Some services provided by the community are discussed here.

Community recreation consists of programs that meet the needs of their citizens. The recreation program in Hempstead, New York, provides busing for its residents to go to the beaches. Photo courtesy of the Town of Hempstead Department of Parks and Recreation.

Serving Community Recreation Needs

Community recreation consists of those programs sponsored by the towns and cities to meet the recreation needs of their citizens. These programs include arts, drama, sports, music, camping, and all types of social events. Some of the objectives of a community recreation program are:

1. to promote democratic values and community pride
2. to meet individual and group needs for all age groups
3. to serve the community without discrimination toward any racial, religious, or socioeconomic group
4. to provide activities for specialized groups such as the handicapped or retarded
5. to provide qualified professional leadership and adequate financial support for their programs
6. to provide adequate facilities where programs can be conducted
7. to improve physical fitness and stimulate the mind through responsible recreation programming

These objectives or goals should also take such factors as general physical health, creativity, socialization, and supplementary education into consideration when formulating a community recreation program. Each of these factors will be discussed here in some detail.

1. *General physical health.* In recent years, physical exercise has been neglected by many people. Teenagers ride to school and their parents ride to work. Watching television and taking car trips has replaced games and athletic activities. It is, therefore, very important that a community recreation program include active sports programs in their planning.
2. *Creativity.* Creativity is often neglected in the schools and in large urban complexes. People of all ages have the need to create but frequently must be motivated toward developing creative ability. This can be accomplished by introducing cultural programs that include art, drama, music, and dance as an integral part of any community recreation plan.
3. *Socialization.* Socialization is the coming together of all members of the community in programs that promote friendship and understanding without prejudice. A good recreational program brings young and old people together in their own groups and in areas of participation where each group can occasionaly interact with each other. Recent community programs have senior citizens acting as foster grandparents to disadvantaged youngsters. Many young people work with the handicapped and mentally retarded as a result of a community group effort. Socialization is also important in encouraging the development of close personal relationships among group members.
4. *Supplementary education.* This includes preschool programs, day-care centers, adult education courses, and courses that discuss the environment

SERVICES FOR SPECIAL GROUPS

Senior citizens participate far more in local agency programs than do preschool children, but ...

they require far fewer personnel, as they typically contribute substantially to their own programs as well as perform services for others in their communities.

SERVICES FOR THE DISABLED

More local resources are directed toward the mentally retarded than the physically handicapped, and more services are provided for youth than adults.

Services for the disabled are provided mainly by part-time personnel.

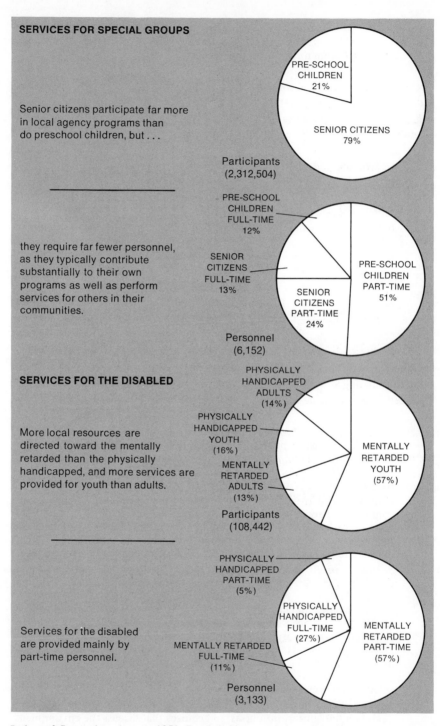

PRE-SCHOOL CHILDREN 21%

SENIOR CITIZENS 79%

Participants (2,312,504)

PRE-SCHOOL CHILDREN FULL-TIME 12%

SENIOR CITIZENS FULL-TIME 13%

SENIOR CITIZENS PART-TIME 24%

PRE-SCHOOL CHILDREN PART-TIME 51%

Personnel (6,152)

PHYSICALLY HANDICAPPED ADULTS (14%)

PHYSICALLY HANDICAPPED YOUTH (16%)

MENTALLY RETARDED ADULTS (13%)

MENTALLY RETARDED YOUTH (57%)

Participants (108,442)

PHYSICALLY HANDICAPPED PART-TIME (5%)

PHYSICALLY HANDICAPPED FULL-TIME (27%)

MENTALLY RETARDED FULL-TIME (11%)

MENTALLY RETARDED PART-TIME (57%)

Personnel (3,133)

Parks and Recreation, August, 1971. Reprinted by permission of the National Recreation and Park Association.

40

and the areas in which people are living. Adult education is vital to any community recreation program. Many adult education courses give students the opportunity to learn the English language, complete requirements for grade and high school graduation, and to receive vocational training. In addition, these courses provide interesting programs in the arts, drama, history, natural sciences, and in many other fields. Community recreation programs also provide for museums, exhibit halls, art centers, zoos, gardens, preservation of historical landmarks, and many other cultural programs.

Community Recreation Services According to Age Groups

It is impossible to list every recreation service provided by every community but a few of the major services are presented here according to the age of the participants. Of course, some activities will overlap regardless of age category.

1. *Preschool and school children*
    a. nursery schools and day-care centers
    b. wading pools, spray pools, and supervised swimming and diving lessons
    c. arts and crafts, music, and story-telling programs
    d. free, organized play programs that include Little League teams for both sexes
    e. supervised park and playground programs after school and during the summer months
    f. day camp, camping, and nature study programs
    g. meeting places for clubs and social events
2. *Teen-agers*
    a. meeting places for teen-age clubs and groups
    b. teen centers for socializing
    c. organized sports, both team and individual
    d. organized community service projects
    e. special-interest groups with qualified supervision
    f. supplementary educational and vocational training courses
3. *Adults*
    a. meeting places for clubs and special-interest groups
    b. organized exercise and recreation programs that concentrate on physical fitness
    c. community sports leagues that encourage team work and competition
    d. cultural activities and discussions on topics of current interest; adult education courses
    e. swimming, tennis, and golf facilities and teaching programs
    f. community celebrations
4. *Senior Citizens*
    a. meeting places that are close to public transportation

YOUTH SERVICES

CIVICS

PHYSICAL EDUCATION

MODERN DANCE   FOLK DANCING

OUTDOOR EDUCATION   HEALTH EDUCATION

HOME ECONOMICS   LANGUAGE ARTS

MATHEMATICS   WOODWORKING

ASTRONOMY   CITIZENSHIP

SKETCHING   SWIMMING

ZOOLOGY   CONCERTS

ATHLETICS   DRAWING

PAINTING   REGULAR   HISTORY

READING   SCHOOL DAY   WRITING

SINGING   SCIENCE

EXTENDED THROUGH

MUSIC   CLUBS

DRAMA   AFTER SCHOOL   MOVIES

SINGING   RECREATION   HOBBIES

DAY CAMP   PROGRAM   RHYTHMS

QUIET GAMES   SWIMMING

SCIENCE ACTIVITIES   SOCIAL DANCING

ARTS, CRAFTS   PLAYACTING

PHYSICAL GAMES   SOCIAL ACTIVITIES

SPECIAL EVENTS   STORYTELLING

CITIZENSHIP ACTIVITIES   PHYSICAL RECREATION

FAMILY NIGHT   SPORTS NIGHT

RECREATION CAMPING

Clock face numerals 12, 11, 1, 10, 2, 9, 3, 8, 4, 7, 6, 5

AROUND THE CLOCK

Reprinted from *Guide for Youth Services Personnel,* 1972, with permission of the Los Angeles City Schools, Youth Services Division.

    b. programs that provide physical-fitness activities

    c. park areas that have benches, card tables, and games that older people enjoy

    d. organized trips both to local areas and abroad

    e. community service activities

    f. hobby clubs and special-interest groups

    g. lectures and courses to provide intellectual stimulation

A community recreation program must be well-rounded and take into consideration the population that makes up the community. Urban and rural areas, East and West Coast communities, large and small cities, all have different needs in terms of community recreation services. It is these different needs that must be met.

Trap and skeet shooting are popular with senior citizens. The Sportsmen's Center also includes areas for small and large bore pistol, field and target archery, and a fly and bait casting pool. The Center is operated by the County of Westchester Department of Parks, Recreation, and Conservation. Photo used by their courtesy.

Urban Recreation

Urban recreation provides many initial problems. The population is large and living space is congested. Areas for recreation are very limited, and in many of our large cities recreation programs have been neglected. Recreation services in our urban areas is very important, especially among the disadvantaged children and young adults. Many teen-agers leave school and are in the streets with no place to go and little to do. Many people are unemployed and are without direction in their lives. Recreation services can provide this needed direction and can help these people utilize their time in a beneficial manner.

The biggest problem of urban recreation is meeting the needs of the inner-city inhabitants. Statistics have found that many people who live in our inner cities rarely take advantage of recreational offerings that may be a subway ride away. A new concept that is meeting this need is the mobile recreation vans that tour city areas in the spring and summer months. New York City has been very successful with this program. They have mobile swimming pools, athletic vans with gym equipment and trampolines, and other recreational equipment. In Boston, inner-city parks have high-intensity lighting to provide nighttime recreation services.

Some suggestions for a successful urban recreation program are the following:

1. *Recreation plazas.* Areas created by closing off streets or sections where demolition has occurred. Services offered should include playground programs, swimming areas, games, and meeting places. Organized play programs and supervised activities should be available.

2. *Park-school development.* This simply means the working together of any city's park and school boards. Park areas can be planned around school areas and existing schools can be used for recreation purposes. Existing schools can offer many recreation services – this will be discussed in the section of this chapter that deals with school recreation (see page 45). The major factor in park-school recreation services is economy of both land and financial resources.

3. *Off-season use of swimming pools.* Swimming pools can be used for fishing, boating instruction, model sail or motor boating exhibitions, scuba-diving instruction, ice skating, and ice hockey.

4. *Auto-hobby shop.* Provides a needed service to young people who have an avid interest in cars, an interesting hobby that can also have a vocational value.

5. *Teen center or coffee shops.* A place for young people to meet and socialize with their peers.

6. *Floating community centers.* Cities near water can purchase luxury ships about to be retired to provide recreational services at a reduced cost. Most ships have swimming pools, shuffleboard courts, gyms, and a wide range of recreational facilities.

7. *Vest-pocket parks.* Briefly mentioned in Chapter 2, these parks are a valuable asset to the inner city if they offer such necessary services as: (a) play areas for young children, (b) basketball courts, (c) flower and vegetable gardens, (d) gym areas, and (e) portable pool sites. An inner city neighborhood may have many such small park areas each offering a different recreation service.

Settlement Houses

Settlement houses exist in urban areas and provide much needed services to the surrounding community. They are sponsored chiefly by charitable donations. One of the most famous settlement houses is the Henry Street Settlement, now called the Urban Life Center, at Henry Street on the lower east side of New York City. This area has a mixed population, including blacks, Puerto Ricans, Chinese, and other ethnic groups. It began in the late nineteenth century and today serves the needs of approximately 25,000 people.

Its services are varied and include educational, vocational, cultural, and recreational activities. Some of the programs that are currently being operated are:

1. day-care centers
2. Camp Echo sleep-away camp
3. dance, music, art, and handicraft programs
4. manpower training programs

5. home-planning workshops
6. senior citizen clubs
7. Urban Training Center for professionals in the field of social work, urban planning, and recreation
8. Community Consultation Center – a mental health facility
9. Community Affairs Center

A settlement such as Henry Street provides services to people who have a real need for recreational activities.

School Recreation

School recreation may be defined as any recreational activity that makes good use of leisure time within the school setting. Some objectives of a good school recreation program are:

1. education for beneficial use of leisure time
2. supervised instruction in recreation activities
3. to provide an outlet for creativity
4. to provide a varied program of activities
5. to provide adequate facilities for recreation programs
6. to work with the community in recreation planning
7. to make good use of the teaching staff
8. to involve as many students as possible

A good school recreation program provides students with instruction and participation in many activities and sports programs. Some recreation services offered include:

1. *games-sports:* archery, fencing, intramural sports, social games, skating, swimming, stunts and tumbling, and table tennis
2. *hobbies-crafts:* ceramics, woodworking, gardening, sewing, painting, metalworking, jewelry-making, cooking, and sewing
3. *music-dance:* social dancing, creative dance, choral and drama groups, band and orchestra groups

Programs should be conducted during school hours as well as after school and during the evening. It is essential that schools offer recreation services on a full-time basis.

In order to meet the recreation needs of the community, school-community programs that utilize school facilities must be developed. In many communities schools are closed on holidays, weekends, during school vacations, and during the summer. A community may be totally lacking in recreational services because it has overlooked the important school facilities. Community groups

The Los Angeles schools provide opportunities for model building. Photo courtesy of the Los Angeles City Schools, Youth Services Section.

that work with school boards can open up schools to provide year-round recreation services. Some of these services may include:

1. intramural sports
2. day camps
3. swimming lessons
4. tennis and golf instruction
5. hobby clubs
6. cultural activities
7. adult education courses
8. meeting places for different age groups
9. gymnasium activities
10. team sports for young people and leagues for adults

All of these services and many more can be provided by the community making use of existing school facilities. It is essential, however, that community and school board members thoroughly plan recreational services to avoid any conflicts due to scheduling or improper care of equipment or facilities.

New York Jets football players work with the Town of Hempstead ANCHOR Program (*A*nswering the *N*eeds of *C*hildren with *H*andicaps through *O*rganized *R*ecreation). Photo courtesy of the Town of Hempstead Department of Parks and Recreation.

RELIGIOUS INSTITUTIONS
AND RECREATIONAL SERVICES

Religious institutions serve an important recreational need in the community. Many people take this recreation service for granted as it has become so much a part of the American way of life. The church supper, picnic, or dance are all recreational activities that help to bring people together to enjoy their leisure time. But, religious institutions provide for many more recreational services than the social ones already mentioned. Some of these services will be discussed in this section.

Objectives of Recreation Services
Offered by Religious Institutions

The objectives of a religious recreation program differ somewhat from a community or school program. In a religious program, religion is intermingled with recreation, and recreation services are frequently used to attract people to the church or synagogue. In most cases, people attending such recreation programs are of the same religion and usually know each other from other church-sponsored functions. Recreation is, therefore, frequently used to achieve a high degree of fellowship among the participants, to teach cooperation, and to develop high moral standards. Some additional objectives of religious recreation programs include:

1. development of individual as well as group skills
2. imparting a sense of identity with a religious group

3. setting of democratic standards
4. development of leadership
5. development of a sense of life and God

To meet those objectives, religious institutions offer recreation services to all age groups. Some of the many services offered include arts and crafts, music, drama, social events, holiday programs, service projects, day-care centers, teen centers, special-interest clubs, camping experiences, and team and individual sports.

Catholic Youth Organization (CYO)

The CYO is a good example of a church-sponsored recreation program for Catholic young people. United Synagogue Youth (USY) is a similar program for Jewish youth. Some of the services of CYO will be given here so that the reader will have a better understanding of a church-related recreation program:

1. Establishes teen-age clubs and youth programs
2. Conducts recreational programs for handicapped youngsters
3. Conducts camps for disadvantaged children
4. Offers day camp experiences
5. Maintains youth centers where daily recreation services are offered
6. Obtains free tickets and passes for athletic events and entertainment functions
7. Sponsors a Scouting and Sea Cadet Program
8. Sponsors drug-abuse programs which provide preventative and educational information
9. Sponsors athletic and cheerleading programs and competitions

These are only a few of the services CYO offers its members. Services vary according to the Archdiocese. USY and other religious youth groups offer similar services with emphasis on guiding young people in the beneficial use of their leisure time.

YMCA, YWCA, YMHA, and Jewish Community Centers

These four organizations and others that are similar differ from church-sponsored groups in that they are semipublic and are aided by community funds. Their membership is open to the public without religious affiliation. However, depending on the type of institution, religious values are stressed, holidays observed, and cultural activities pertaining to the sponsoring religion are presented. The YMHA is the Hebrew equivalent of the YMCA.

Generally speaking, all of these organizations offer similar recreational services. Some of these services include:

1. cultural programs
2. special-interest groups
3. senior citizen programs
4. nursery schools and day-care centers
5. day camps
6. swimming lessons
7. adult-education courses
8. team-sports programs
9. drama workshops
10. community service projects

One YMHA, the 92nd Street Y in New York City has gained recognition for its cultural programs that include drama, music and dance performances, art exhibitions, and lectures and readings by well-known authors, poets, and celebrities. These cultural programs are just one of many recreational services provided by this Y.

Some communities have Jewish Community Centers that are primarily recreational in nature. They are open to the public and offer many of the same recreation programs as the YMCA and YMHA.

YOUTH SERVICES

Youth services are those recreational programs that are aimed chiefly at young people from preschool to high school age. Most recreational services fall into this category, as young people need direction to utilize their leisure time in a beneficial manner and to encourage recreational pursuits that will become a part of their adult lives. Some of the youth services that will be discussed here include the White House Conference on Children, playground programs, teen centers, youth groups, and camping programs.

White House Conference on Children

This conference, concerned with the needs of children and youth, has been held at ten-year intervals since 1909. The most recent conference was held in 1970–71 and was attended by 3,700 delegates. All major problem areas facing children were discussed, but for our purposes we will discuss those problems concerning children and recreation. The major objectives of the forum dealing with recreation are:

1. Elimination of prejudicial attitudes that hinder leisure opportunities
2. A commitment to establish leisure service to all children without regard to race, sex, economic status, or locale
3. Coordination of activities between institutions and communities
4. Encouragement of family participation in planning leisure activities
5. Promotion of different forms of leisure activities
6. Promotion of better relations between children, their families, and all the people of the community

Playground Programs

These programs are very important to the youth of a community. Playgrounds offer many different kinds of services. Some playgrounds offer extensive summer programs for all age groups, and playground directors and group leaders provide experienced recreational supervision. These summer programs usually involve games, sports, athletic competitions, day-camping experiences, drama and dance programs, swimming, track-and-field meets, and arts-and-craft activities. One playground program in Maryland sponsors Family Nights, when community members come to see the activities that their children have participated in and to enjoy special events such as carnivals, movies, picnics, talent shows, or movies.

Playgrounds in many communities have a year-round schedule and sponsor indoor activities in colder weather. Some playgrounds use school or community center facilities to sponsor arts and crafts, drama, dance, indoor sports, and social events. Many playgrounds sponsor trips to see plays, museums, or historical sites. Some activities may also include bicycle trips, overnight hikes, camping trips, and participation in community events such as the 4th of July or a community anniversary celebration.

Community and Teen Centers

Most communities have a community center that provides recreational services to all the members of that community. All age groups are served through nursery schools, day-care centers, clubs for older children, teen groups, adult activities, and senior-citizen programs. Some of the objectives of a community center are:

1. To bring together people from different areas of the community
2. To promote community unity
3. To provide services for all people regardless of race, religion, or financial status
4. To provide programs that will benefit all people

Some services offered by community centers include gymnasium activities, drama and dance groups, games such as billiards and table tennis, arts and crafts, kitchens, libraries, swimming pools, and meeting rooms. Community centers are often used as a central place to hold fund-raising social events, celebrations, community picnics, and fireworks on July 4th. The importance of the community center varies with the size of the community and the other recreation facilities available.

Teen centers

Teen centers are primarily social in nature and provide recreational outlets through teen clubs, groups, or informal gatherings. A teen center may be housed in a separate facility or may utilize a room in a community center or other community building such as a school or firehouse. The major objectives of a teen center are:

1. To direct young people toward beneficial and enjoyable use of leisure time
2. To keep teen-agers within the community
3. To help them to develop characteristics of leadership and community responsibility
4. To develop positive social values among young people

One county in Maryland has more than twenty teen clubs that participate in community service activities as well as in other social events. These clubs work together on certain programs and participate competitively in sports. They also come together at different times for dances, parties, and other social events. This particular county sponsors an annual teen conference at which delegates from the different teen clubs come together to discuss mutual problems and to organize events for the coming year.

Because teen centers are in competition with every other recreational facility in the community, it is very important that these centers offer enough diverse services to attract members. A purely social progam is not usually sufficient to attract the majority of teen-agers in the community. Therefore, most teen centers have well-planned programs that encompass social events, trips, drama and music programs, art classes and exhibits, and discussions on problems common to teen-agers. A well-rounded program must be supervised by a full-time recreation staff. The size of the staff depends on the number of teen-agers attending center activities.

Teen centers report a wide variety of services offered. Some of the social events include: talent shows, family nights, swim parties, picnics, hay rides, group attendance at concerts and plays, bicycle hikes, and camping trips. Weekend trips to cultural or historical points are also a part of their programs. Service programs may include: clothing collections, recycling collections, time donated to hospitals and other institutions, collecting for campaign drives, and sponsorship of scouting troops and other organizations for young children.

Camping programs are an important part of some recreation programs. Clear Creek Camp. Photo courtesy of the Los Angeles City Schools, Youth Services Section.

Camping

Camping programs are widespread in the United States today. Camps exist as day camps, overnight camps, and weekend or short camping experiences. Camping, in this context, may be defined as a group living together in a natural environment under the supervision of trained personnel. Camping provides many recreational services to youth that they may not have been exposed to otherwise.

Some of the objectives of a good camping program are:

1. Learning how to live in a natural environment
2. Developing camping, creative, and athletic skills
3. Learning about healthful living through constructive use of leisure time.
4. Developing leadership skills and the ability to live closely with other people

Camps may be sponsored by organizations or agencies such as the Boy Scouts, Girl Scouts, Y's, settlement houses, and similar groups. These organizations are most important in providing camping experiences to disadvantaged children as well as to those who can afford to attend camp.

The majority of camps are sponsored by private or commercial enterprises that operate camps on a profit-making basis. These camps, which are usually expensive and offer a variety of camping activities, may concentrate on a particular sport such as swimming or tennis, or a specialty such as drama or music. In recent years, many unusual camp specialties have appeared. One can glance through the classified section of a large city newspaper and see advertisements for travel camps (home and abroad), diet camps (weight loss is the primary factor), scuba-diving camps, work camps (projects such as farming or building), study camps (concentrate on school work), foreign-language camps, and canoeing camps. These are only a few of the specialties offered.

There are also public camps sponsored by communities, state and national parks, government agencies, and school groups. Many of these camps fall into the day-camp category. The major objective of these camps is to extend the benefits of camping to as many children as possible.

Churches and religious groups also sponsor camps. These camps are often at sites owned by the religious organization and are usually short-term sleep-away camps that attempt to serve many children in the course of one camping season. These camps also offer the camping experience to disadvantaged children. Included in these organizations are the Jewish Welfare Associations, CYO, the Salvation Army, and the agencies of most religions.

Generally speaking, camping offers activities that may include: nature study, ecology programs, all sports and games, athletic competition, arts and crafts, drama, music, camping skills, boating, swimming, dancing, and folklore. Short-term camps and day camps may concentrate on only a few of these services, depending on the time allotted and facilities available.

THERAPEUTIC RECREATION SERVICES

Therapeutic recreation may be defined as recreation services rendered to people who are physically or mentally ill, handicapped, disabled, or retarded. These services are provided in many settings that include hospitals, nursing homes, institutions for the mentally ill, sheltered workshops for the handicapped or retarded, and numerous public and private institutions that provide rehabilitation to persons with handicaps. For our purposes, a handicapped person may be defined as an individual who is unable to compete successfully in all areas of life. A person's ability to compensate for his handicap is a major objective of recreation therapy.

In this section of Chapter 3, the different recreation services offered to handicapped and sick people will be briefly discussed.

Therapeutic Recreation in Hospitals

Hospitals provide a wide variety of therapeutic services and employ the greatest number of professional recreation therapists. Veterans' hospitals and

Recreation for the handicapped. Wheelchair basketball, Valley Junior College. Photo courtesy of the Los Angeles City Schools, Youth Services Section.

military hospitals have well-organized recreation programs. The size of a hospital is usually the determining factor in the type of recreation services that are offered. For example, a recent survey showed that over ninety-six percent of hospitals that had over 1,000 beds had well-organized recreation programs. Some services provided by hospitals include: television, movies, reading, arts and crafts, social events, music and drama, games and sports, dancing, hobbies, and patient participation in hospital newspapers, radio stations, and organized entertainment programs.

The objectives of any hospital recreation program are the same as for institutions for the mentally ill, handicapped, or retarded. These objectives are:

1. Aid the physical, mental, and emotional health of the patient
2. Develop morale and fitness of the patient
3. Help patients to constructively use leisure time and to enable them to carry on some of these activities upon leaving the hospital
4. Help the individual satisfy social needs despite his handicap or illness

Many hospitals extend their recreation programs to include outside activities. One hospital, the Institute for Physical Medicine and Rehabilitation in New York City, takes many of its patients to baseball games, concerts, theatres, movies, and sites of interest. This program helps patients to develop confidence in their ability to cope with the world around them.

Recreation for the Physically Handicapped

Physically handicapped people may have impaired vision, hearing, or speech; neurological problems; and orthopedic or crippling conditions. As one can see, there are many types of handicaps, all with different causes, and good recreation programs must meet the needs of the individual patient.

Programs for the handicapped differ according to the settings and patients involved. General activities may include swimming, arts and crafts, games, wheelchair basketball, trips, puppet shows, magic tricks, and camping experiences. Much success has been achieved in camping programs for the handicapped. Some camps specialize in the treatment of certain diseases or handicaps. Camp Kno-Koma and Camp Nyda are two camp sites that provide recreation services to diabetics while teaching them how to care for their handicap. The Easter Seal Societies have sponsored numerous day and resident camps for handicapped children. Even severely handicapped children can successfully participate in camping programs.

Recreation for the Chronically Ill

Chronically ill persons are those individuals with diseases or conditions that cannot be cured. These patients include persons with cardiac, diabetic, tubercular, or cancerous conditions. Many of these conditions may not incapacitate the patient but may limit the type or degree of his activity. Chronically ill persons are usually older but may also include children and young adults. Although recreation therapy must fit the individual patient, painting, music, outings, all crafts, cookouts, drama groups, and nature study groups are often popular among the chronically ill.

Recreation for the Mentally Retarded

Mentally retarded persons have a lower than "normal" intelligence and therefore find it difficult to cope with their environment. Depending on the degree of impairment, they may or may not be institutionalized. There are more than five million retarded persons in the United States today.

There is a wide variety of services offered to the retarded. Some services are in residential facilities, whereas others are offered at sheltered workshops and centers for the retarded. Retarded persons enjoy crafts, music, dancing, sports and games, swimming, camping, and all social events. Generally speaking, most mildly or moderately retarded people can successfully participate in any recreational activity. In recent years, many counties and states have held competitive athletic events for retarded persons. These were well-attended and provided a chance for the retarded persons to show special achievement in a particular activity.

INDUSTRIAL RECREATION SERVICES

Industrial recreation may be defined as those programs provided by a work setting to promote better use of leisure time among employees. Some of the objectives of industrial recreation programs include:

1. Development of leisure interests that can be carried over into life outside of the industrial complex.
2. Improvement of company morale; reduction of absenteeism and job boredom
3. Promotion of employee recreation with the involvement of family members
4. Promotion of better relations between employees and improvement of labor-management relations
5. Improvement of industry-community relations

It has been estimated that there are about 30,000 companies with active recreation programs, and about thirty-four million employees participate in these activities. Recent surveys have found that extensive recreation programs in many large companies are best administered by the employees themselves. This may be accomplished by employee associations working with personnel management. Many companies do employ a full-time recreation director and full or part-time staffs, but this depends on the size of the company.

The recreation services offered by industry vary greatly, depending on size, number of employees, company policy, and ability and willingness of a company to support recreation services. Some of the many services offered may include golf, tennis, boating, swimming, all team sports, gymnasium activities, physical fitness and weight-control programs, health clubs, trips, camping sites, and hobby or special interest clubs. Companies are often represented in sport leagues such as softball, basketball, or bowling leagues. These leagues meet other industrial leagues in competitive games. Some companies, such as IBM, have large country clubs with many recreational facilities and services available to all employees and their families.

CULTURAL RECREATION SERVICES

Cultural recreation includes those services offered by art museums, natural history museums, concerts, dance presentations, theatres, movies, and many other cultural programs. Cultural programs of all types have been steadily gaining in popularity; many new concert theatres have been appearing. The

Garden State Arts Center in central New Jersey offers a wide variety of classical, popular, and childrens' programs to its patrons. Another example is the Los Angeles Cultural Arts Center. This contemporary structure serves the Los Angeles area with a variety of theatre, drama, music, and dance programs. Perhaps one of the best-known cultural activities is sponsored by the New York City Parks Department. Their Shakespeare in the Parks programs have allowed millions of people to view Shakespearian plays with fine casts in open-air settings. The recently opened John F. Kennedy Center for the Performing Arts in Washington, D.C. filled a great need for cultural programs in our nation's capital.

Some of the centers and programs previously mentioned are large-scale operations, but almost every small community sponsors some cultural programs in conjunction with libraries, museums, community centers, or private organizations. Many community newspapers list cultural activities in a weekly digest of what is happening around town. Cultural interests of all types provide an educational and enjoyable way of using leisure time.

ARMED FORCES RECREATION SERVICES

The Armed Forces provide many recreation services for the military and civilian personnel and their families. The Armed Forces Recreation Society (AFRS) unites professional recreation workers in different service branches to establish common recreation goals for military and civilian personnel. The objectives of the Armed Forces' recreation programs include:

1. Beneficial use of leisure time for members of the Armed Forces and their families
2. Bringing personnel together in a relaxed atmosphere
3. Strengthening morale of members of the Armed Forces
4. Offering a diversion from the pace of military life
5. Providing opportunities for self-expression and promoting physical fitness

Activities vary in different parts of the country and according to the size of the particular military installation. Most bases have separate clubs for officers and enlisted men, and a wide variety of services are offered to all military and civilian personnel. Some activities include sports, cultural programs, library and study groups, social events, and craft shops. Most bases have bowling alleys, movie theatres, field houses, gymnasiums, libraries, swimming pools, service clubs, tennis courts, golf courses, auto repair shops, and outdoor recreation facilities.

MOST IMPORTANT PERCEIVED BENEFIT OF ARMY RECREATION ACTIVITIES
(Sample Size = 22,563)

RANK	BENEFIT	% AGE GROUP				Total	% EDUCATIONAL LEVEL			
		-21	21-25	26-35	36+		-HS	HS	HS+	Degree
(1)	Provides a change of pace from the military environment	33.9	37.7	28.6	25.4	34.6	24.3	34.2	40.1	45.4
(2)	No Benefit	12.9	11.6	11.2	13.6	12.1	16.6	12.6	9.2	7.5
(3)	Helps me to keep physically fit	10.7	10.1	13.3	16.0	11.0	11.0	11.9	10.0	8.8
(4)	Allows me to do something related to my civilian occupation	12.3	8.4	6.4	4.6	9.2	14.9	8.2	7.8	6.5
(5)	Gives me something to do in my spare time	7.6	8.0	10.6	11.2	8.4	8.4	9.1	7.5	6.5
(6)	Gives me an opportunity to meet people with interests similar to mine	7.3	6.9	12.5	13.6	8.1	10.9	8.6	6.3	4.1
(7)	A benefit other than above	6.7	7.4	10.6	10.9	7.8	7.4	7.9	7.6	7.3
(8)	Provides an opportunity for self-expression and creativity	4.7	6.2	5.1	3.8	5.5	3.6	4.5	7.4	9.5
(9)	Gives me something familiar to do in what is otherwise a very unfamiliar environment	3.9	3.7	1.7	.9	3.3	2.9	3.0	4.1	4.4

Parks and Recreation, August 1971. Reprinted by permission of the National Recreation and Park Association.

QUESTIONS AND EXERCISES

1. Explain the seven major areas of recreation services. How may these areas be interdependent?

2. What are some of the major objectives of a community recreation program? Are there any other objectives that you think should be considered in planning for community recreation?

3. Discuss some ways to institute a successful urban recreation program. If you live in or near an urban area, report on some of its recreation services.

4. What are some of the programs offered by the Henry Street Settlement? Do you think that settlements such as Henry Street have their place in providing recreation services?

5. Discuss some of the objectives of school recreation programs. Interview local school recreation personnel to determine what job opportunities exist for recreation professionals.

6. Does your community work with the schools to provide total recreation service? Detail some of the programs cosponsored by the schools and the community.

7. What are some of the objectives of religious sponsorship of recreation services? Do you think religion has a place in recreation services?

8. Discuss some objectives of the White House Conference on Children.

9. What types of teen activities does your community provide? Briefly discuss programs, personnel, and attendance at community teen programs.

10. What are some of the objectives of a good camping program? What are some of the major types of camps?

11. What is meant by the term *therapeutic recreation?* Give some objectives of a hospital recreation program.

12. What is meant by the term *cultural recreation?* What types of cultural recreation programs are offered in your community?

SELECTED REFERENCES

"Armed Forces Recreation," *Parks and Recreation.* Vol. VI (August, 1971).

Batcheller, John, and Sally Monsour, *Music in Recreation and Leisure.* Dubuque, Iowa: Wm. C. Brown Co., 1972.

Breaking Through on the Lower East Side. New York: Urban Life Center, Henry Street Settlement.

Ebbeck, Frederick N., "Learning From Play in Other Cultures," *Childhood Education.* Vol. 48 (November, 1971).

Furlong, William Barry, "Our Kids Tell Us About Drugs," *Today's Health.* Vol. 49 (February, 1971).

Goodridge, Janet, *Creative Drama and Improvised Movement for Children.* Boston: Plays, Inc., 1971.

Herrold, Zadia, "School Recreation . . . Fact or Fiction," *Illinois Journal of Health, Physical Education and Recreation.* Vol. 1 (Winter, 1970).

Kraus, Richard, *Recreation Today.* New York: Appleton-Century-Crofts, 1966.

Levy, Joseph, "Recreation at the Crossroads," *Journal of Health, Physical Education, and Recreation* Vol. 42 (September, 1971).

Lutzin, *Making Teen Centers Succeed.* Albany: State of New York, Division for Youth, 1971.

Lynch, G. L., "Role of School as Recreation Centers," *American School and University.* Vol. 38 (July, 1966).

Pomeroy, Janet, *Recreation for Physically Handicapped.* New York: The Macmillan Company, 1970.

Reek, Jeanne, et. al., *Folk Dance and Lore of Norway.* Madison: Wisconsin House, 1971.

Staley, Edwin, ed., *Leisure and the Quality of Life.* Washington, D.C.: American Association for Health, Physical Education and Recreation, 1972.

part II
history and philosophy
of recreation

Chess in the park. Hempstead, New York. Photo courtesy of the Town of Hempstead Department of Parks and Recreation, Recreation Division.

4

CHANGING HISTORICAL
AND PHILOSOPHICAL
CONCEPTS OF RECREATION

Recreation has played a significant role in the life of man from the beginning of prehistoric times. This chapter traces the evolution of recreation, starting with primitive societies and concluding with contemporary developments. Interwoven with each historical period, the reader will find related recreational philosophies characteristic of the thinking prevalent at that time.

THE DEVELOPMENT OF RECREATION

In this chapter, one can see how recreational activities and philosophies developed throughout time. In the first part of this chapter, the reader will gain an awareness of the recreation movement, beginning with primitive man and proceeding to the earliest organized civilizations. Following this discussion, the Classical Age will be discussed. Then, the period known as the Middle Ages is discussed, followed by the significant contributions of the Renaissance. How recreation came to America and developed into its modern-day, organized form will be the subject of the remainder of this chapter.

Recreation during the prehistoric age was directly related to man's fight for survival. Cave paintings and drawings in early times depicted such forms of recreation as hunting, spearing, wrestling, and fishing. These activities were concerned with the mastering of skills necessary for man's survival. The differentiation between work and play was not always clear. Ancient people did not have the time or the necessity for inventing new outlets for their leisure time. They had time to reinforce only those skills directly related to survival in their challenging environment. These skills were basically utilitarian – for example, gardening, and herb collecting. Crude forms of art and music were developed at a later time, showing that the emphasis of recreation changed from labor to more pleasurable leisure pursuits.

Recreation during the early Egyptian and Mesopotamian civilizations was designed for the rich and ruling classes. With the advent of these civilizations, recreational activities were engaged in by the wealthy and ruling classes during their leisure time. The organization of stratified society allowed little time for any persons but the wealthy to participate in recreation. Since the Egyptian pharaoh was believed to be divine, the peasants and slaves were forced to devote their lives to pleasing their ruler. This life-style, which mainly involved work, left them little opportunity to engage in recreation. In contrast, the rich had opportunities to enjoy the cultural contributions of other civilizations. The invention and use of papyrus as a means of recording information encouraged the development of libraries for the rich. Of course, the rich and ruling classes also enjoyed other types of recreational activities, such as having their subjects entertain them in various acrobatic stunts as well as their own participation in hunting and other activities.

The ancient Greek civilization provided an opportunity for development of both mind and body. During this ancient period (2500 B.C.–500 B.C.), man's striving for intellectual improvement was considered to be an important form of recreation. There were, of course, other activities; for example, the Greek philosopher, Plato, was interested in the benefits of music and gymnastics. He believed there were spiritual and physical rewards to be gained from the pursuit of recreation. A milestone in the development of recreation was the inception of the Greek Games, which began from a religious motivation and were performed at regular intervals in honor of the gods. The Olympic, Nemean, and Isthmian Games, for example, served to unify the country through the means of athletic and other forms of competition, including such events as foot races, wrestling, chariot races, musical contests, recitations, and rowing. Equal importance was given to accomplishments in the intellectual fields.

Open-air amphitheaters were constructed where music, dance, and art festivals took place. Plato established the Academy for intellectual pursuits devoted to preserving a life of philosophic leisure. The cultural pursuits of the ancient Greek civilization emanated from here for many years.

Ancient Greek children played with many objects familiar to us today. These implements of recreation consisted of such equipment as marbles, hoops, and kites.

The ancient Romans did not adhere to the Greek concept of recreation. Opposed to the Greek concept of being "doers," many of the Romans were spectators. Those persons who participated in recreation events in ancient Rome were slaves and condemned political and religious prisoners. Recreational activities took place, for the most part, in the *Circus Maximus.* Many of these activities were destructive and barbaric, pitting man against man and man against beast. The *Ludi* or public games provided entertainment such as chariot racing, gymnastic contests, and military reviews.

The reasons for Roman spectator recreation was in order to fill the vast amount of leisure time of the unemployed masses. One explanation for this condition was the importation of cheaply produced foreign goods. The Roman tradesmen and farmers could not compete profitably with this type of market situation, so they lived on government doles, and most of their time was spent in the city attending the spectator events.

Early Roman civilization provided limited opportunities for active recreational participation. Roman *thermae,* or baths, afforded a medium for socializing and exercising, and various ball games were enjoyed within the bath houses. Physical activities took place in the *Campus Martius,* or parade grounds, which might be considered as the forerunner of modern parks and play fields. Participants included the aged, the young, and the physically handicapped.

Other forms of recreation in which the Roman populace engaged were gambling and cockfighting. Still another characteristic of the society at that time was the orgy, a function that promoted feasting and pleasure-seeking.

As can be seen, the balance was unequal between active and passive forms of ancient Roman recreation. For the most part, the life of leisure for the Roman was an inactive one based on satisfying his natural and instinctive drives. It was in sharp contrast to the ancient Greek philosophy in which the development of the intellect within a sound body was a primary concern.

During the Dark Ages recreation was at a low ebb. The church dominated the lives of its people during the Dark Ages, that period following the fall of Rome when the Teutonic barbarians overran the Roman Empire. The abstinence from worldly pleasures was the main goal of life during this period. The establishment of monasteries further maintained this philosophy of asceticism, in which the practice of adherence to the policies of self-denial was predominant. A main form of recreation for monastery monks was gardening, with their botanical knowledge being shared with the townspeople. In the early universities, formal recreation was not considered a part of the curriculum, and many students during their free time indulged themselves in drinking and gambling.

Recreation during the feudal period was primarily related to social class. During feudal times the amount of leisure available was directly related to social standing. The class system consisted of lords and nobles, peasants and serfs, and guildsmen and clergymen. The upper class of lords and noblemen enjoyed the most leisure time. During the period between battles, they were actively engaged in such activities as mock combat, with jousting and tournaments helping to develop their tactical skills. The ladies were occupied primarily with domestic activities, such as embroidering and household concerns, but were invited as spectators to watch the various tournaments. Within the upper class, the young men of wealth used their leisure time to perfect their talents in becoming chivalrous knights as well as in pursuing the arts. The young men were tutored in reading, singing, and playing musical instruments. This cultural emphasis was balanced by such physically active recreative pursuits as riding, use of weaponry, hawking, and armor care and handling — all of which prepared him for the demands of war.

The recreational activities of the peasants, such as the harvest dance, were related to their agricultural duties; in quarter-staff tilting, long wooden poles were carried by the peasants on horseback while they tried to upset their opponents from their mounts.

The serfs who tilled the manor's land engaged in such recreational pursuits as pageants, races, bowling, cockfighting, and archery contests. Such activities were performed out-of-doors, close to the source of their work.

The guildsmen or craftsmen were largely self-sufficient in their choice of vocation and recreation since they were not bound to the feudal master, but instead were independent workers. Their enjoyment of leisure and work was exemplified by the singing of work songs that served to stimulate accomplishment in their crafts. An important form of recreation that was instituted by the craftsmen was the development of the guild carts, mobile units that travelled throughout the city and brought mystery and miracle dramas to the towns-people.

The Church during the Middle Ages fostered cultural forms of recreation. Clergymen believed in involving themselves with esthetic forms of recreation. They were actively concerned with the religious forms of art, literature and drama, and usually frowned upon any open expressions of physical competency, including spectator sports, which the church felt were a misuse of time more profitably spent in following intellectual pursuits.

The Renaissance (fourteenth to sixteenth centuries) offered man the opportunity to achieve a balanced existence. This period of "rebirth" after the Middle Ages instituted, among other things, the revival of classical art and literature. Relating this concept to recreation, the Renaissance also reemphasized the Greek ideal of the unity of mind and body. During this period, the church was in favor of man finding happiness in his work as well as in his leisure. The Pope, in fact, considered recreation as a definite necessity in man's daily life.

Recreational activities varied in accordance with social class. Many wealthy families, who acquired vast fortunes from foreign trading, became patrons of artists and also enjoyed formal balls and banquet parties. They also spent part of their leisure hunting on game preserves and devoted many hours to spectator activities such as the opera, exhibitions, and the theater.

The middle class tried to imitate their wealthier counterparts by participating in less extravagant balls and festivities; they also enjoyed gardening and hunting. Children's play often stressed intellectual and creative activities, such as the studies of art, literature, science and music.

The Renaissance is also known for its humanistic approach toward society. The desire for knowledge and self-improvement included a recognition of the importance of recreation. The Renaissance philosophy exemplified in many ways the modern attitude toward recreation with its emphasis upon a balanced life. Vergerio stated in his treatise, *De Ingenious Moribus et Liberalis,* "man cannot give all his efforts to work alone." Recreational activities have a definite place as a part of man's normal existence.

Recreation in the Modern European period followed the American pattern. Although the philosophy of the Renaissance gave new impetus to the importance of recreation, many problems involving the work ethic, religious convictions, and the continuing demand on each person's time to engage in activities essential to subsistence delayed the development of recreation as a strong and dynamic profession.

Since the growth of recreation in Europe in modern times took some of its impetus from America, the historical and philosophical discussion in this chapter now focuses on the United States and some of the historical milestones that have occurred in this country to mark recreation's progress.

DEVELOPMENT OF RECREATION IN AMERICA

The first colonists in America faced a situation similar to the one that greeted primitive man. Life was a struggle for survival – one had to battle the elements as well as the wilderness. This fight to perpetuate the species left little time for recreation, and the early settlers enforced strict rules against idleness. The Puritan Ethic, as we have come to refer to it, stressed that idleness, nonproductive use of leisure time, was sinful. Settlers who did engage in recreational pursuits were made to feel guilty. This guilt complex did much to slow down, or even reverse, the forward trend of the recreation movement.

Recreational pursuits that were sanctioned included various "bees" where many families and friends would gather for purposes of house-building, corn-husking, and canning fruit. Quilting parties were also popular and functional as well as serving to stimulate the production of homespun clothing. The colonial period, as can be seen from these activities, stressed the productive use of leisure time.

The recreational pursuits of the pioneers differed from those of the Pilgrims. The hardy pioneer, like the Pilgrim, engaged in many communal work projects. However, unlike the Pilgrim, the pioneer would wrestle, dance, and play games following the completion of his work. On cold winter nights, he would often turn to drinking and gambling. These activities, plus others such as card playing and bear-baiting, resulted in more prohibitive laws and accompanying punishments.

Recreation following the Revolutionary War was a mixture of the simple and the brutal. The majority of the American population during the third quarter of the eighteenth century still lived on farms or in small communities. Recreation for these people consisted of outdoor activities such as hunting and fishing, and social gatherings such as country dancing and fairs. In contrast, the frontiersmen indulged in hunting of a more barbaric type, such as ring hunts, in which animals were surrounded by a ring of hunters and then gunned down; rifle marksmanship, log-rolling, gambling, and drinking bouts. British sailors are credited with introducing boxing and gouging – a man-to-man form of combat, in which biting and gouging the eyes of one's opponent were permitted. Another cruel activity prevalent during this period was gander-pulling, in which horsemen would try to pull off the greased head and neck of a live gander that was suspended from a tree.

The increase in reading material helped to counteract the church's influence concerning recreation. Until the nineteenth century, the church had opposed sports and recreation and equated idleness with sin. With the increased circulation and availability of newspapers and other reading material, however, the public could see and read for themselves the many forms of recreation open to them. As a result, many persons broke away from tradition-ridden taboos regarding the use of leisure time and assumed their own responsibility for their selection of recreational activities. Among these, minstrel shows, circuses, and amusement parks gained widespread acceptance. The change in emphasis from active to passive recreation, however, deprived many Americans of necessary physical activities.

Organized recreation received a great impetus from the Boston Sandgardens. Professionals largely agree that the recreation movement received its start with the establishment of the Boston Sandgardens in 1885. The concept was borrowed from the public parks in Berlin, where piles of sand were available for youngsters to play in. The Massachusetts Emergency and Hygiene Association started its experiment as a private project, using volunteers to supervise the activities. Later, paid matrons were used, and after that, teachers and other trained personnel were employed. From Boston, the playground idea grew and spread to such cities as Philadelphia, Milwaukee, Pittsburgh, Denver, Minneapolis, New York, Chicago, Providence, and Baltimore. Although the Sandgardens initially included only sandpiles for the children, in time they also incorporated play areas with various apparatus as well, so that older youngsters might be attracted to these recreational activities and locations.

Recreation for the poor and underprivileged was an historical phase of the recreation movement. In 1886, the Neighborhood Guild in New York City introduced the settlement-house movement. In 1889, Jane Addams established Hull House in Chicago, which later included land for the first model playground. Recreation programs in such play areas included apparatus, sports activities for older children, and supervised games of low organization.

The Industrial Revolution was significant to the recreation movement. With the coming into existence of factories, industrial expansion, the mass production of goods, and other allied developments, recreation was needed to provide for the increased leisure time that this mechanized age provided. America, as one of the great industrial nations of the world, found that its ability to turn out manufactured goods in great quantities not only made it a wealthy nation economically, but at the same time raised some social problems in regard to how its citizens should spend their free time after work.

The nineteenth century saw the beginnings of state and national preserves and park developments. The first state parks were established in California, New York, Michigan, Minnesota, and New Jersey during 1870-1890. The first state forest park was established in the Adirondack mountains in New York State on 800,000 acres in 1885. The advent of the automobile stimulated a growth in other than urban recreational facilities, and in order to meet the travel needs of people, more parks were opened.

The years between 1900 and 1914 contributed to the growth of community recreation. The first playground under the auspices of a municipal government was established in Los Angeles in 1904. The birth of the Playground and Recreation Association of America, later called the National Recreation Association, took place in 1906. Its purpose was to stimulate the organization of recreation and, among other accomplishments, it distributed information to the public concerning community recreation services.

Other significant community recreation organizations that were started included the Boy Scouts of America, The Camp Fire Girls, and the Girl Scouts of America. Private camps also flourished during this period, along with community camps.

Social and civic centers began to appear during these years. More recognition was given to children's needs for organized recreation. The thought that schools were used solely for education was changing; the public began to see the schools also as places for recreation.

GROWTH OF RECREATION
DURING THE WAR YEARS

Organized recreation played a vital role during World War I. The lack of fitness of draftees in World War I led the United States War Department in 1917 to request the Playground and Recreation Association to mobilize its resources into the War Camp Community Service. This organization initiated recreation programs in over 600 communities located near military centers and another fifty in strategic industrial centers, and clearly demonstrated the value of organized recreation to the community.

Following World War I, recreation increased in importance. In the decade following World War I, many new parks, community houses, swimming pools, beaches, golf courses, picnic areas, skating rinks, and bowling alleys were constructed. The public began to realize that a well-organized recreation program could accomplish much in the way of a better life-style for Americans. Concurrently, an emphasis on legislation for recreation was in evidence, and public appropriations for play facilities rose to almost thirty million by 1922. Furthermore, educational institutions joined the recreation movement by mandating compulsory physical education programs. Schools broadened their curricula to include intramurals along with hiking, winter sports, social affairs, and other recreational activities.

As the nation prospered, the recreational movement gained added momentum. The mass production of the automobile allowed the tourist industry to provide man with a mobile form of recreation as thousands of persons flocked to the movies and other places of entertainment to spend their leisure time.

Presidents of the United States also recognized the importance of recreation. In 1924, President Coolidge called the National Conference of Outdoor Recreation. Five years later, President Hoover's Research Committee on Social Trends gave special consideration to recreation as a use for leisure. These and other developments accented the need for trained leaders. In 1926, the National Recreation Association began a one-year graduate course designed specifically to train recreation leaders. The National Recreation School, as it was known, was principally responsible for educating recreation executives.

The Depression of the 1930s resulted in an increased emphasis on recreation. The modified workweek, shortened to give more jobs to more people, resulted in more leisure time for all. The depression resulted in a downturn in business and some commercial recreation programs had to be closed as a result. In light of the shortage of recreation programs, voluntary and community recreation agencies did the best that they could, but fell short of the demand. As a result, the national government, through its federal agencies, gave the recreation movement momentum by providing jobs for those persons who were out of work, by building new or refurbishing old recreation areas and facilities, and by providing monies for employing recreators to provide leadership for programs throughout the country. As a result of federal intervention, such agencies as the following contributed to the recreation needs of Americans: the Federal Emergency Relief Administration, the National Youth Administration (NYA), the Works Projects Administration (WPA), and the Civilian Conservation Corps (CCC). Among other things, these agencies gave people jobs and were responsible for building and improving such facilities as parks, picnic areas, roads, and trails. The WPA and the NYA also hired recreation leaders and held institutes for training both volunteers and recreation workers alike.

The WPA program was a "grass-roots" program aimed at increasing community involvement. Various works projects were developed in the field of community public recreation. Their objective was to stimulate mass recognition of, and action in, community recreation. The Works Projects Administration had previously concentrated on organized games and sports for children and youth. This was broadened to include an increased emphasis on, and participation in, a cultural program of esthetic and intellectual activities. Professional artists, whose areas of expertise included art, music, drama, and writing, were added to the recreation movement. An important feature of the WPA experiment was its attempt to develop a community or grass-roots leisure program by integrating physical activities, education, and art programs.

Recreational expansion as a result of federal assistance provided many new jobs and also resulted in many new and better facilities. WPA and Public Works Administration funds financed the construction of school sports facilities, swimming pools, tennis courts, and athletic fields. New positions were created, such as jobs as camp and community center personnel, craft specialists, swimming instructors, consultants, and plant, program, and facility managers.

Federal programs also made it possible for small as well as large communities to benefit from recreation programs. Facilities were built, personnel hired, and services provided in many of the nation's small counties, cities, towns, and villages.

The outdoor recreation movement gained momentum during the 1930s. Federal funds that financed state park and forest systems contributed to a sharp rise in state outdoor-recreation developments. Forty-six Recreation Demonstration areas, initiated under the National Park Service in 1936, were later turned over to federal and state agencies. The state's work in protecting and improving game resources was accompanied by an increase in the already popular outdoor sports of hunting and fishing. Private agencies added skiing to the selection of outdoor activities.

Colleges and universities recognized that recreators need special preparation. A conference concerned with the training of recreation leaders was held in 1937 and was sponsored by the University of Minnesota and the recreation division of the WPA. The impetus for this development had been given by the WPA and its leadership training program for supervisors, leaders, and lay personnel participating in its program. This program, and the techniques developed, influenced recreation methods and materials in thousands of communities.

With World War II came the realization that recreation was indispensable. The physical examinations undergone by draftees showed the poor physical condition of our population. Programs geared toward improving both physical and mental health of servicemen were undertaken by the USO, American Red Cross, Army Special Services Division, the Welfare and Recreation Section of the Bureau of Naval Personnel, and the Recreation Service of the Marine Corps. The objectives of these organizations included relieving war-induced tension, bolstering morale, and decreasing the psychological impact of the serviceman being separated from home. The worth of this work was demonstrated by the

Outdoor recreation includes a study of animal life. Photo courtesy of the Los Angeles City Schools, Youth Services Section.

The outdoor recreation movement has forged ahead in recent history creating the need for new centers to provide for this activity. Clear Creek Outdoor Education Center, Los Angeles. Photo courtesy of the Los Angeles City Schools, Youth Services Section.

increased efficiency of the fighting force, a program for the relaxation and diversion from work responsibilities for servicemen, and improvement of conditions for millions of Americans living in congested areas.

Three groups were outstanding in providing leisure-time activities during this war period. The first of these were groups that functioned under the auspices of the Armed Forces – the Army, Navy, Merchant Marine, and Red Cross. The Special Services Division of the United States Army was empowered to provide facilities, programs, and monies for the recreation of the soldiers. The Navy Welfare and Recreation Section offered personnel, facilities, equipment, and funds for recreation programs at sea and on the land. The United Seaman's Service was responsible for the Merchant Marine and served the men of the country's civilian fleet, which transported goods to the Armed Forces. The American Red Cross was officially requested by the War Department to provide recreational centers, posts, facilities, programs and other recreational opportunities for soldiers overseas.

The second group that contributed so importantly to the war-time recreation movement was the United Service Organization (USO). This agency was comprised of six divisions: the Jewish Welfare Board, the Salvation Army, Catholic Community Services, Young Men's Christian Association, Young Women's Christian Association, and the National Traveller's Aid. Its purposes were to service the leisure needs of the armed services in community settings and to provide recreation for industrial workers engaged in the war effort.

The Federal Security Agency also played a key role in the recreational programs that were developed during the second World War. This agency helped communities to initiate, organize, develop, and maintain recreation to meet the increasing demands of the war effort through such means as surveys, publicity, publications, and by providing the motivation and support for communities to initiate their own recreation services.

The contribution of recreation to a nation at war proved its worth during World War II. Since that time, it has also proved its worth in other confrontations that have developed, including the Vietnam War. It is a matter of historical record that the nation's servicemen and women have been helped enormously as a result of their participation in the recreation programs that were provided for their use during these national emergencies.

The momentum gained by the recreation movement during wartime was continued in peacetime. Those persons who had assumed wartime leadership roles in the recreation movement during World War II became advocates for new community recreation programs. Many cities had discovered, as a result of the war, the value and need for recreation programs. Also, millions of dollars worth of facilities built to meet wartime recreation needs were available for peacetime use. Furthermore, the extended evidence of recreation activity on the community level bore witness to the notion that recreation and leisure had become a national concern and necessity.

RECREATION IN MODERN AMERICA

From the middle of the twentieth century until the present, the American people have seen many changes take place as a result of the emphasis on recreation. Some of these changes and meanings will be discussed here.

Leisure pursuits of Americans have changed. During the period from 1955 to 1960 alone, one-twelfth of the total income was spent on recreation activities. The public during these years showed a renewed interest in actively participating in such activities as tennis, bowling, and golf. In fact, money spent in active sports participation far exceeded expenditures for spectator sports during this five-year period. Today, Americans are actively engaged in a diversity of recreational activities. Outdoor activities in particular, and especially water-based activities, are very popular.

The federal government has promoted outdoor interests. The National Park Service initiated a long-term project, designated "Mission 66," to further extend the offerings of the national park system. In 1956, Congress requested that the Forest Service survey recreation use and needs, which opened the way for Operation Outdoors, a program designed to rehabilitate national forests. In 1958, Washington was the scene of the first national conference to research the matter of outdoor education. Also, during this same year Congress created the Outdoor Recreation Resources Review Commission, whose three-year survey led to the establishment of the Bureau of Outdoor Recreation in the Department of the Interior in 1962. In 1960, state park attendance figures had reached nearly 260 million. Recreation activities today include all types of pursuits, ranging from bicycling along wooded trails to arts and crafts, scuba diving, and camping. Chapter 8 of this book will discuss these activities in greater detail.

Recreation is concerned with mental and physical fitness. The Kraus-Weber tests, which measured muscular strength and flexibility of American as well as European children, indicated that this nation's youngsters were weak by comparison. This revelation initiated a vast national fitness program in which the nation's recreation programs have actively participated. The interrelationship between mental and physical health was recognized in the Washington Conference on Recreation for the Mentally Ill, sponsored by the American Association for Health, Physical Education and Recreation in 1957. In 1961, a conference to explore curriculum needs in therapeutic recreation showed that the concern for mental fitness within the context of recreation programs was an important consideration.

Recreation has played a key role in providing for the mental and physical fitness of Americans. The President's Council on Physical Fitness and Sports and hospitals and mental health agencies have all worked closely with recreation to integrate the programs offered.

The needs of youth are a major concern of the recreation movement. The

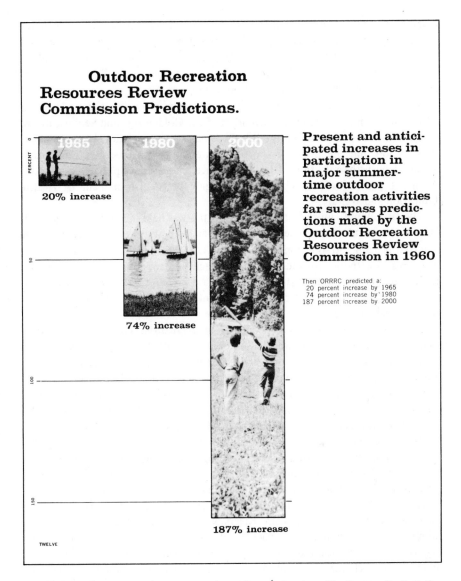

Outdoor Recreation Resources Review Commission Predictions.

20% increase

74% increase

187% increase

Present and anticipated increases in participation in major summertime outdoor recreation activities far surpass predictions made by the Outdoor Recreation Resources Review Commission in 1960

Then ORRRC predicted a:
20 percent increase by 1965
74 percent increase by 1980
187 percent increase by 2000

The Federal Government has promoted outdoor interests with the result that the predictions for outdoor recreation in the future is great. From *Outdoor Recreation Trends*, Department of the Interior, Bureau of Outdoor Recreation, Washington, D.C., April, 1967.

first conference to study the needs of the nation's youth was held in 1909. The 1960 golden anniversary conference had as its theme, "For each child an opportunity for a creative life in freedom and dignity." More than 7,000 people attended this conference. Recommendations were made relating to health, religion, education, and related topics. Some of the recommendations included community program development, encouragement of leisure-time reading, greater stress on the arts, and an increased effort to research the value of recreation. From these beginnings, the recreation movement has continued to emphasize the needs of children and young people.

Recreation programs for the aged are receiving attention today. The year 1960 saw the Fourth Annual Convention of the Golden Age and Senior Citizens in New Orleans. Subsequently, this became a formal national organization. Recognition that the needs of the older population must be met was further accented with the selection of Dr. Donald Kent to be the Special Assistant for Aging as part of the special staff on aging in the Department of Health, Education and Welfare.

The first White House Conference on Aging was held in Washington in 1961. Prior to this conference, federal grants had enabled states to conduct their own studies on aging. At the conference some 3,000 delegates recommended more programs of activities for the aging, better facilities, cooperative planning, better leadership, more research, and more adequate preparation for retirement. This concern for the nation's older population continues to have a high priority in the nation's recreation programs.

The cultural explosion had its impact on recreation. The National Cultural Center for Performing Arts was made possible by a 1958 congressional act. The center was situated on a ten-acre site on the Potomac River in Washington, D.C. Joseph Prendergast, Executive Secretary for the National Recreation Association, was appointed by President Eisenhower and served on the advisory committee for this center. In 1962, the opening of the Lincoln Center in New York also evidenced the increased attention being given to cultural interests.

The increased national interest in music, art, concerts, exhibitions, and other cultural interests is affecting recreation. Programs are including specialists in the various arts, additional appropriations are being made for this purpose, and programs are allocating more time and leadership for these activities.

Recreation is international in scope. In 1956, the International Recreation Association was founded. Tom Rivers was appointed Director General to administer the international phase of the world recreation movement. Also significant was the beginning of the first International Cooperative Community Recreation Exchange, wherein America exchanged recreation personnel with foreign countries.

Recreation extends its influence into the religious sphere. The first National Workshop in Recreation for Leaders in Religious Organizations was sponsored by the Indiana University Department of Recreation in 1952, with the purpose of clarifying a recreation philosophy for members of all faiths. Recreation programs as part of churches and religious agencies have continued to grow. In contrast to the opposition recreation received from the church in the Dark Ages, today it is recognized that recreation can play a very important role in the total offering of religious agencies.

States join forces to meet recreational needs of their citizens and visitors. On April 1, 1969, the states of Vermont and New Hampshire signed a Plan of Cooperation whereby the recreational services of each state are to work cooperatively. This is the first such formal agreement between the recreation services in two states, and it is expected to develop into a trend throughout the country as the demand for recreation services increase. The Vermont-New Hampshire plan of cooperation calls for an interchange of publications, discussions between state directors of recreation, and leadership training programs in recreation.

Federal government attempts to preserve and improve the beauty of America. The national government recognizes that our technology is rapidly swallowing up areas of natural beauty and therefore is taking the necessary measures to preserve our environment. Among some of its accomplishments are planning land acquisition for conservation purposes, conducting research, preserving wildlife, retaining and improving scenic and historical sites, improving water and waterways, and controlling pollution of streams and rivers. More detailed information on this subject is discussed in Chapter 5 under "Recreation and the Environment."

Community-school cooperation helps administration of recreation programs. Two examples of such cooperation exist in Flint, Michigan and Los Angeles, California. In Flint, Michigan, as a result of the philanthropy of Charles Stewart Mott and the Mott Foundation, recreation programs exist in the schools, which bring together people of all backgrounds. The program includes recreational activities from roller skating to an international program that involves approximately 1,000 athletes and their families in both Flint, Michigan, and Hamilton, Canada. In Los Angeles, the city school district, through its Youth Services Section, sponsors a program in which millions of people participate each year. More than 550 recreation sites are used and more than 4,000 full-time and part-time personnel are involved in the leadership phase of the program.

The National Recreation and Park Association gives leadership to recreation. This new association combines the efforts of the leading recreation and park people in furthering recreation in America. Concerned with both natural and man-made beauty in America and the human environment, it is attempting to help Americans have a better and healthier place in which to live, work, and enjoy their leisure. Its goal is to provide good parks and playgrounds and to instill the need for proper use of land and water.

The future of recreation depends on meeting certain challenges and priorities. One problem faced by recreation today is in the area of ecology — that balance between nature's resources and our technological production. Our beaches, for example, are being eroded and polluted. The dumping of industrial wastes, oil-tank spills, and improper care may mean that these beaches will cease to exist for recreation purposes unless certain controls are established. Other aspects of the environment also must be cared for, as discussed in Chapter Five.

There must be more efficient use of available recreation resources. One area that requires attention is that of vandalism. In New York City alone, more than two million cases of vandalism are reported annually. This concern for vandalism was pointed out by Richard M. Clurman, who was sworn in as Parks, Recreation and Cultural Affairs Administrative Commissioner of Parks on January 4, 1973. Mr. Clurman said that if areas need to be constantly rebuilt because of destructiveness, the maintenance forces will be selectively withdrawn. He went on to say that if the public wishes to remain apathetic, certain areas will remain neglected.

Recreation is needed at all socioeconomic levels of the population. An urgent need at present is among the ghetto and slum-dwelling segments of the nation. One place where they are trying to meet this need is New York City. An example of what they are trying to do is the initiation of a mobile program in which vans go into underprivileged areas with arts-and-crafts equipment, marionettes and puppets, roller skates, weights, volleyballs, trampolines, rock bands, animals and other equipment and materials, and supply the youngsters with recreational experiences they had not had previously. Another innovation is the closing off of streets and other designated areas from traffic and congestion so as to provide a recreation program for the inhabitants during specified times.

Increased attention must be given to the recreational needs of the handicapped. For too long, the atypical individual has been neglected in the recreational scheme of things. They, too, must receive meaningful experiences in recreation to assure their harmonious growth as human beings. The need for specialists in this area has never been greater than at present.

Space-age technology forecasts a need for recreation. As astronauts are confined for increasingly longer periods of time in their space capsules and space platforms, recreation assumes greater importance. Recreation must accept the challenge of providing vital sensory stimulation and mental diversion from long hours in space when common earth-noises, such as birds chirping, winds rustling, or children shouting, are absent. Recreation is also important for the increased physical challenges that space travel necessitates.

QUESTIONS AND EXERCISES

1. Trace the history of recreation from ancient times to the discovery of America.
2. Compare the kinds of recreational activities you engaged in today with the type engaged in by early man.
3. List and discuss five problems that affect the growth of recreation today. Why are they problems and what solutions do you propose for solving them?
4. Research the growth and development of recreation in your own community and prepare a report on your findings.

5. Identify what you consider to be five key milestones responsible for the growth of recreation as a dynamic profession. Justify your answer.

6. Compare the growth of recreation in Europe with that of America.

7. How did the economic depression of the 1930s in the United States contribute to the growth of recreation?

8. Interview representatives of the armed services and determine the contribution that recreation makes to the life of a serviceman or a servicewoman.

9. What contribution did recreation make to our fighting man in the late Vietnam War?

10. What should be the role of recreation in the ghetto areas of our large cities? Plan a recreation program that you feel would interest and benefit the youth of the inner city.

SELECTED REFERENCES

Carlson, R. E., et. al., *Recreation in American Life.* Belmont, Calif.: Wadsworth Publishing Co., 1972.

de Grazia, Sebastian, *Of Time, Work and Leisure.* New York: The Twentieth Century Fund, 1962.

Doell, Charles E., and Gerald B. Fitzgerald, *A Brief History of Parks and Recreation in the United States.* Chicago: The Athletic Institute, 1954.

Dulles, Foster Rhea, *A History of Recreation.* New York: Appleton-Century-Crofts, 1965.

Kraus, Richard, *Recreation and Leisure in Modern Society.* New York: Appleton-Century-Crofts, 1971.

National Recreation and Park Association, *Parks and Recreation Magazine,* all issues.

President's Council on Youth Fitness, *Physical Fitness Elements of Recreation: Suggestions for Community Programs.* Washington, D.C.: U.S. Government Printing Office, 1962.

Report to the President and Congress by the Outdoor Recreation Resources Review Commission, *Outdoor Recreation in America.* Washington, D.C.: U.S. Government Printing Office, 1962.

Van Dalen, Deobold B. and Bruce L. Bennett, *A World History of Physical Education.* Englewood Cliffs, N.J.: Prentice-Hall, Inc., 1971.

5

RECREATION

AND THE ENVIRONMENT

According to Webster, the word *environ* refers to those elements that surround or encircle. Therefore, the word *environment* refers to "the aggregate of all the external conditions and influences affecting the life and development of an organism." It includes the atmosphere and the air we breathe, the water we drink, the land in which we grow our crops, as well as the sounds from planes and automobiles that grate upon our ears day and night. In addition, the environment involves human beings and any other living thing or part of nature that inhabits the earth. Finally, the environment, besides including those realities that surround us, also relates to such problems as malnutrition and infection that continue to plague mankind, as well as chemical pollution and increased mechanization that are causing so much concern in our own country.

MAN AND HIS ENVIRONMENT

Man has adapted the environment to meet his own needs. Ever since the beginning of time, the environment has been adapted for the purposes and needs of mankind. When the first crude hut was built for shelter, the first coat made for protection, and the first fire kindled to provide warmth, the environment was being adapted for the purposes of human survival. As people have multiplied on the earth and as the industrial revolution has taken place, environments have been altered on a much larger scale. Forests have been felled to make way for highways, wild land brought under cultivation to raise crops, marshes drained to build cities, and the air filled with atomic particles to develop military power.

Man, while shaping the environment to suit his own needs and purposes, unfortunately, did not see the full consequences of his action. He failed to realize that many of his actions were wastefully exhausting valuable national resources, killing wildlife, making the atmosphere dangerous to breathe, and poisoning the water that is necessary for life. Furthermore – a matter of great importance to the student of recreation – man could not fully realize that his actions were destroying or restricting the way in which he could use the environment to spend the many leisure hours that had increased as a result of industrial progress.

There is a reciprocal influence between man and his environment. Ever since the time of Herodotus, a Greek historian called the "father of history," profound thinkers have noted a close interrelationship between man and his environment. In recent years the word *ecology* has achieved popular usage in our vocabulary. Ecology, the mutual relationships between organisms and their environment, is of great concern to man today because it shows that physical, biological, and social forces acting on human beings give direction to their development. In the final analysis, ecology determines to a large degree what man actually is and becomes.

Environment is now a public concern. Concern for the environment has taken on an added dimension since the start of the last decade. Public responsibility for the environment is readily seen in the interest that now exists, not only on the part of the government, but also on the part of the average citizen. In addition, the "teach-ins" in colleges and universities, the "earth days" that are scheduled, and the books and articles that are written on the subject, show further interest in the environment. Indeed, today the environment is looked upon as a national public responsibility and everybody's business.

Recreation has a major stake in the environment. Interest in the environment has also been voiced by recreation leaders throughout the nation. Play and recreation represent a genuine human need; in order to satisfy this need, usable parks, rivers, streams, coastlines, lakes, mountains, and playgrounds are needed. The increase in activities in which the American people desire to spend their increased leisure hours means a greater use of present natural resources, as well as the need to set aside additional resources for future programs. Recreation, therefore, has a large stake in the environment. It also follows that any student considering recreation as a career must clearly understand the important role of the environment in recreation, and, in addition, must help preserve a quality environment that will be conducive to the best interests of man.

THE PRINCIPAL COMPONENTS OF THE ENVIRONMENT

Three aspects of the environment, namely, air, land, and water, will be considered in order to show more directly what is happening to the environment, and, in turn, the implications of environmental changes for recreation.

The air we breathe is essential to life – as well to recreation. Air is an invisible, odorless, and tasteless mixture of gases that surrounds the earth and all living creatures. It is composed of nitrogen, oxygen, a small amount of carbon dioxide and traces of other gases. The air in its pure state also contains varying amounts of water vapor.

The atmosphere is several hundred miles in depth and represents the entire mass of air surrounding the earth. Most of the total air mass is concentrated in a layer some twelve miles thick around the earth's crust. As the distance from earth increases, the air gradually decreases in density and finally merges into empty space.

Man needs to take air into his lungs and extract the available oxygen in order to live. Lack of oxygen, even for a few seconds, means death. Man not only needs pure air to breathe, he also needs clean air for other reasons. Impure air such as "smog," can, for example, affect his comfort, his eyesight, as well as the very homeostatic balance or steady state of his health. One of the dangers of mining, for instance, is that sometimes men become trapped below the earth's surface where clean air is unavailable and as a result these workers lose their lives. In a similar way, but on a much larger scale, when the earth's atmosphere becomes polluted with coal burning, automobile exhausts, or atomic particles, it can have a damaging effect on man's welfare. It can cause disease, discomfort, and death, just as readily as coal gas causes these maladies below the earth's surface.

Since recreation is closely tied in with man's welfare, it depends largely on a clean atmosphere. Man needs clean air so that he can safely enjoy his many recreational pursuits, so that he can enjoy nature's resources to the fullest, so that wildlife, including birds, fish and animals, can exist, reproduce, and continue to be a valuable part of this nation's heritage, and also so that outdoor recreation activities will continue to contribute to his health and welfare.

Land is a chief source of food and of recreational benefits. Land is the solid part of the surface of the earth, the ground or soil furnished by nature. Land is the wealth of any nation. It is where the crops are grown, the forests exist, and the minerals are buried. The soil resources of the United States are bountiful and rich and the envy of the rest of the world. They are so extensive that a small number of farmers have used only sixty percent of the arable land to give most American people a high-quality diet, and still export millions of tons of food to other peoples of the world.

With such great expanses of land and rich harvests, it is easy for Americans to become complacent about this important resource. This apathy should not exist for long, however, when one realizes that millions of acres of land are being bulldozed each year; parcels of the best farm land are being replaced by highways. Of great importance to recreators is that much land that provides excellent sites for recreation is being eliminated by an industrialized and materialistic society.

Recreation has a stake in the preservation of land resources. There is a need not only to better care for crop land in order to prevent erosion, eliminate harmful pesticides and fertilizers, and to control dust storms and wind damage, but also there is a need to set aside more land for better outdoor living, such as more playgrounds and recreational areas, wildlife refuges, and national parks.

Human beings are dependent upon water for personal, industrial, and recreational purposes. Sea gulls patrol this quaint South Carolina harbor waiting for a handout. Fishing boats along the coast bring restaurants their daily supply of fresh fish. Photo courtesy of South Carolina Department of Parks, Recreation, and Tourism.

Humans depend on water for personal, industrial, and recreational purposes. As is well known, water is the liquid that comes down from the clouds in the form of rain and the substance that forms rivers, streams, lakes, and seas. Man uses water to drink, as a cleansing agent, and for sanitary purposes. Industry relies on water to produce power, transport goods, and to dispose of wastes. Recreation depends on water for many activities, including boating, fishing, and swimming. Water-based activities are one of recreation's most popular attractions.

Water, pure water, is essential to man. The water that is used today is the only water that will be available for the years to come. According to the U.S. Department of Interior, there will be no more water tomorrow than there is today. Therefore, it must be used over and over again and be kept free of contamination. What man does with this valuable resource will determine the degree and amount of usable water future generations will have.

Although there are ample amounts of water — it covers seventy percent of the earth's surface — this fact is based on the assumption that it does not become polluted and continues to be usable by mankind. Unfortunately, the world's water is becoming contaminated. Barry Commoner, well-known environmentalist, points out that contamination has caused the oxygen content of water samples to drop from 2.5 ccs per liter in 1900 to 0.1 cc today. This represents a threat to the life that exists in water as well as to human life. Highly industrialized nations like the United States are responsible for much of the pollution, with the result that the nation's and the world's water is in danger, thus having grave implications not only for recreation, but also, for our personal and industrial welfare.

IMPORTANCE OF
A QUALITY ENVIRONMENT TO MAN

A quality environment is a must for man if he is to continue to enjoy the mode of living to which he has been accustomed. This is true for several reasons.

A quality environment is essential since man is in constant interaction with his environment. Ecology tells us that organisms are constantly interacting with their environments and that this interaction must be kept in proper balance. In other words, the steady or homeostatic state must exist. If not, disruption and damage occur. For example, fish in a pond depend on their environment for their existence. They must receive adequate oxygen from the water. As vegetation and vegetable debris build up at the bottom of the pond, these may absorb oxygen, reducing the oxygen content of the water. If there is a natural flow of water into or out of the pond, changes in this flow will change the ecology of the pond as well; and if life forms in the pond change as a result of pollution, the pond itself will change. Constant interaction of various aspects of the environment may result in disequilibrium or a failure to maintain the steady state, causing disruption and even death.

Just as the fish in the pond depend on various aspects of their environment, so mankind depends on its environment. To live a happy, healthy, and productive existence requires that the various environments be kept in proper balance. They must maintain the steady state for a healthful existence.

A French political philosopher once observed when he visited the United States during its early history that the American people possessed vigor and their country had a wealth of inviting streams, beautiful forests and plains, and clear skies. He pointed out, as though he could see into the future of this country, that such a nation would not likely perish for lack of strength or insufficient resources, but that it could very well fall if its strength were misdirected or its resources abused.

A quality environment is essential since it affects man's physical and mental state. Problems of health, poverty, and nutrition can be traced to environmental influences. The fact that many people enjoy better health today than did previous generations is largely due to a better understanding of the relationship between man and his environment. For example, today we know better how to combat disease, protect against the extremes of temperature, and supply the nutritional elements that our bodies need. Under such conditions, an optimum state of physical and mental fitness exists.

The study of ecology has revealed that the various physical, biological, and sociological forces interacting with man help to mold his nature for better or for worse. Unfortunately, our complex industrial society has now reached the point where it is creating many unstable ecological situations. The present dangers caused by the pollution of man's environment produce a risk that may alter man's life to the extent that his physical and mental states are adversely affected. Smog, for instance, is resulting in some respiratory ailments, and too much noise is affecting the mental state of some people. The only answer to the dilemma is to curb pollution and ensure a quality environment.

A quality environment is essential for man's very survival. In order to live, man must have an adequate supply of clean air that will provide him with sufficient oxygen for his life process. The food he eats must meet satisfactory nutritional requirements. The water supply must be sufficient so that there is enough to drink, to bathe in, and to care for other bodily needs. Other requirements must also be met. Unless man's biological and psychological mechanisms can keep up with the pace of the times, all mankind will suffer. Life itself depends on a quality environment.

PRESENT AND FUTURE IMPORTANCE
OF THE ENVIRONMENT TO RECREATION

Without the many resources that a quality environment provides, recreation will take on a form different than what we know today.

Recreation has a major stake in the environment. Swimming, hiking, camping, outdoor photography, skiing, and golf, are just a few of the recreational activities that depend on the environment. Enjoying a walk through the woods, experiencing the serenity of a placid lake, witnessing the beauty of a range of mountains, and participating in other recreational experiences, have been sources of great pleasure to man over the years. The environment provides the open spaces necessary for hunting, the wooded areas and forests conducive to relaxation, and the sites necessary for family picnics and barbecues. The continuance of such recreational activities depends on an environment that provides suitable settings for these experiences.

Recreation must consider the environment in planning for the future. The population growth, increased speed and efficiency of transportation, higher family incomes, technological advances, and increased leisure time mean that

Recreation has a major stake in the environment. Water and beaches represent a very valuable resource. Hunting Island State Park, South Carolina. The park offers camping and recreational facilities, rental cabins, a nature trail and excellent shell hunting in a subtropical island setting. Photo courtesy of South Carolina Department of Parks, Recreation, and Tourism.

more environmental resources will be needed for recreational facilities. America, as one of the most affluent nations in the world, has been blessed with an abundance of natural recreational resources. However, extending the nation's frontiers and achieving a high industrial output has taken its toll. The time has come when steps must be taken to preserve the land's beauty and rustic character for its recreational and aesthetic values. The great surge of interest in skiing as a recreational pursuit and the great number of people who visit beaches and shorelines to surf, fish, scuba and skin dive, water ski, and operate power-boats and outriggers necessitate the setting aside of facilities and resources to provide for these popular pastimes. When a person realizes there are approximately 100 million swimmers, fifty-seven million fishermen, fifty-two million boaters, six million canoeists and five million sailors in our midst at the present time and that this number is constantly growing, the need for additional resources is very much in evidence. Projections for the number of participants in major water-based recreation activities indicate an increase of as much as sixty-five percent by 1980 and about 190 percent by the year 2000. As an example, by 1980, the Bureau of Outdoor Recreation of the Federal government estimates there will be 170 million swimmers alone.

ENVIRONMENTAL DAMAGE AND POLLUTION

Pollution may be defined as the presence of harmful substances that exist in undesirable amounts. It is a danger to our health and limits the use of our environment.

Americans are polluting their environment. They throw away one million old cars, forty-eight billion cans, twenty-six million bottles, four million tons of plastic, and fifty-eight million tons of paper in a typical year. This is only part of the pollution picture. In addition, land space is rapidly vanishing, lakes and rivers are filled with wastes, and beaches and coastlines are polluted with garbage and oil. And, there is still more pollution. The increase in "No Swimming – Water Contaminated" signs is alarming. The presence of smog over the skies of our larger cities results in such radio and TV pronouncements as : "Air Conditions Unsatisfactory."

Fish and wildlife have not escaped the contaminating influence and as a result some species are becoming extinct. Yet, automobiles and factories continue to spew their gases into the air. Radioactive fallout is present in the atmosphere. Insecticides, aerosol sprays, and some fertilizers are causing damage. Noise is increasing at an unabated rate.

In order to paint a complete picture of the extent of pollution in this country, air pollution, land damage and pollution, and water pollution will be separately discussed.

AIR POLLUTION IS THE NUMBER ONE
ENVIRONMENTAL PROBLEM

Coal burning industries and the automobile are two of the main sources of air pollution. Sulphur oxide particles from factories damage human lungs, carbon monoxide and hydrocarbons from automobiles slow reactions and damage the heart, nitrogen oxides from high-temperature combustion engines and furnaces increase the susceptibility to influenza, and photochemical oxidants from motors irritate eyes and increase asthma attacks. The result is damage to human health. There are also changes in respect to sunlight and climate. Cities create thermal mountains, making cities warmer and wetter. LaPorte, Indiana, for example, which is downwind from the Chicago steel mills, has had increases in rain and snow.

Governmental estimates point out that dirty air costs each person in the United States eighty dollars per year in terms of damage to human health, residential property, materials, and vegetation. The grand total cost is 16.1 billion dollars each year.

When health, sunlight, and climate are affected adversely, recreation also feels the pain. Participation in activities in the out-of-doors is reduced because some people feel that under such polluted conditions their health is in danger. Pollution also affects the activities in which a person engages, the degree of safety in participating in these activities, as well as the enjoyment accruing from them. Driving, for example, is an popular form of recreation and necessary in getting to outdoor recreation settings; yet, carbon monoxide makes driving dangerous. A day of breathing ten parts per million of this gas dulls mental performance, slows reactions, and makes people more accident prone. In heavy traffic, concentrations of seventy to 100 parts per million are frequent.

Noise pollution of the air affects man's physical, mental, and social welfare. An article in a recent popular magazine stated that Americans live in the noisiest country on earth and that noise pollution is as detrimental to the environment as excessive amounts of carbon monoxide. Motor vehicles represent a major source of noise production, with construction running a close second.

Urban noise is doubling every ten years. An estimated thirteen million Americans live near an airport and consequently suffer from the roar of jet engines. Seventeen million Americans work in dangerously noisy occupations. One hundred fifty million Americans in urban and suburban areas are exposed to excessive noise each day that degrades their quality of living.

Noise pollution is detrimental to one's health and hearing. Forty-three rock musicians with an average age of twenty-two were tested by Dr. Rayford C. Reddell of the San Francisco Hearing and Speech Center. He found that twenty percent of them had the hearing of seventy-year-old men. Young people who listen to these concerts face the same hazards. Sound levels at rock concerts and discotheques have been measured up to 130 decibels, equal to the roar of a jet fighter's engine. Another example of the toll that noise pollution takes is the number of man-hours lost because employees stay home, take sick leave, or even quit their jobs where such conditions exist.

Recreation should be concerned with noise pollution. Since one of the objectives of recreation is improved health, activities that are detrimental to one's hearing and health should be discouraged. Furthermore, the setting for recreation activities should be such that participants, at least during their leisure hours, may enjoy freedom from excessive noise.

LAND DAMAGE AND POLLUTION

The concentration of population in urban areas represents a challenge to man. Americans are crowding into urban centers as a place to live. The U.S. Census shows that one-half of our people live within fifty miles of the West and East Coasts. Furthermore, although the United States has only fifty-eight people per square mile, seven out of ten of them are living on two percent of the land. About one-half of the nation's counties lost population during the past decade – a further indication the trend is continuing. Such overcrowding breeds crime, results in substandard housing, fosters poor schools and drug abuse, and raises a question about suitable recreational activities.

A major challenge faced by such concentrations of population is the need to provide adequate recreation programs for the multitudes that inhabit these areas. The need for creative thinking is important since programs must be planned and carried out without the large expanses of land that rural and other areas have available to them. Model-city programs and urban development in the future must take into consideration the recreational, as well as housing, educational, and other needs of the people who live in these places.

Land use and pollution represent a threat to wildlife. Birds and animals are struggling to survive amidst the pollution that exists from coast to coast. About 100 species are gradually becoming extinct. New York's official state bird, the bluebird, and Louisiana's state bird, the brown pelican, are very few in number. Birds of prey like hawks, eagles, and ospreys are declining at rates as high as twenty percent per year.

DDT is destroying the egg-shell quality of many species. Poisoning kills coyotes and other predators. Mercury has been found in pheasants, ducks and other game birds, as well as swordfish, tuna, and other fish. Thousands of sea otters were killed in the waters off Amchitka Island in the Aleutians following a nuclear test blast. Lake Michigan beaches have noted a decline of sea gulls – one explanation, the heavy use of DDT and other chemical substances. One writer explains, "Washed down from the cherry orchards by rain, those long-lived pesticides have entered the lake's food chain. When gulls eat fish, they also take in a concentrated dose of poison. As a result, they lay eggs with such thin shells that most of them do not hatch."

Even the wild horses are in trouble. There were millions of these animals in 1900 but now, only about 16,000 wild horses barely subsist in arid brush country in ten Western states. A major reason for the decreasing numbers is that they are being slaughtered as a source of pet food. Thankfully, ecologists and conservationists are helping to bring a halt to such meaningless killing.

Mankind, as a result of doubling the population every fifty or sixty years, together with modern industrial development, has proved a menace to wildlife. The expansion of cities, the construction of electric power dams, the unbridled use of poisonous chemicals in agriculture and industry, the cutting down of wide stretches of forests, and the millions of people who go into wildlife territory seeking to enjoy nature have imposed heavy pressures on the nation's wild birds and animals. There is a need for better wildlife management and for parks and sanctuaries. There is a need to protect the rights of wildlife since they represent a valuable national resource.

PROBLEMS OF WATER POLLUTION

The three principal sources of water pollution are municipal, industrial, and agricultural wastes. Advances in technology and expansion of cities that are already too large have resulted in the pollution of rivers and lakes. The lack of adequate sewage treatment facilities in many cities is a major contributor. In some communities, domestic wastes, such as human wastes, detergents, and household greases have not been disposed of adequately. The result of such inadequacies is reflected in a survey of a cross section of 969 cities, which showed that in forty percent of them the water was inferior in quality and in nine percent of them it had reached the stage of being dangerous.

Industrial wastes abound in each state, contributing, according to government figures, sixty-five percent of the water pollution in this country. Municipalities, on the other hand, contribute twenty percent, and agriculture contributes an additional fifteen percent.

Industry frequently discharges its waste products directly into lakes and rivers. Some industries need large amounts of water as part of their processing and cooling production-processes. When the water is returned to the streams it is warmer than before, with the result that more dissolved oxygen is needed to decompose the waste. Chemical wastes and toxic agents from factories have also been found in rivers and other bodies of water. Tankers transport petroleum across the seas. Oil spillage has ruined beaches, killed wildlife, prevented swimming and damaged the landscape in many parts of this country, as well as in other parts of the world. The technological progress in this country has created many polluting conditions that may get worse before they get better.

Agriculture, with its animal wastes, eroded soil, fertilizers and pesticides, contributes to water pollution. Furthermore, where improper farming procedures have been used, such as when trees have been removed carelessly, the result has been that soil erodes and waters thereby become polluted.

Recreation is deeply affected by water pollution. In such pursuits as scuba and skin diving, boating and other water activities, pollution has resulted in participation being curtailed. French undersea explorer, Jacques Costeau, who has been close to the sea for many years, points out that approximately thirty years ago he could see underwater for about 300 feet, but today, he says, the visibility has shrunk to 100 feet. Costeau also estimates that fish and plant life in the seas have declined some thirty percent to fifty percent in the last twenty years.

Fishing is an important recreational activity, yet toxic materials are a growing worry to fisherman, particularly lead and mercury. The amount of mercury in fish is expected to rise because more microorganisms are being produced by increased wastes, mainly from industry and agriculture. The microorganisms move up the food chain into fish, and man eats the fish. Heavy doses of mercury can result in nervous-system damage, even death. Lead, long a factor in urban air pollution, has now been found in the oceans.

Another concern to recreation is the threatened coastlines of America. Much of the U.S. coastline is being spoiled by pollutants. The Department of Interior reports severe to moderate modification of seventy-three percent of the 53,677 miles of U.S. tidal shoreline. Between 1950 and 1969, nearly 650,000 acres were lost to dredging and filling alone. According to the natural estuary study compiled by the Interior Department, more than one-fourth of the 1,400,000 acres designated as shellfish areas is polluted. An example of the pollution is New England's beautiful shoreline, which is caught between population and industry, and whose effluents are fouling the water with untreated sewage and industrial wastes, creating sludge beds and a reduction of oxygen levels of the water. New York City's coastline, largely because of overpopulation and the resultant uncontrolled runoff of sewage, has resulted in forty percent of the harbor bottom being covered with sludge. Miami Beach and North Miami, Florida, send out more than fifty million tons of untreated sewage each day, resulting in a shore line that the Floridians call, because of the smell, "The Rose Bowl." The 3,350-mile tidal shoreline of Texas is dotted with oil refineries and chemical plants that cause industrial pollution on a wide scale.

ACTION TOWARD SOLUTION
OF ENVIRONMENTAL POLLUTION

Many steps must be taken if the pollution of the environment is to be held in check. First, there must be preventive action now rather than waiting and trying to repair the damage after it has occurred. Furthermore, where preventive measures have not been applied over the years, we must now use the means of cure. This means massive amounts of money must be spent, many pollution-abatement laws must be passed, and a total national commitment for action must be made. Walter J. Hickel, former Secretary of the Interior, points out that we must follow new principles of living, such as the following:

1. The right to produce is not the right to pollute.
2. New things must not be injected into our surroundings until we have carefully researched their possible impact.
3. Industries using good-quality water in their factories must return an equal amount of good-quality water to rivers and lakes.
4. Water, land, and air are no longer free for the taking and using in any manner most appealing to the taker and user.
5. Anti-pollution laws must be universal, and polluters must be prosecuted.

Environmental pollution is regarded as a world problem. Since many countries of the world are experiencing problems similar to those we have in the United States, and since, for example, the pollution of many bodies of water, such as oceans, border on more than one country, pollution is a global concern.

Such world-wide concern makes possible a sharing of efforts and a unified approach to the solution of the problem of pollution. The General Assembly of the United Nations provided evidence of this world concern when it called a World Conference on Problems of the Human Environment and aired the ecological concerns of the peoples over the face of the globe.

The federal government is playing a prominent role in protecting the environment. The signing on January 1, 1970, of the National Environmental Policy Act of 1969 signaled the acceptance of environmental concern as a legitimate public policy for the United States. This act declared that it is the policy of the federal government to use all practicable means to create and maintain conditions under which man and nature can exist in productive harmony and fulfill the social, economic, and other requirements of present and future generations of Americans. This act also established a Council on Environmental Quality to conduct research and promote environmental quality. As a result of this legislation, other bills followed, including those designed to close up the waterways, provide for the monitoring of land, water and air resources, and establish standards to be met by industry and other agencies. Examples of this legislation include: auto makers must manufacture vehicles within the near future that will be ninety percent pollution free; tough emission standards were set for new steam power plants, sulfuric and nitric acid plants, cement plants and large incinerators; and funds were appropriated for air pollution research. Other legislation, designed to save the world's whales, declared eight species endangered, stopped whale-product imports, and ordered an end to U.S. commercial whaling. In another action, the U.S. seized contaminated fish and filed suits against major mercury producers.

The various states are active in curbing pollution. State-wide zoning laws have been enacted to control land development and building, and land has been placed under good conservation management. In cooperation with the U.S. Department of Agriculture, states have established watershed programs for flood prevention and erosion control and at the same time provided for water recreation needs. State scenic recreation river systems have been established. Concern has also been shown for effective flood plain regulation and basic river planning in order to expand water-based recreation opportunities.

Many voluntary agencies are contributing their resources. A sampling of voluntary agencies that are helping to do something about the pollution problem include the Izaak Walton League, Defenders of Wildlife, Soil Conservation Society of America, Wildlife Management Institute, and the American Conservation Association.

Cities are helping to solve their own environmental problems. Chicago has cut its sulfur dioxide by fifty percent and has passed legislation giving it the power to shut down factories, traffic, and airlines in pollution emergencies. New York has ordered some 2,500 buildings to shut down their incinerators and have their refuse carted away. It has also reduced sulfur dioxide by having Consolidated

Edison, the utility that supplies its gas and electricity, convert to low-sulfur fuels, as well as increasing sharply the production of electrical power in nuclear plants outside the city. In addition, it has set up monitoring stations covering a 320-square-mile area to sound the alert in possible emergency situations.

Individual citizens and industry are becoming involved. One significant way in which individuals are helping to clean up the environment is through recycling, that is reclaiming and reusing materials such as paper, glass and metals. In Madison, Wisconsin, a year-long salvage drive saved fifty percent more paper for recycling than in the previous year. Over seventy million cans were returned throughout the nation in a three-month period.

Industry and research are showing that recycling can be economically sound and in so doing will improve the quality of living and conserve irreplaceable resources. Industry, under recycling, uses junked cars to provide more than one-half the steel used in new cars, and used paper already saves 200 million trees a year. In the future, garbage may be processed into crude oil. Much more research is needed to show the way to economically feasible methods for reclamation and reuse of refuse. In the meantime, the nation's citizens and industries are being urged to Reduce, Reuse, and Recycle packaging materials.

Another method by which waste is being reduced is reflected in a new word, *rejase,* which refers to reusing junk for some other useful means. For example, a beer barrel becomes a chair, old railroad ties are converted into benches, tin cans become lamps, telephone-cable spools are transported into patio tables, light bulbs become handy sock-darning eggs, and junked cars are dumped offshore to act like coral reefs, attracting fish and fishermen.

Each person and industry, of course, has a responsibility in cleaning up the environment. This includes avoiding waste in the home and factory, using household cleaning products carefully, conserving water and electricity, avoiding excessive refuse, providing proper waste disposal, and helping to make the community a cleaner and more beautiful place to live.

Environmental education is important. If the environment is to be saved, the people who make up this country must understand and appreciate our natural resources and how they can be preserved and protected. This means a dynamic educational program. In recognition of the importance of educating the public regarding the environment, pilot projects are being conducted, research is being accomplished, and curricula are being established. Approximately 4,000 school systems in the United States provide for environmental instruction. A National Council of Environmental Education to coordinate the work of all agencies and organizations interested in the environment is being considered. The National Education Association and the National Park Service are conducting workshops in various parts of the country to show both teachers and park management people how to handle nature study projects in the parks. The Bureau of Sports' Fisheries and Wildlife, which runs the nation's 320 wildlife refuges, has established an educational program.

Environmental education is important. In the Los Angeles schools, students have an opportunity to plant trees in burned-out areas. Photo courtesy of the Los Angeles City Schools, Youth Services Section.

Outside the government, most of the national conservation organizations are developing environmental education programs. The National Council of the State Garden Clubs is providing teachers in public, parochial and private schools with material needed to make environmental education an integral part of their instruction. The National Audubon Society has printed more than 100,000 copies of a textbook on nature study for the fourth to sixth grades. The National Wildlife Federation is providing environment pamphlets for grade schools, secondary schools, and colleges. The National Recreation and Park Association and the American Association for Health, Physical Education and Recreation have sponsored a Symposium on Outdoor Recreation and Education, in which it brought together the nation's outstanding authorities in recreation education and environmental planning.

ENVIRONMENTAL CHALLENGE TO RECREATION

The scientific progress of man has resulted in many advances being made in respect to controlling disease, reducing infant mortality, and prolonging life. Industrial production has advanced to where we can produce material items at an astounding rate of speed. Machines do the work of many people and, as a result, leisure time has been increased. The automobile is providing transportation so that we can see things in distant places that never before were possible. The comfort Americans enjoy is the envy of people all over the world.

Yet, despite this progress, accessible outdoor recreation and adequate environmental facilities for recreational use do not exist in sufficient numbers, and those that do exist are being threatened. The automobile, although a blessing in getting us to national parks, at the same time is threatening our atmosphere with its exhaust emissions. The forests that once were so plentiful are being threatened by super highways and unlimited construction. The coastlines are filled with wastes.

The noise and fast pace of life in America's crowded cities, their polluted atmospheres, rising rate of crime, and tension-producing existence suggest that quality living should provide opportunities for their inhabitants to recreate after hours of work and during vacation periods. Recreation is an essential to their welfare — physically, mentally, socially, and spiritually. However, in order for recreation to realize its potentialities in the city as well as in other settings, environmental problems must be solved. The conditions presented by an urbanized environment present a challenge to recreation that involves comprehensive planning, imagination, and dedication. City and suburban planners concerned with urban renewal and housing designs must be made aware of the need to include recreational facilities within their complexes. Land and water areas must be set aside for parks, green spaces, and woods. Hiking trails, children's play areas, and scenic spots must be preserved and developed. Noise, confusion and automobile traffic and other menaces to the environment must be controlled. The president of the United States stated the challenge in meaningful words when he said: "The great question of the seventies is, shall we surrender to our surroundings, or shall we make peace with nature and begin to make reparations for the damage we have done to our air, our land and our water?"

QUESTIONS AND EXERCISES

1. Define the term *environment*. What are the component parts of the environment? How does the environment affect mankind?
2. What stake does recreation have in the environment? Be specific and give facts to support your answer.
3. What is the relationship, if any, between America's industrial progress and present-day problems concerning the environment?
4. Prepare an essay on the statement, There is a reciprocal influence between man and his environment.
5. Research five articles that have to do with the environment and report on them to the class.
6. What are today's principal environmental problems concerned with (a) air, (b) land, and (c) water?

7. What has been the government's role in protecting the environment? Be specific.
8. Prepare a position paper outlining constructive steps that the recreation profession should take in protecting the environment.
9. What are some steps that each citizen of the United States could take to provide for a better environment?
10. What is the relationship between health and the environment? Between health and recreation?

SELECTED REFERENCES

American Association for Health, Physical Education and Recreation, *Environment and Population: A Sourcebook for Teachers.* Washington, D.C.: The Association, 1972.

American Association for Health, Physical Education and Recreation, *Man and His Environment: An Introduction to Using Environmental Study Areas.* Washington, D.C.: The Association, 1970.

Audubon Magazine, all issues, but with particular reference to the following: January, 1971; March, 1971; and May, 1971.

Commoner, Barry, *The Closing Circle.* New York: Alfred A. Knopf, 1971.

DeBell, Garrett, *The Environmental Handbook.* New York: Ballantine Books, Inc., 1970.

Galbraith, J., *The New Industrial State.* New York: Houghton Mifflin Company, 1969.

Hurley, William D., *Environmental Legislation.* Springfield, Ill.: Charles C. Thomas, 1971.

Jensen, Clayne R., and Clark T. Thorstenson, *Issues in Outdoor Recreation.* Minneapolis: Burgess Publishing Company, 1972.

Major policy statements by President Richard Nixon with commentaries by Richard Wilson: *We Must Move Now Against Pollution,* A comprehensive message to the Congress of the United States. Charles Publications, Inc., 1970.

Marx, Wesley, *The Frail Ocean.* New York: Ballantine Books, Inc., 1967.

Matthews, William H., *A Guide to the National Parks.* Garden City, N.Y.: Natural History Press, 1968.

McClellan, Grant S., *Land Use in the United States.* New York: The H. W. Wilson Co., 1971.

Mitchell, John G., and Constance Stallings, *Ecotactics: The Sierra Club Handbook for Environment Activists.* New York: Pocket Books, 1970.

Muir, J., and R. Kauffman, *Gentle Wilderness.* New York: Ballantine Books, 1968.

Odum, E., *Ecology.* New York: Holt, Rinehart & Winston, Inc., 1969.

River of Life — Water: The Environmental Challenge. Conservation yearbook no. 6, U.S. Department of the Interior, Washington, D.C.: U.S. Government Printing Office.

The Conservationists' Magazine, all issues, but with particular reference to the following: January, 1971; February, 1971; and March, 1971.

Tupper, Margo, *No Place to Play.* Philadelphia: Chilton Books, 1966.

6

SOCIAL FORCES

AFFECTING RECREATION

IN TODAY'S SOCIETY

Society is constantly changing. People live differently today than they did just five years ago. Today we are much more aware of the problems in our cities, the problems of people who are disadvantaged, the growing crime rate, the increase in civil disorders, the energy crisis and the numerous cultural changes that affect all of us. All of these problems and conditions that affect our society in turn affect recreational services and settings. For example, a decaying city is given federal appropriations for urban renewal in some slum areas. New housing, schools, and shopping centers must be included in any rebuilding plan. But what about recreational facilities? A rebuilding program that does not include planning for recreational needs is a futile one. Inhabitants of inner cities have special recreation needs that must be considered prior to any reconstruction program.

In this chapter, the recreational needs of different segments of our society will be seen through discussions of cities and their inhabitants, the problems of crime and civil disorder, and cultural changes that include emphasis on the family, youth, the aging and aged, and the special problems of women in contemporary society.

THE CRISIS IN OUR CITIES

Cities have always posed a serious problem to city, state, and federal governments. In recent years, greater numbers of middle-class people have been moving away from the cities, leaving the cities to big business and to the disadvantaged members of the population. Many urban renewal programs have

The old sections of the nation's cities provide a picture of urban life prior to the "Crisis in Our Cities." A horse-drawn carriage tour through one of the oldest streets in Charleston, South Carolina. Photo courtesy of South Carolina Department of Parks, Recreation, and Tourism.

been started, but the cost of these programs is so high that some projects are never completed. One program in San Francisco was started in the 1950s and today only twenty percent of the project has been completed. Yet, more and more cities are asking for federal aid for urban renewal. In 1960, there were 365 projects under way, and in 1970 there were 1160 projects involving over 1000 cities. The federal government has been unable to keep up with financial requests for urban renewal projects.

You may be asking what urban renewal has to do with recreation. The purpose of any urban renewal project is to provide adequate housing for its inhabitants. These projects should include adequate recreational areas, including parks, playgrounds, swimming complexes, and community centers to meet the needs of the people that will live there. A "total" redevelopment program can only be successful when all basic needs of people are met. Recreation is one of these needs.

Model Cities Program

The Model Cities Administration of the U. S. Department of Housing and Urban Development (HUD) was conceived to make grants available to local governments to plan, develop, and carry out programs to restore decaying areas of certain cities through coordinated use of federal, local, and private funds. Recreation is an important factor in Model Cities planning. In 1970, the Model

Cities Administration awarded several contracts for technical assistance in the area of recreation and culture. Recreation experts meet with local officers of cities in the program to plan recreational facilities to meet the needs of the population of the cities under urban renewal. The major goals of the recreation experts are:

1. improve the quality of the neighborhood
2. develop innovative recreation programs
3. effect institutional change

Recreation-culture workshops are also conducted with Model Cities staff members, local citizens, recreation-culture agency members, and federal officials. These workshops provide open discussion of problems, approaches, and operating techniques. In Savannah, Georgia, the technical assistance of the National Recreation and Parks Association (NRPA) helped this city to plan its first recreation program in a model neighborhood that included mobile recreation units, staff training and development groups, and a black cultural arts program. In all, over twenty-five cities have been helped by NRPA consultants to plan a wide range of recreation and cultural development programs.

The Importance of Community Involvement

Community involvement is essential to the success of any recreation program. This is true in suburban areas as well as in our cities. In past years, suburban programs almost always involved the community, but this has not always been the case in largely populated urban areas. In inner cities, administrators from federal, state, and city governments often made all the decisions while the people that were to be served by urban renewal or other programs were neglected. This fact has been widely publicized in recent battles over "home rule" in matters of education and recreation services.

A recent forum conducted by the NRPA found that:

1. Park and recreation planning should be oriented to the needs of small units of population and neighborhoods.
2. Community participation must be sought before any decisions on park and recreation planning can be made.
3. Community involvement should be present in the implementation as well as in the planning of programs.
4. Park and recreation programs should be oriented toward a goal of solving pressing urban problems.

In the early 1970s, community members of inner-city neighborhoods are demanding and getting greater community control of recreation programs.

Citizens have become aware of community problems and have been working with recreation administrators to create social reform in their neighborhoods.

There are implications for both community residents and administrators in the administrative decentralization of recreation programs. Some of the implications for residents are:

1. to influence employment patterns and gain training for careers in recreation management
2. to provide citizen bargaining power
3. to gain more frequent and satisfying recreation experiences as the result of being involved in the planning and implementation of programs
4. establish models to inspire community members in new areas of employment and social action

The implications for administrators are that they can now bring about the

1. necessary impact on community life,
2. creation of a new job market and work force of and for the community,
3. creation of valid methods of evaluating recreation programs,
4. assessment of leisure-time patterns of community members.

An administrator of a community recreation program must first meet with community leaders and assess what the responsibilities of the community will be in any recreation program. As the project progresses, community members should make the administrator aware of their satisfaction and dissatisfaction with the program. Mutual agreement should accompany major changes. Once the program is on its feet, major responsibility should be put in the hands of community members. Training and hiring programs should be held in the community for its members. In this way, community involvement provides jobs and keeps interest going in the established programs.

An example of successful community involvement in a recreation program is that of Orlando, Florida's Washington Shores Recreation Center. In the heart of Orlando's black ghetto, this center had no recreation programs for its young people. In 1966, Dr James Smith organized a day-care center for the children of working mothers. The community and Dr. Smith realized the inadequacies of this program, and in 1968, they began discussing a self-sustaining center to be operated for and by the black community of Orlando. The initial money was raised within the black community and was more than matched by contributions from the white business community of Orlando. The programs concentrate on children of preschool, elementary, and junior-high-age, and team and individual sports are stressed. There are study facilities and a tutorial program staffed by college students. The program currently operates on a break-even financial basis, and federal funds have as yet not been requested.

High-Rise Recreation

So far in this chapter much of our discussion has centered on the decaying areas of our cities. However, many cities have an abundance of low-middle income, high-rise housing, and higher income, private apartments and condominiums abound in most urban areas. In most of these apartment-house complexes, no organized recreation program exists. One community is trying to change this: Arlington County, Virginia, a suburb across the Potomac from Washington, D.C., has recently instituted an Apartment Recreation Activities program for its approximate 115,000 apartment dwellers. Meetings are held to plan recreation programs and such activities as arts and crafts, slimnastics, jogging, yoga, and other programs are being introduced. Often, apartment dwellers with expertise in a particular field volunteer to lead and organize their specialty group. Programs like this are an excellent method of promoting recreation and socializing among apartment dwellers who frequently never have opportunities to meet one another.

FOCUS ON THE DISADVANTAGED

The term *disadvantaged* has been used before in this chapter, but has not been adequately defined. *Disadvantaged* is a general word used to describe a person or groups of people who may be culturally, economically, physically, or socially deprived. The physically disadvantaged have been previously discussed in the section of Chapter 3 that related to therapeutic recreation. Most disadvantaged people live in inner cities, but disadvantaged people who fit one or

Girls playing football as part of recreation program. Community Center, North Little Rock, Arkansas. Photo courtesy of the North Little Rock Recreation Department.

more of the conditions previously mentioned may be found in any part of the country. For example, the American Indians are one of the most disadvantaged groups even though the majority of them live on reservations in the western parts of the United States.

Generally, disadvantaged people have inadequate housing that is infested with roaches and rodents, has poor plumbing and heating, and absentee landlords. Inadequate nutrition and health is often a problem, and many people are unemployed and are frequently illiterate. Schools may be substandard and recreational facilities nonexistent. Narcotics addiction and crime, which are often fostered by this deprivation, are a growing concern in disadvantaged communities.

The leisure time of the disadvantaged is much different from that of the upper- or middle-income person. Since many disadvantaged people are unemployed or have left school at an early age, they have more leisure time than the higher income groups. However, they have neither the money nor the facilities to use this time beneficially. Many disadvantaged people do not participate in commercial types of recreation. They usually do not own a car, rarely take vacations or attend spectator events, social functions, or cultural activities. This is due as much to a lack of money as to a lack of a constructive concept of personal leisure. One study conducted among disadvantaged youth in Boston showed that these people tended to reject organized constructive recreation activities that were made available through public or voluntary organizations.[1] Some of the reasons for this rejection included lack of interest on the part of the youths' families and disapproval by older youths in the community.

What Government Can Do

The federal, state, and local governments as well as voluntary and semipublic agencies all have much to contribute to the disadvantaged segment of the population. In the past, most federal and state provisions for recreation have been for people who could get to recreation areas on their own and were knowledgeable concerning camping, boating, swimming, and other outdoor recreational activities. Not only were these people knowledgeable, but they were also financially able to pay for services and equipment necessary to benefit from these recreational facilities. Most federally owned land is remote and not near any of the great metropolitan areas, particularly those cities along the eastern coast of the United States. When a state park does exist near a large city, it is often difficult to get there by public transportation. Many inner-city residents lack knowledge of the city's transportation system and often speak a foreign language, which creates problems of confidence and incentive in seeking out distant sources of recreation.

[1]C. Tait and E. Hodges, Jr., M.D., *Delinquents, Their Families and the Community* (Springfield, Ill.: Charles C. Thomas, Publisher, 1962).

South Carolina is a state that has provided for the recreation of its citizens. South Carolina's Grand Strand. Photo courtesy of South Carolina Department of Parks, Recreation, and Tourism.

In recent years, attendance at national parks has often been limited by raising entrance fees and requiring reservations for use of camping grounds. This was done for conservation and beautification purposes, but the results directly affect the disadvantaged in our population. For example, raising the entrance admission at a national park from one to three dollars will not affect the middle-income family but will deter the low-income family. The very idea of reservations is middle-class in orientation, and disadvantaged people usually live from day to day and may have little experience in how to get the necessary information in order to make a reservation.

The local government has a great responsibility to provide suitable recreation to all members of the population. Unfortunately, studies have shown that middle- and upper-income groups are usually favored in recreation programs. Even when programs are open to the entire community, they are often based on middle-class values and interests, and costs are higher than most low-income families can afford. For example, community swimming and tennis complexes are appearing in many of our smaller cities and townships. They are open to all, but the disadvantaged family often cannot afford the $100–$300 annual membership fee required to join the facility. In New York and Connecticut, a number of public recreation departments have taken over private country clubs and have opened membership to the community — or to those persons who can afford the membership fee. Even if a disadvantaged family could afford membership, in many cases they would not have the necessary transportation to reach the facility.

Voluntary agencies also must share in the responsibility for inner-city recreation programming. Y's, Boys' and Girls' Clubs, and settlement houses have

Los Angeles provides many recreational services through its youth services program. Photo courtesy of the Los Angeles City Schools, Youth Services Section.

been doing good jobs where they exist. However, it has been increasingly found that when areas begin to deteriorate and the middle-class population leaves, voluntary agencies often leave with them.[2] This is an unfortunate reality of disadvantaged areas.

To sum up this section, one can say that federal, state, and local governments can improve recreation for the disadvantaged by:

1. considering the cultural and social values and financial abilities of these people in all recreation planning
2. involving community members in planning and staffing of facilities
3. planning programs that suit the age and interests of participants
4. providing transportation to distant recreation sites
5. taking the non-English-speaking resident into consideration by providing multilingual information concerning recreation facilities

[2] Richard G. Kraus, "Recreation for Rich and Poor," *Teachers College Record,* 67, No. 8 (May, 1966).

Compensatory Recreation

Compensatory recreation is simply a plan to provide the greatest effort in recreation programming for the disadvantaged segment of the population. This effort is to compensate for social and economic hardships suffered by disadvantaged persons.

It has been found that disadvantaged youth usually have a poor self-image. Their environment makes it almost impossible to achieve necessary goals. The disadvantaged grow up to expect defeat and frustration and they are rarely disappointed. A meaningful recreation program can help these young people to think more of themselves and their futures. It is important that any recreation program provide suitable adult models that young people can relate to.

One way of providing meaningful recreation experiences to the disadvantaged is to plan recreation programs that meet the needs of the community through self-help programs and hiring practices that include community members. Community Action Programs established by the Economic Opportunity Act of 1964 emphasized direct involvement of the disadvantaged in their own education. The Job Corps and Neighborhood Youth Corps (NYC), both established by the same 1964 Economic Opportunity Act, promote hiring of the disadvantaged in community programs. The Job Corps is a residential training program that provides remedial education, training, recreation, and counseling to disadvantaged youth between the ages of sixteen and twenty-one.

The Neighborhood Youth Corps has an in-school program for disadvantaged youth in grades nine through twelve and an out-of-school program for unemployed youth over sixteen years of age. This program helps to provide part-time work and on-the-job training. One of the areas that NYC members frequently work in is recreation. The Washington State Parks hired over 1,000 NYC members to work in the parks under the guidance of park rangers. These young men and women cleared forest trails, built fire trails, and constructed roads, footbridges, and campsites. They were taught how to repair roofs, help in office procedures, and act as lifeguard aides, tour guides, and park assistants. They were paid a standard hourly wage for a thirty-two-hour week. After leaving the NYC, many found better jobs because of the skills they had learned while working in the state parks. In most cases, these youths improved their self-image, which altered negative attitudes toward their future.

What the Professional Recreator Can Do

A person trained in the discipline of recreation must be instilled in his college experience with an understanding of the cities and their disadvantaged population. Many middle class people who enter the field of recreation have little experience with the values and culture of the many groups of people that form the disadvantaged. Students majoring in recreation should take courses that will enable them to learn about the urban disadvantaged. Minority-group cultural implications and their special problems of leisure time should be required course work. Of course, the best way to learn about these people and their problems is to work with them in planning and instituting various recreation programs. Volunteers are always needed in urban areas and this is a good way to get first-hand experience.

It is also important to recruit more minority and disadvantaged students for careers in recreation services. Few minority members choose to enter a career in recreation. A 1969 study showed that only 2.4 percent of black students enrolled in a nontechnical curriculum that would include recreation.[3] One of the reasons that helps to explain this low figure is that the course offerings in recreation curriculums neglect the minority and disadvantaged groups. If the curriculums are upgraded and a realistic effort is made to recruit the disadvantaged, then the result will be seen in inspired urban recreation programs.

IS RECREATION A FACTOR IN THE INCREASE OF CRIME AND CIVIL DISORDERS?

Crime and *civil disorders* are grouped together in this chapter because of the role that inadequate recreation plays in the increase of these "diseases" of our society. Every day newspapers are reporting increases in one or both of these categories. A recent press release showed that serious crime in the United States had risen six percent in 1971, and this was the *smallest* increase in the six previous years.

You may be asking yourself what recreation has to do with crime and civil disorder? This will be explained in greater detail in this section, but a brief answer to this question can be seen in some of the conclusions of the Kerner Commission Report on Civil Disorders.[4] The Commission discovered that inferior recreation services ranked fifth in importance as a reason for the civil disorders of 1967. In three major cities, lack of recreational facilities was given as the most important grievance that led to specific civil disorders.

Role of Increased Leisure Time in Crime

In this chapter, leisure among disadvantaged groups was discussed. Many low-income people are unemployed; with little to do, they occupy their minds with criminal activity. Persons who are addicted to drugs must have money in order to meet their daily drug need. The increase in drug addiction in recent years

[3]James F. Murphy, "Recreation Education – A Social Concern," *Parks and Recreation,* Vol. 9 (September, 1970).
[4]*Report of the National Advisory Commission on Civil Disorders* (Washington, D.C.: Government Printing Office, 1968).

Gun control has been a subject of much concern throughout the nation. Photo courtesy of the Los Angeles City Schools, Youth Services Section.

points to the need to mentally escape the environment, and this addiction adds to the drastic increase in serious crime.

Studies that have been conducted to show the relationship between delinquency and recreation have found that delinquent youth spend less time in organized recreation programs than nondelinquent youth. It has also been found that most delinquency occurs during leisure time, and wholesome recreation tends to prevent this social deviation.[5]

Recreation
and Increase in Gang Delinquency

Gang delinquency can be defined as groups of young people, usually of the same sex, who form large structured groups and engage in antisocial behavior. Twenty years ago gangs were common to inner-city areas, and recently they have been making a comeback; violence by youth gangs has risen sharply in our major cities; New York, Chicago, Los Angeles, and Philadelphia all report increases in gang activity. Chicago reports 700 gangs in existence in 1972. Recently a special force on gangs reported to John Lindsay, former mayor of New York. The results of their report led to a one-million-dollar allocation for job training, placement, recreation, and remedial education. Some of the new breed of gangs are nonviolent and have goals of neighborhood improvement, such as eviction of pushers, neighborhood cleanup, and voter registration.

[5]Martin H. Neumeyer, *Juvenile Delinquency in Modern Society* (D. Van Nostrand Co., Inc., 1962).

Citizen Involvement and Law Enforcement

Citizen involvement in law enforcement is a fairly new concept, and it can and does work in many communities. In Indianapolis in 1961, Dr. Margaret Marshall was fatally beaten by a teen-age purse snatcher. Following this attack, Indianapolis citizens decided to do something to make the streets safe after dark. Women belonging to thirty women's clubs were organized to form the Women's Anti-Crime Crusade. A Special Committee on Law Enforcement was formed, and a Crime Alert program, which guaranteed anonymity to callers concerning crimes, was put into action. Along with this, the city administration introduced new recreation programs and kept playgrounds open. These acts helped to reduce delinquency.

Youth patrols have become increasingly popular in recent years. Many of these patrols were started during the riots of the 1960s. One of these groups called the "White Hats" (because of their helmets) was decisive in quieting Tampa, Florida, during civil disturbances in 1967. Following the disorders, they continued as advisors to the Commission on Human Relations and continued unarmed patrols. These patrol programs are important because they promote better relations between the police and youth, relate well to delinquent youth, and help maintain order in the community. Some of their duties include:

1. patrolling business areas at night
2. escorting women home from work
3. reporting dangerous conditions in their neighborhoods
4. breaking up fights

Atlanta, Georgia, initiated an experimental Junior Deputy Program in the summer of 1968 and continued it. The police department in this community has a general youth program that involves more that 2,000 young people in recreational programs.

Relationship between Leisure Time and Civil Disorders

Civil disorders have been a major news story in the past decade. The 1960s is also referred to as the "age of leisure," and many studies point to a causative relationship between increased leisure time and civil disorders. Many factors come into play when considering a cause and effect relationship. It is well known that persons with too much leisure time and too few recreational outlets have much energy – that must seek an outlet. In addition, anger sometimes builds when realization of inadequate facilities comes to the forefront.

An excellent example of the relationship between recreation and civil disorders was the 1964 "riots" in Jersey City. During the summer when the riots occurred, several housing-project playgrounds were closed for economy reasons. Lack of playgrounds and other recreation facilities was one of the major grievances cited by Negro leaders as contributing to the cause of the riots. In a time of federal and state economy on all fronts, it is unfortunate that recreation programs are frequently the first to be cut back. Administrators easily forget that although many middle- and higher-income people have the resources to seek recreation services, this is rarely true in our large urban areas where recreation is needed most desperately.

Park and recreation professionals definitely have a major responsibility in improving urban conditions. Educational experiences in the universities must be updated to include urban studies and exploration of recreation programs needed and desired by communities. Improvement of youth-oriented and counseling programs is basic to prevention of future civil disorders.

RECREATION AND CULTURAL CHANGES

Cultural change is an accepted fact in today's world. Society is constantly moving and changing, as reflected in shorter workweeks, increased automation, family disruptions, increased drug problems, increased leisure time, and the women's liberation movement. All of these cultural changes and many more have their influence on recreation and its settings and services.

Recreation and the American Worker

Changes in the structure of the American economy have affected work in all areas of industrial, professional, and civil service. From 1960 to 1970, the American worker has gained about fifty hours a year in free time. Some of this time is in additional holidays and vacation days, and the remainder is in reduced working hours. In addition, automation has influenced the shorter workweek. Many companies are already on a four-day workweek, and some trade unions have also adopted this plan. More vacation time, more long weekends with Monday holidays, and shorter workweeks all result in increased leisure time for the working person. Many persons will have to learn about beneficial and enjoyable use of leisure time. Free time is frightening to some people in that they have never had leisure interests and do not know what to do with this added time. It is important that leisure not be looked at as something that has been earned because of hard work but rather as an integral part of one's life and a very necessary part.

An interesting cultural change relating to work is how certain segments of the youth culture fail to identify with the work ethic. In certain circles, persons with full-time "regular" jobs are frowned upon and status is derived from freedom from work. Many young people who feel this way will concentrate on a hobby or avocation from which they can sometimes derive an income. In recent years, young beggars have been seen in great numbers on city streets. Most would prefer to beg than to work in a nine-to-five, restrictive job. Some of these young people do use their leisure time to explore arts, crafts, music, and dance activities, while others do not spend their leisure in a constructive manner.

Urbanization and Population:
Their Effect on Recreation

Americans crowd into urban areas in increasing numbers. In 1970, approximately sixty-five percent of Americans lived on only nine percent of the land and 140,000,000 Americans lived in just 215 metropolitan areas. The East and West Coasts are heavily populated, while much land remains undeveloped in the remainder of the country. The population growth, coupled with the unequal growth of certain areas of the country, has led to an unprecedented demand for land for recreational use. Unfortunately, recreational land is not available in or near the metropolitan areas where it is desperately needed. Legislation to protect existing undeveloped land must be passed so that all usable land in these high-population areas is not turned into more houses and industrial sites. Especially in a period of increased leisure time, recreation must be made more accessible to those who need it the most — the metropolitan-area dwellers.

Recreation and the American Family

Perhaps the cultural changes in the American family have been the greatest in recent years. The divorce rate is presently about fifty percent, and this results in many children living in one parent's home. In general, children engage in few activities with their families. As the children get older, they want to be with their friends rather than in the presence of the family. One of the problems here is that leisure activities often differ among family members, and so they all go their own ways. Between school, work, and different leisure activities, the family rarely participates together in any one thing. This situation tends to keep the family apart both physically and emotionally.

There are many recreational activities that the entire family can enjoy. Some of these include: bicycle trips, camping trips, picnics, bowling parties, swimming activities, tennis, hiking, jogging, fishing, and numerous other activities. If a family finds itself going different ways all the time, it should set aside one night a week or an afternoon on a weekend to do something together. Communication and understanding is found to increase when the family enjoys each other's company.

Recreational Needs of the Aging Person

More and more people are retiring at an earlier age and are more physically fit than ever before. This segment of the population has very special problems that may include loneliness, sickness, or lack of interest in their lives. There are about twenty-five million Americans today who are sixty-five years of age or older. Some of the facts about this group in our population include:

1. Women outnumber men by considerable numbers.
2. There are more foreign-born and Caucasian persons among the older population than in the lower-age groups.
3. Single, divorced, and widowed persons make up about half of this population.
4. Most older persons live alone.
5. They are predominantly persons with less than a high-school education.

Older people have a great amount of free time and, because they are usually retired, live away from their families, and have fewer responsibilities than they did as younger people, they sometimes have a sense of being unwanted. They need opportunities for self-expression and meaningful service. Some recommendations of one early White House Conference on Aging were:

1. Greater opportunities are needed in areas of voluntary service, recreation, and citizen participation for all aging persons regardless of race, creed, or economic status.
2. Older persons should be encouraged to maintain ties with younger persons individually and in groups.
3. More family-centered projects should be emphasized.
4. Activities should be directed toward the aging ill and handicapped whether institutionalized or homebound.
5. Sufficient income to permit greatest enjoyment of recreation services should be provided.

The 1971 White House Conference on Aging also discussed leisure activities as they pertained to recreation needs of this segment of the population.

Increasingly, many older persons join Senior Citizens or Golden Age Programs and many retire to adult-only communities. These clubs and retirement communities usually offer numerous recreational facilities as well as one-day excursions and organized travel tours that take the person's age into consideration in tour planning. Many volunteer programs involving the elderly have met with great success — for example, foster grandparent programs, VISTA activities at home, and Peace Corps activities abroad. Many older volunteers work with handicapped and mentally retarded youngsters and get out of these relationships as much as they put into them. New programs for retired business people involve them in counseling younger people going into their first business venture. All of these activities are both gratifying to the older people involved and very helpful to the rest of the community.

QUESTIONS AND EXERCISES

1. Explain why recreation is an important factor in urban renewal programs.
2. In what ways is community involvement essential to recreation programming?
3. What were some of the findings of the National Park and Recreation Association's survey concerning community involvement?
4. What is high-rise recreation? Do you have any suggestions for more effective programs in this area?
5. Who are the disadvantaged members of our population? What are some of the problems faced by the disadvantaged in relation to recreation?
6. What are the responsibilities of all levels of government as well as nongovernment agencies in planning recreation for the disadvantaged segment of our population?
7. Explain the term *compensatory recreation.* What programs are utilized in compensatory recreation?
8. Do you think that students majoring in recreation should be familiar with urban problems? What other courses of study would be helpful to their professional preparation?
9. What were some of the conclusions of the Kerner Commission on Civil Disorders in relation to recreation planning?
10. If you were a recreation leader assigned to an inner-city gang, what types of recreation programs would you try to institute, and how would you go about working with this group?
11. How does leisure time affect the American worker in contemporary society?
12. Discuss recreation planning and administration in relation to (a) the American family, (b) the aged, and (c) women in today's society.

SELECTED REFERENCES

Furlong, William Barry, "Our Kids Tell Us about Drugs," *Today's Health,* Vol. 49 (February, 1971).

Gilbert, Douglas L., *Natural Resources and Public Relations.* Washington, D.C.: The Wildlife Society, 1971.

Gold, Seymour M., *Urban Recreation Planning.* Philadelphia: Lea & Febiger, 1973.

Gray, David, "Compensatory Recreation," *Parks and Recreation,* Vol. 2 (April, 1967).

———, "The Changing Pattern of American Life," *Parks and Recreation,* Vol. 1 (March, 1966).

Hodgson, J. D., "Leisure and the American Worker," *Journal of Health, Physical Education and Recreation,* Vol. 44 (March, 1973).

Hormachea, Marion N., and R. Carroll, eds., *Recreation in Modern Society.* Boston: Holbrook Press, Inc., 1972.

Hutchinson, I. J., "Leisure Time and the Riots, are We Contributing?" *Parks and Recreation,* Vol. 4 (July, 1969).

Jansen, Donald, "Youth Gangs' Violence," *New York Times,* April 16, 1972.

Jensen, Clayne R., and Clark T. Thorstenson, *Issues in Outdoor Recreation.* Minneapolis: Burgess Publishing Company, 1972.

Kraus, Richard G., "Recreation for Rich and Poor: A Contrast," *Teachers College Record,* Vol. 67 (May, 1966).

Marcuse, Peter, "Is the National Parks Movement Anti-Urban?" *Parks and Recreation,* Vol. VI (July, 1971).

Martin, David L., "Competitive Sports: Are They Wasting Dollars and Ruining Youngsters Too?" *American School Board Journal,* Vol. 160 (August, 1972).

Murphy, J., "Recreation Education: A Social Concern," *Parks and Recreation,* Vol. V (September, 1970).

Nesbitt, J., et. al., eds., *Recreation and Leisure Service for the Disadvantaged.* Philadelphia: Lea & Febiger, 1970.

Report of the National Advisory Commission on Civil Disorders. Washington, D.C.: U.S. Government Printing Office, 1968.

Weinandy, Janet E., et al., *Working With the Poor.* Syracuse, N.Y.: Youth Development Center, Syracuse University, 1965.

7

RELATIONSHIP

BETWEEN LEISURE TIME

AND RECREATION

The term *leisure* has been used many times in this book. As was discussed in Chapter 1, *leisure* and *recreation* are not synonymous words. By this text's definition, *leisure* refers to a time element, i.e., the amount of time an individual is not working, his free time after his formal responsibilities and necessities of life have been cared for. *Recreation,* you recall, was defined as the activities one participated in during his leisure time. In this chapter, leisure will be discussed in detail in order to find out more about how much leisure time we have, how we can be educated for the beneficial use of leisure time, how leisure time and its uses differ among different social classes, what the economics of leisure are, and how new trends in leisure-time activity affect the economics of leisure.

AVAILABLE LEISURE TIME

There are many people who manage to take care of their needs and responsibilities, but still do not have leisure time. The free time may exist, but the individual may have no interest in leisure-time activities or he may not have the ability to make use of this time. One must be able to express his interest, make use of his abilities, and take advantage of situations that would contribute to beneficial use of leisure time.

There are many men and women who are so completely absorbed in their daily activities that they have no interest in anything else. When these people retire, have longer vacations, or more time away from the job, they become ill at ease and are frequently depressed. Leisure time to these people is not pleasureful, but a very real burden. Have you ever known people who dread weekends, especially long ones? Work is the only way they know of to use their time. Of course, financial ability and social class does enter into this picture in a very important way. If a person's total energies, both emotionally and physically, are involved in the very act of survival for himself and his family, then leisure time may be practically nonexistent. Such a person neither has the resources nor the interest in doing very much with the little free time he may have. This aspect of leisure will be discussed in more detail later in this chapter in the section concerning social classes.

How Should Leisure Time Be Used? Of course, there can be no one answer for this question. Different people with very different needs and goals will use their leisure time in many diverse ways. Many people, however, do not stop to think about the way they are using their available time. Some individuals use their leisure time in the same manner as they did when they were children or young adults. They have never explored the many leisure activities open to them. Their use of leisure time has become a habit and if they are "good" at a particular activity, they may not want to risk not being as "good" at something new.

Leisure-time activities should be beneficial in themselves and therefore beneficial to the participant. Watching television, for example, may be good on some occasions, but it generally does not contribute to improving our health, knowledge, ability to carry over activities to other realms of our life, or add zest, interest, or enthusiasm to our life. Spectator activities, in general, are not as beneficial to a healthy, outgoing life, as are participatory interests. Leisure time should be a time when we can improve ourselves and the richness of our lives through worthy pursuits.

Leisure time should also be used to contribute to the development of the complete or integrated personality. A person, for example, who works at hard, physical labor all day would hopefully use some of his leisure time to explore the less physical aspects of life that might include cultural programs, adult education classes, or the less physically demanding athletic programs. On the other hand, the person who is seated behind a desk for most of the day might seek out leisure pursuits of a body-developing, physical nature. These activities would provide physical outlets that the job does not allow. The goal of this use of leisure time is the development of a balanced personality having both physical and intellectual sides.

How Much Leisure Time Do We Actually Have? Just as there are several different schools of thought as to the definition of leisure time, so too are there divergent opinions on whether the amount of leisure time available to us is increasing or decreasing.

The rationale frequently used to support the view of an increase in available leisure time is that of the shorter workweek. This shorter workweek, whether in the form of a shorter workday or fewer workdays per week, is primarily the result of technological advances in labor-saving devices and government and union labor legislation. The average seventy-hour workweek of a hundred years ago is currently below forty hours, with predictions from experts in the field that this will be around twenty hours in the not too distant future. Some workers have already achieved a twenty-five-hour workweek and many workers are in a four-day work schedule. In addition, the growth of leisure time is a direct result of extended vacation periods and increased days off due to an increase in holiday time, i.e., new legislation that provides for four holidays in addition to Labor Day to fall on Mondays. Growth of leisure also results from attractive pension plans that encourage earlier retirement. In recent times of high unemployment, many large corporations as well as the federal government have encouraged earlier retirements by upgrading persons and allowing greater benefits at an earlier age. This concept helps the organization to retain most of its younger employees.

It seems apparent from the previous discussion that leisure time is indeed increasing. However, many experts in the field, while acknowledging this premise, have shown that leisure time is in reality decreasing. What is meant by this somewhat confusing statement? In simple terms, it means that while the amount of hours available for leisure activities have been increasing, so have been the demands on these hours. Demands may include work-related activities such as a second job, increased commuter hours, more work to be completed after work hours, or an increase in business-related trips. Nonwork-related demands may be community- or home-oriented. PTA, church, community service, organizational meetings, and social functions make high-priority demands on available free time. Home demands include time spent with children and spouse, house maintenance, car repairs, and a multitude of daily, unplanned demands for leisure time. For example, it has been pointed out that the average executive spends a total of fifty-five hours a week on work-related activities, including time spent at home on business matters and business entertaining. This does not include commuting (over five hours per week) or business travel (which may run as high as thirty hours per week).[1] In the time since this study was made, commuting times, due to increased traffic, poorer commuting facilities, and homes further from urban complexes, have probably increased. It is not unusual for a man or woman to commute two or three hours or more per day. In many cases, this lengthy travel time not only shortens available leisure time but also tends to discourage a person's desire to use the remaining time in active recreation activities.

The homemaker's time has also, in essence, not increased. A study conducted by Kathryn Walker found that the total time used in caring for a family was not less in 1967-68 than it had been forty years earlier. Time spent in food

[1]Sebastian de Grazia, *Of Time, Work, and Leisure.* New York: The Twentieth Century Fund, 1962.

preparation and cleaning had diminished, but time spent in marketing had increased.[2] In addition, the modern homemaker is very much involved in community activities, frequently has a part-time or full-time job, and spends more time in chauffeuring children to and from activities than ever before.

Thus, it becomes clear that available leisure time is in reality decreasing for a large number of people. Even students feel this burden due to an increase in school work, school-related functions, and political and social activities. There are probably very few members of contemporary society who are not suffering from the effects of loss of available leisure time. The working man or woman in the lowest income bracket and the people who are supported by public welfare tend to have the greatest bulk of free time. Of course, their burden is apparent, and therefore they do not benefit substantially from this additional time. This factor and other aspects of leisure and society will be the topic of the next section of this chapter.

LEISURE AND SOCIETY

Earlier in this chapter, leisure was defined as that time remaining after formal responsibilities and activities necessary for preservation of life have been accomplished. This free or leisure time has been steadily increasing as man needs less time to care for his responsibilities and the necessities of life. With the abolishment of slavery, child labor, and sweat shops, and with the increase of protective devices, mechanization, and improved transportation, most people have more time to avail themselves of leisure pursuits. In addition, workweeks and workdays have become shorter, and social security, annuities, and pensions have been introduced to help accommodate the increase in leisure time.

How did man adjust to this increase in available leisure time? Some men utilized it for self-improvement, others for greater financial gain, and still others ignored it completely — not really knowing what to do with it. How a man reacts to and uses this time is frequently a function of the social class he finds himself in. In this section of Chapter 7, social class and leisure will be discussed in relation to the existing social classes, their leisure-time activities, and their potential for education in the more beneficial uses of leisure time.

Meaning of Social Class

People find themselves in different social classes by virtue of similar age, educational and socioeconomic backgrounds, and interest patterns. In our society, there is no written document that divides people into social classes, but people usually align themselves with other people having similar characteristics. Why people do this has long been discussed and evaluated. The major reasons

[2]Geoffrey Godbey, "Leisure: Nearing the Receding Horizons," *Parks and Recreation,* Vol. VI (August, 1971).

seem to include a desire for security, a feeling of being at ease with persons who have similar backgrounds, and a general fear of what is unknown. Of course, social class does not preclude persons having friends or acquaintances outside his class distinction. When this occurs, there is a good chance that both persons' values and therefore their use of leisure time will be affected. For purposes of this discussion, social classes will be divided by economic status into lower, middle, and higher socioeconomic groups.

Use of Leisure Time
by Different Social Classes

It is interesting to note that both the very rich and the very poor probably have the most time available for leisure use. This is so because the very rich usually have few job responsibilities and a staff of household employees and other help to aid them in their responsibilities, so that much free time remains. On the other hand, the very poor are usually unemployed or underemployed, so that they also have a great amount of leisure time. Of course, their leisure-time use differs greatly by virtue of their financial and educational resources.

Both the upper and middle classes seem to participate in most of the recreational activities that we are most familiar with: outdoor and commercial recreation, social and civic organizations, travel, water-oriented activities, cultural pursuits, reading, classes, and movie- and television-viewing. The degree

Senior citizens spending their leisure fishing. Photo courtesy of the County of Westchester Department of Parks, Recreation, and Conservation.

to which they participate is usually directly related to income. For example, a middle-class family may take one family-oriented vacation a year, while their upper-class counterparts may take two or three vacations and also go away for frequent weekends. Both of these classes are usually fairly well-educated and aware of public and private recreational offerings. The middle classes may make better use of semipublic organization programs than will the members of the upper classes. Middle-class children are more likely to attend "Y's" and community centers and go to Scout- or "Y"-sponsored summer camps, while upper-class children attend private recreation clubs and go to more expensive commercial camps. The very wealthy may have an entirely different leisure outlook that includes a compulsive pursuit of fun that takes them any place where they can find a pleasurable source of entertainment. These people, often referred to as "jet setters," travel thousands of miles to a yacht party or other social functions.

In recent years, recreation has become an important essential of real-estate offerings for the very wealthy. Advertisements for apartments and condominiums in major cities frequently point out such innovations as heated swimming pools, health spas, handball courts, tennis courts, gyms, clubrooms, ice-skating rinks, and numerous other on-premise aids for using leisure time.

But, this "total living" dimension is now being offered to the middle classes in suburban garden apartments and townhouse complexes. Most of these developments offer swimming pools, tennis courts, parks, playgrounds, nursery schools, theaters, and restaurants all within the complex itself. The Twin Rivers development in East Windsor Township, N.J. is a stunning example of this centralized concept of living. Twin Rivers offers a multitude of different housing forms, including apartments, condominiums, town houses, and detached homes. There are all types of recreational facilities, schools, a shopping center, industrial park, theater, and restaurants all within the development. It is currently about seventy-five percent complete and is expected to house more than 10,000 people by the middle 1970s.

A very sizable segment of our population exists under conditions of extreme poverty. The majority of these people are over sixty-five or under eighteen. As was discussed in Chapter 6, these people are often members of minority groups, are politically and socially inactive, tend to be lonely, uninvolved, and apathetic, usually do not belong to unions or social and fraternal organizations, and are frequently reluctant to use public or semipublic recreation facilities.

How do they use their leisure time? Certain points are self-evident. The urban family living on less than $5,000 per year usually does not enjoy most forms of private and commercial recreation. They frequently do not have cars and their leisure involvement may tend toward drinking alcoholic beverages, drug use, vice, gambling, and crime. Michael Harrington, in his book, *The Other American,* points out that in Harlem, a ghetto area of New York City, bars do a good early afternoon business, men crowd around the streets just walking or talking, and crap games and violence abound. The violence is a consequence of enforced idleness. The lower socioeconomic groups often have the most leisure time available and the least available resources. Review the sections of Chapter 6 concerning the disadvantaged to refresh your memory concerning the special leisure-related problems of this group.

Playing horseshoes is an economically low way to spend leisure hours. Bell Vets Park. Photo courtesy of the Los Angeles City Schools, Youth Services Section.

ECONOMICS OF LEISURE

Economics is basic to any discussion of leisure time. The term has already indirectly entered our discussion concerning leisure and social class. Available leisure time and the uses it is put to are often directly related to socioeconomic status. This use of the word *economic* is on a personal or family level; but there is another use of the word as it relates to leisure. Economics in this other sense relates to leisure as a big business, i.e., the amount of money spent annually in the pursuit of leisure and the way in which this money is spent.

In this section of this chapter, we will examine the multibillion-dollar recreation industry, how it came about, and where the money goes. In addition, we will explore some of the implications that leisure economics have for the professional recreator and his programs.

The Leisure Boom

The term *leisure boom* is used to describe a leisure economy that spent approximately $105 billion dollars in 1972. This amount has almost doubled in seven years from a 1965 figure of $58.3 billion to the present figure. It is interesting to note that this figure exceeds the cost for our national defense. It is also greater than the total outlay for new home construction and far larger than the combined incomes of all American farmers. It is estimated that this figure will more than double before 1980. The reasons for this increase in leisure spending are much the same as the reasons for increased leisure time. Greater spending is enhanced by longer vacation periods, more lengthy weekends, shorter workweeks (about 2,000 companies have a four-day workweek), and earlier retirement programs. Perhaps the most important factor in increased leisure spending is the rapid rise in personal income. Personal income in 1972 was estimated around 920 billion dollars, a fifty percent increase since 1967. Of course, this is not all "disposable" income — income that may be spent after taxes, social security, and other deductions are made. Another factor that must be considered is the problem of inflation and how it affects the value of the dollar. Personal incomes certainly did increase greatly during this period of time; however, so did inflation. This is an interesting point to ponder, considering how much the American family still manages to spend on leisure-oriented activities.

Expenditures for Leisure

Americans spend more than fifty billion dollars for recreational equipment and admissions to sporting events, cultural programs, and other commercial leisure activities. Total purchases of leisure equipment have increased by more than fifty percent in the past five years. In Chapter 8, we will be discussing outdoor recreation and its importance as a leisure-time activity. Outdoor recreation is one of the reasons for the great boom in leisure spending. More and more people want to "return to nature" and they are doing it by purchasing more camping equipment, recreational vehicles, boats, and water-sports equipment.

Recreational vehicles are a large source of leisure spending. The 1972 estimates for recreation vehicles are more than 1.8 billion dollars, of which motor homes of all types account for approximately 720 million dollars. These homes, equipped with facilities for sleeping, cooking, eating, and bathing, cost an average of $10,000 and are definitely for those who wish to camp in style.

Other recreational vehicles include travel trailers (approximately $3,400 each), tent trailers, campers, and pickup covers. It is anticipated that in 1978, there will be nearly 7.5 million camping vehicles in use in the United States. That number is nearly double the number used in 1972. The strain on our camping areas is already showing, as the Department of Interior has had to begin to limit visitors to the wilderness areas.

Recreation vehicles come in all sizes and shapes and include snowmobiles, dune buggies, minibikes, and bicycles. More than 600,000 snowmobiles were sold in 1972. Many persons own their own, while others rent or lease them when on vacation. Most resort areas own a number of these vehicles and provide

Bicycle riding has become a popular recreational activity in recent years. Myrtle Beach, South Carolina. Photo courtesy of South Carolina Department of Parks, Recreation, and Tourism.

open areas for their use. Bicycles seem to have made a big comeback in recent years. Some give the antipollution crusade the credit for their return. Sales in 1971 were over 8.5 million bikes, and the Department of Interior reports that more than thirty-seven million Americans participate in bike-riding. With the energy crisis, more persons will be riding bicycles.

Minibikes, too, are making their economic impact felt. These bikes cost between $200 and $400, and more than two million of them were owned by the end of 1971. This figure is ten times as great as the 1965 figure.

Additional Expenditures for Leisure

Second only to combined figures for recreation equipment and admissions to commercial and cultural events is money spent on radios, TVs, records, and musical instruments, for a total of over ten billion dollars in 1972 as opposed to 8.5 billion in 1967. When you add the amount spent on reading matter, clubs and fraternal organizations, garden materials, race tracks, and other personal consumption activities, the fifty-billion-dollar total is reached.

The remainder of the 105-billion-dollar sum is made up by a whopping forty billion dollars for travel within the United States, 7.5 billion for travel abroad, 5.5 billion in vacation lots and land, and two billion for second homes.

Vacation homes and vacation land lots are large sources of leisure-time spending. These areas will be explored in greater detail in the next major section concerning trends in leisure activities.

How the Leisure Boom
Affects Recreation as a Profession

Accompanying the national leisure boom was an expansion in the field of recreation services during the 1960s. A national study reported that in 1968 there were approximately 1.4 million full- and part-time workers in the field of recreation. It was also estimated that there would be a serious shortage of trained recreation personnel in the not too distant future. Many colleges and universities attempted to meet the growing need for recreators only to find that in the past few years budgetary cutbacks have had a damaging effect on the number of city and state recreation positions.

There are a number of reasons for these cutbacks. In the forefront, however, is the economic crisis of the early 1970s. Contributing to this crisis was the serious inflation problem, a recession that caused a rise in unemployment and serious social problems with high costs to all levels of government. Included in these social problems are spiralling welfare and urban renewal costs and increases in the cost of education, housing, and law enforcement. In addition, high costs of solving the problems of pollution, civil-service strikes, and running municipal governments have contributed to the lack of funds available for recreation services. This is a blow to the professional recreator and to the people themselves. As was pointed out in Chapter 6, poor recreation facilities was a major reason given for increased crime and civil disorders.

The federal government has also been forced to cut back funds for programs and services related to recreation and parks. Although the National Park Service expanded in terms of facilities and attendance during most of the 1960s, it was forced to accept budgetary restrictions in 1968. These restrictions necessitated shorter park seasons, shorter hours, new entrance fees, limited services, and combined supervisory staffs which looked after groups of smaller parks. It is interesting to note that following these restrictions, crime rose 67.6 percent in the National Parks in 1969, as opposed to a national increase of sixteen percent.

Support has also been withdrawn from other federal programs that are related to recreation. The greatest cutbacks came in March of 1970 when the Office of Economic Opportunity announced it would no longer support Summer Community Action Programs that emphasized recreation, camping, and cultural enrichment programs for the urban poor. In 1973, the Office of Economic Opportunity itself was threatened by severe cutbacks, but this is still under investigation.

Necessity of Establishing Priorities

A consideration of priorities is most important. Revenue sharing is now returning about eleven billion dollars annually to the states. How will the states use this money? Recreation should be an important factor in financial budgeting.

We have already discussed the great amount of money that Americans spend on leisure-related activities. However, why are Americans unwilling to support public- and voluntary-agency facilities and programs? Some of the money currently being spent on private recreation should be diverted to meet the needs of the public. Nevertheless, when new tax bills are introduced, they are met with a resounding "no." The taxpayer is unwilling to pay any more for services, but he is quite willing to spend 105 billion dollars on personal leisure. Again, the word *priorities* must be considered. What is more important and what will a reduction of facilities and personnel mean to the American way of life in the years to come?

Another way to overcome austerity budgets in the recreation field is to try to use present facilities and employees and bring more volunteers into the programs. Programs that charge minimum fees can also help to support themselves, and careful planning by professionals can eliminate some of the "fat" in programming, so that what remains is still effective.

TRENDS IN THE LEISURE ECONOMY

As noted earlier, the leisure economy keeps rising, and certain trends or new ways to spend this money are becoming more apparent. The trend toward recreational vehicles has already been mentioned and this trend has added to the recreation boom as well as to recreation enjoyment.

Skiing is another sport which has grown in participation in recent years. Ski resorts, once catering only to the very rich, are now proliferating around the country and drawing people from most socioeconomic levels. In 1971, more than 4.25 million skiers spent 1.3 billion dollars on equipment, lodging, travel, ski-lift tickets, and entertainment. This figure was cited by the Ski Industries of America. It is predicted that skiing will be a two-billion-dollar industry by the middle 1970s. Ski clubs, tours, and social organizations that organize ski trips are all contributing to the growth of this sport, which keeps attracting thousands of new skiers every year.

Water-oriented sports are enjoyed by millions of Americans. According to a recent study by the U.S. Bureau of Outdoor Recreation, swimming, fishing, and boating in that order ranked second, sixth, and seventh in the number of participants in major outdoor recreational activities. Water-skiing has grown rapidly in recent years, and the American Water Ski Association estimates that eleven million people tried the sport during 1971. More than forty-five million dollars were spent on water skis during that same year. Other water-oriented sports that contribute to the leisure boom are surfing and skin diving. There are more than 1.5 million surfboard users and more than a million skin divers. Estimates cite that skin divers spent more than thirty million dollars on related equipment in 1971.

Another trend, which will be elaborated on in Chapter 13, is the movement toward playing tennis. Tennis players now number over ten million, and they buy fifty million dollars worth of tennis equipment each year. Tennis growth can also be seen in the number of indoor tennis courts that have been built, along with the increase in active tennis programs, lessons, and even residential tennis camps for people of all ages.

Golf has long been a very popular recreational activity, with an estimated 12.25 million golfers who spend more than three billion dollars a year on greens fees, club memberships, and golf equipment.

Golf has long been a very popular recreational activity. Dunes Golf and Beach Club, Myrtle Beach, South Carolina. Photo courtesy of South Carolina Department of Parks, Recreation, and Tourism.

The quest for vacation homes and land has soared in recent years. In 1971, more than two million American families owned vacation homes, and this number is expected to increase annually by 200,000 more homes. This number of homes accounts for about two billion dollars of leisure money expenditures, and the figure is expected to double in the next eight years.

In addition, vacation land sales are at an all-time high. The American Land Development Association estimates sales exceeding 650,000 lots with a total value of approximately 5.5 billion dollars. Many of the land development corporations offer amenities along with the purchase of land. These special attractions may include golf courses, swimming pools, community clubhouses, riding trails, and developed ski areas where feasible.

The trend toward travel both at home and abroad has been with us for a number of years now and continues to increase both in number of people travelling and amount of money spent in this pursuit. The American Automobile Association (AAA) estimates that forty billion dollars will be spent on domestic travel alone, and Americans will drive more than 300 billion miles to and from vacation areas.

Foreign travel attracts about six million Americans who spend more than 7.5 billion dollars a year in this pursuit. Even with the recent devaluation of the American dollar, travel abroad is on the increase. Special charter flights, airline tours, travel clubs, and reductions in air fares have greatly contributed to the growing popularity of foreign travel.

EDUCATION FOR LEISURE

Most people assume that use of leisure time cannot be learned. People feel this way because they have never been taught how to beneficially use their available free time. In recent years, some learning experiences have begun to take

Firemen cooperate by opening hydrants so children can enjoy their leisure on a hot day. Community Center, North Little Rock, Arkansas. Photo courtesy of the North Little Rock Recreation Department.

place. Schools have been concentrating more on leisure-time activities, especially those with some carry-over potential for later life. Industry has also offered more opportunities for use of leisure time. Adults are being reached through adult education programs and other programs sponsored by civic organizations. However, there is still a wide gap to be filled by proper education in the use of leisure time. This gap becomes evident as the members of the drug culture increase, crime statistics increase, and more and more persons hang around street corners during leisure hours. Who should be responsible for leisure time education and what should be taught in such programs? These are some of the questions that we will try to answer in the following sections of this chapter.

Responsibility of the Parent

A child's first exposure to use of leisure time occurs within the family. It is their pattern of recreation that will, to some extent, be adopted. If one sees only mother doing homemaking activities and father working around the house or watching television, then one will have a very narrow view of what reacreational activities are available.

Leisure skills and interests do not suddenly appear one day; they must be nurtured through knowledge and participation. Some of the things a parent can do to encourage an active interest in beneficial use of leisure time include:

1. *Participate in activities yourself.* Provide a good example by becoming involved in leisure-time experiences that you have already had a desire to

Parents have a responsibility for the wise use of leisure time by their children. One way is to acquaint them with the programs available for recreation. Sprain Ridge Pool. Photo courtesy of the County of Westchester Department of Parks, Recreation, and Conservation.

do. Encourage your child to observe you and participate in the activity if at all possible. For example, if you bowl in a weekly league, take your child with you occasionally. This will be beneficial to both of you in many ways. However, be careful not to force your leisure activities upon the child.

2. *Support his interests.* Do not always expect him to have the same interests as "most" of the other children. If he has an unusual hobby or interest, encourage him by learning about it yourself and if possible by participating with him.

3. *Open your home to your child's friends so that they may explore leisure interests together.* An open home is conducive to exploration of leisure-time activities.

4. *Acquaint your child with programs available within the community, such as Boy and Girl Scouts, "Y's," community centers, and park and recreation facilities.* Help to schedule his time so that he can best avail himself of these services.

5. *Take your children to educational and cultural programs.* There are many community offerings of theater, concerts, and other cultural events for children. In addition, his horizons can be widened by visiting zoos, museums, parks, sporting events, and church- and civic-related programs.

6. *It is important not to overschedule a child's day.* If the child is pressured by too many activities, he will not be able to derive enjoyment from any one of them.

7. *Provide for family-centered activities.* There are many leisure-time pursuits that can be enjoyed by the entire family. Picnics, camping trips, swimming sessions, and day trips are all educational, recreational, and, most importantly, enjoyable to all.

Many parents tend to leave the leisure aspects of their child's life to the schools or community groups. However, many schools are inadequate in leisure education and very often children do not avail themselves of community offerings.

Responsibility of the School

"Education has no more serious responsibility than making adequate provision for enjoyment of recreative leisure not only for the sake of the immediate health, but still more if possible for the sake of its lasting effect upon the habits of the mind," wrote John Dewey, one of our foremost educators.

It is important to educate children to have a sense of values concerning the time they have to use during a day. To do this, they must first find out how they are presently using this time and what they can do to change their existing schedules. They should ask themselves such questions as: Why am I doing this? Is this what I really want to do? Are there any alternatives? How do I find out about them? Many teachers have introduced activities to help children answer these questions.

Frequently children are asked to keep a "time diary." This is simply a chart the child keeps for one week that breaks the week down into half-hour segments. The child is asked to record his comings and goings during that weekly period. The teacher should not ask to see these charts as they should be kept personal, and there also should not be an atmosphere of inquiry or right or wrong attached to the diary. The diary is kept so that the child may:

1. discover where he is wasting time
2. find out the activities he enjoys most
3. see the difference between what he says and what he does
4. gain perspective concerning those activities which *must* be done and those over which he has some freedom of choice

At the end of the week, some of the major activities may be listed, discussed, and their values explored. The children will usually come to very valid conclusions about their use of leisure time on their own.

Another activity that can be done in the classroom is a weekly evaluation. Five copies of a form are given to each child, one to be filled out each week for the next five weeks. Questions that may be included on these forms are:

1. Did you do anything this week that you had been thinking about?
2. Did you devote more than two solid hours to any one activity?
3. Did you plan for any future activities?
4. How could the week have been better?

The teacher may use these forms to spot problem areas, encourage certain activities, provide impetus for discussions about leisure time, and have students exchange sheets anonymously to get views about the activities of others.

Another interesting concept is that of value cards. Students are asked to turn in a weekly card concerning the quality of living they have done during the past week. The topic is open-ended and allows for great freedom of expression. It also provides valuable views of leisure-time use.

To help children plan for their free hours, it is helpful to have them jot down their leisure-time plans prior to holidays, weekends, and vacations. This activity will start the child thinking about the best way to use this time, and he might discover some ways that he had not thought of before. There are many similar exercises for children to help them gain some concept of the time they have to use and how to go about doing it. Parents and recreation leaders can also use these suggestions in helping children to plan their daily activities.

Physical education teachers have their own responsibilities in educating for leisure time. Physical education classes should devote more time to activities that have a carry-over value. Some schools already include golf, tennis, bowling, archery, and other such activities in their curriculums. It is essential that students be exposed to activities that they can participate in now and in later life. There are at least five important areas of leisure-type activities that should be included in physical education programming. These areas include:

1. outdoor recreation encompassing such activities as camping, hiking, and cycling
2. water-related activities including swimming, boating, and diving
3. sportsman activities such as riflery, skeet shooting, and fishing
4. winter sports such as skating, sledding, and skiing
5. individual and dual games including bowling, tennis, golf, badminton, table tennis, and handball

It is understood that all of these activities cannot possibly be offered in one year, but they could be scheduled so that over a four-year period, a child would have an opportunity to participate in most of these activities. In addition, some activities can be carried on in after-school programs. These activities may be sponsored by the physical education department or students can seek out a sponsor and form their own clubs. The sponsor or leader may be another teacher in the school with a keen interest in a particular leisure-related activity. Informal clubs can plan to participate in their activity on a weekly basis, and, in addition, they can gather literature about the activity and attend exhibitions. A tennis club, for example, can plan trips to major tennis exhibitions and attend and enter community tennis competitions. The club can sponsor films pertaining to tennis and invite guest lecturers to help them learn more about the game.

The role of the physical education teacher and his programs have been discussed extensively, but leisure education is also served by other teachers and departments in our schools. Cultural programs of all types can be offered as an extracurricular activity and these programs involve people in many aspects of music, drama, and dance. Many schools have frequent theater productions that involve the outside community as well as the students. Students and others who are not interested in acting and singing can find behind-the-scenes work very satisfying. In addition, there are many clubs that cater to all interests, including language clubs, advanced study groups, fiction- and poetry-reading groups, carpentry and automotive shops, and numerous other activities that provide an education for leisure-time use.

The recent trend toward year-round schools is bound to have an impact on leisure-time education. Many more possibilities are opened to the students who will have more frequent, shorter periods off from school rather than the normal week-long vacations and free summers. Students will now have time off throughout the year and can greatly benefit from programs that will educate them for participating in leisure activities during their free periods.

Role of the Recreation Professional

The role of the professional recreator is vital in education for leisure time. It is the professional who can aid in the creation of programs that are both beneficial and also have carry-over value for a person's later life. In order to educate people in the best uses of leisure time, the professional must first have strong leadership abilities coupled with very real interest in people as individuals. Programs must be planned to meet the needs of the people they are being planned for. This is best accomplished by meeting with representatives of the community and taking their interests into consideration prior to planning specific programs. Existing programs should be continuously evaluated in terms of interest patterns and individual and community needs.

In Chapter 8, "Planning for Total Recreation Programs," the role of the professional recreator is discussed in great detail. In this chapter, you will learn more about how the recreator can plan his programs to meet the needs of education for leisure time.

The Journal of Leisure Research

The *Journal of Leisure Research* is a publication designed to acquaint park, recreation, and conservation leaders with the latest research in the area of leisure. It is published by The National Recreation and Park Association and was started in 1969. The publication includes articles on completed research, abstracts, scholarly inquiries, summaries of research in specific areas, letters to the editor, and book reviews. The objectives of the publication are to:

1. stimulate research
2. disseminate research results to the field
3. enhance the image of the profession
4. alert the field to leisure-time innovations
5. encourage professional advancement
6. become the leading research journal in the field
7. provide the resource for textbooks and practitioner publications

The major topics discussed include:

1. philosophical and historical foundations
2. urban environment
3. natural resources
4. management practices
5. economics
6. education
7. human behavior
8. planning and design
9. legislation
10. miscellaneous topics of interest to the field

Publications such as this one are most beneficial in learning about how to educate for leisure time. This information, once disseminated to recreation professionals, can then be incorporated into present and future leisure programming.

Responsibility of the Community and Federal Government

From the preceding chapters, it should be apparent that both the community and federal government have a responsibility and an obligation to educate for leisure. They do this through the myriad services that were previously discussed. (Review the sections of Chapter 3 concerning the community and federal government.) However, in addition to offering services, it is important that their programs be well publicized so people know about them. Failure of certain programs is frequently due to public apathy arising from the people being unaware of offerings. In general, all programs should be constructed with education and carry-over potential in mind.

QUESTIONS AND EXERCISES

1. Define *leisure* and *recreation* according to this text. Do you have any other definitions of these terms? Explain your answer.
2. Why are some people unable to use their available leisure time? How can these situations be changed?
3. What is meant by the statement, "Leisure time, though apparently increasing, may in reality be decreasing."
4. What is meant by the phrase "education for leisure"? Who are some of the people who have a responsibility toward this education?
5. What should the parents' role be in leisure education? Does the school have a role also? If so, what should it be?
6. Keep a "time diary" for one week and evaluate your own use of time in relation to some of the statements made in the text.
7. What is the role of the professional recreator in education for leisure? If you were a professional in the field, what suggestions could you make to help educate people in more beneficial uses of leisure time?
8. Define *social class*. Do social classes use leisure time differently? Explain your answer.
9. What is meant by the concept of *total living?* How does this concept affect use of leisure time?
10. What is meant by the term *leisure boom?* What are some of the reasons behind this boom?

11. How has the boom affected the recreation profession? What are some of the reasons behind cutbacks in recreation programs?

12. Briefly discuss some major trends in leisure that have had an important influence on the economy.

SELECTED REFERENCES

Bliven, Bruce, "Using Our Leisure Is No Easy Job," *The New York Times Magazine,* April 26, 1964, p. 19.

Degen, Carl G., Jr., "Communication/Interpretation," *Journal of Health, Physical Education and Recreation,* 43 (March, 1972).

Erickson, Ellwood, "The Innocence of Leisure," *Journal of Health, Physical Education and Recreation,* 43 (March, 1972).

Godbey, Geoffrey, "Leisure: Nearing the Receding Horizon," *Parks and Recreation,* Vol. 6 (August, 1971).

Gray, David, "The Changing Pattern of American Life," *Parks and Recreation,* Vol. 1 (1966).

Hodgson, J. D., "Leisure and the American Worker," *Journal of Health, Physical Education, and Recreation,* Vol. 43 (March, 1972).

Hoffer, Eric, "Leisure and the Masses," *Parks and Recreation,* Vol. IV (March, 1969).

"The Journal of Leisure Research," *Parks and Recreation,* Vol. III (September, 1968).

Kaplan, Max, "New Concepts of Leisure Today," *Journal of Health, Physical Education and Recreation,* Vol. 43 (March, 1972).

Kraus, Richard, "The Economics of Leisure Today," *Parks and Recreation,* Vol. VI (August, 1971).

————, "Recreation for Rich and Poor," *Teachers College Record,* 67 (May, 1966).

"Leisure Boom: Biggest Ever and Still Growing," *U. S. News and World Report,* April 17, 1972.

Leisure: Will Your Child Be a Doer – or a Viewer. Publications Division of the National Education Association, 1201 Sixteenth St., N.W., Washington, D.C. 20036.

Lieberman, Phyllis, and Sidney Stone, "A School's Responsibility: Worthy Use of Leisure Time," *The Clearing House,* Vol. 38 (April, 1965).

Miller, Norman P., and Duane Robinson, *The Leisure Age.* Belmont, Calif.: Wadsworth Publishing Company, 1963.

Moebley, Tony A., "Educating for Leisure," *Parks and Recreation,* Vol. III (November, 1968).

Murphey, James F., "Recreation Education – A Social Concern," *Parks and Recreation,* Vol. V (September, 1970).

Nash, Bernard E., "Retirement as Leisure," *Journal of Health, Physical Education and Recreation,* Vol. 43 (March, 1972).

Staley, Edwin, ed., *Leisure and the Quality of Life.* The American Association for Health. Washington, D.C.: Physical Education and Recreation, 1972.

Strobbe, John E., "The Year-round School and Recreation," *Journal of Health, Physical Education and Recreation,* Vol. 43 (March, 1972).

part III
the recreation program

Reptile Study, Clear Creek Camp. Photo courtesy of the Los Angeles City Schools, Youth Services Section.

8

PLANNING FOR

TOTAL RECREATION PROGRAMS

Recreation programs are intended to satisfy a need for constructive use of leisure time. Programs are designed for people of both sexes, all ages, differing racial and economic backgrounds, and those persons having special interests or needs. Recreation programs are sponsored by such agencies or groups as the government, schools, churches, civic groups, hospitals, and public or semipublic organizations. A complete discussion of agencies that run recreation programs was given in Chapter 3.

In this chapter, the principles of recreation programming will be discussed along with a closer look into community, school, and outdoor recreation programs. In addition, specific programs that are presently being used, or have been used, will be discussed in relation to the particular needs, interests, and age groups that are being serviced.

PRINCIPLES AND PROBLEMS
OF RECREATION PROGRAMMING

Before outlining the principles involved in recreation programming, it is necessary to formulate a working definition of the word *program*. For our purposes in this text, program will be defined as the total activity experience of the person involved, which includes both his needs and interests. For example, if an excellent football program is offered to a group of senior citizens, it will probably be a failure since it can only meet the needs and interests of the people for whom it was designed; successful programming usually involves in the decision-making process the people for whom the program was designed. This was true, as you recall, in our discussion of the importance of community involvement in Chapter 6; see page 100. Some basic considerations in program planning should include the following points:

1. The importance of creativity and discovery
2. Achievement of a degree of mastery over oneself and one's environment
3. Achievement and satisfaction in participation
4. Pleasure and enjoyment of oneself and fulfillment through group social encounters

Basic Principles

Throughout this text, different elements of program planning have been discussed. Here these principles are unified into a cohesive summary of the major considerations for any recreation plan or program.

1. *The individual needs of each participant must be acknowledged.* Programs must be designed with the participant as an uppermost factor. Age, sex, interests, special needs, or disabilities must be taken into consideration. Many programs are wasted because these factors have not been considered in preliminary planning.
2. *Programs must meet the values of our society and the needs of the community being served.* Sound democratic values are basic to good recreation programming. Community interests and needs must be taken into consideration. Inner-city areas, for example, have a varied population make-up and different needs and problems from those of a middle-class suburban population.
3. *Recreation programs should be diverse and well-balanced.* Variety is the best drawing card for any recreation program. If people can find creative, challenging activities, they will participate in the offerings of the program. Any sound program must provide varied offerings on all levels of participation. For example, guitar lessons must be on a beginning level for most people, but the same teacher could also arrange an intermediate or advanced class if there were enough people interested.
4. *Recreation programs should be offered at many different times to meet the needs of most people.* It is necessary to coordinate the schedule of offerings with the greatest number of people to be served by a particular program. School-age and teen-age programs should be conducted in late afternoon hours and/or on weekends. School vacations are an excellent time for more concentrated program activities.
5. *Competent leadership and adequate financial planning is essential to successful programming.* Leaders who have rapport with the participants in the area being served are an integral part of any recreation program. Good financial planning will help to assure the longevity of a program while also allowing for greater participation. Both of these topics will be discussed in detail in Chapters 9 and 10 of this book.

Some activities in the recreation program in North Little Rock, Arkansas.

Problems in Recreation Planning

Howard G. Danford, in his book, *Creative Leadership in Recreation,* points out that many recreation leaders are guided by unsound practices in evolving recreation programs.[1] Some of these practices are mentioned here:

1. *The traditional approach.* The program is continually offered in the same basic manner over the years. Because it may have been successful in previous years, leaders see no reason to change it now.
2. *The current practice approach.* This is the copying of programs that have had some success in other communities or in different areas of the country.
3. *The expressed desire approach.* This approach relies on surveys to indicate the programs desired in a particular area.
4. *The authoritarian approach.* This method relies solely on the recreation leader and his staff to decide on what activities to include in a recreation program.

As you read each of the approaches, some of the problems inherent in the approach probably occurred to you. If we examine each approach separately, the fallacy involved becomes more apparent.

The *traditional approach* relies on the continued success of a program. The fallacy here is that as the people involved in the program change, so must the program. This approach also does not allow people to explore and find success in different activities and to explore new avenues of recreation.

The *current practice approach* relies on success in other communities. "If the program works there, it should work here," is the theme of this approach. The obvious fallacy is that the make-up of communities is different from one part of the state to another, let alone from one area of the country to another. A successful program in one area can be a total failure in a different area. It is important for a recreation leader to learn from different programs and try to use the best ingredients of many different program offerings.

The *expressed desire approach* relies on the people to tell the recreator what they want in a program. This certainly can be advantageous in many cases. However, a recreation leader must be aware that many people suggest only what they feel secure about or are familiar with. A well-rounded program must be diverse and incorporate new fields of interest.

The *authoritarian approach* leaves all decision making to the recreation administrators. This is as inappropriate as leaving all the decisions to the participants. The recreator may have a good textbook knowledge of what a recreation program should comprise, but he must also find out about the special needs and interests of the people he is serving.

[1]Howard G. Danford, *Creative Leadership in Recreation* (Boston: Allyn and Bacon, 1964).

None of the approaches are all bad or all good. Each has something constructive to say about successful programming as long as the fallacies are understood and taken into consideration. Programs must be constantly evaluated, updated, and most importantly have meaning for the community that will participate in them.

Fallacies of Recreation Programs

What is the purpose of a recreation program? Generally speaking, recreation programs are intended to fulfill a need for a constructive and creative use of leisure time. Frequently, the success of a recreation program is judged by the attendance or the amount of money a program generates. Programs that attract publicity are often interpreted as successful. For example, some community recreation programs sponsor beauty contests for children of different ages, i.e., beautiful baby and Jr. Miss America contests. Some communities sponsor competitive sporting events for young children. These types of programs may draw large crowds and get much local newspaper and radio coverage, but are they worthy, beneficial recreation programs? They may not fit our original definition of recreation as a creative and constructive use of leisure time. This is one type of fallacy in recreation programming.

Another common fallacy is to assume that busyness in programming is necessarily beneficial. Many high school and junior high school students have so many activities to keep up with that frequently they don't have the time to enjoy these pursuits. If one is restricted to a half hour of tennis, because she has to go to a dance class, then she probably isn't getting that much out of either activity. Recreation programs should extoll that value of finding a few activities which are constructive and enjoyable. Greater amounts of time spent on these activities will result in better accomplishment and more carry-over interest into later life.

Another program fallacy that is frequently overlooked involves the segregation of special-needs groups. These groups such as the handicapped, retarded, and senior citizens are usually not included in the general recreation programs. Instead, they are grouped according to their special needs. There are many camps for the handicapped and the retarded, but they are usually separate from the camps for so-called "normal" children. Other social and cultural programs for the handicapped, too, are usually separate, and programs of all types for the re-tarded are almost always separate, often held in a different building from other community programs. Senior citizens are another excellent example of separat-ism being carried to extremes. They have their own clubs, social functions, and trips and rarely participate with the rest of the community. Even the new trend toward senior-citizen retirement communities segregates these people right out of the mainstream of life. If anything tends to alienate people more, it is this flagrant segregation of activity programs. Recreators must begin to bring these groups together whenever possible so that they can benefit from each other's company in recreational settings.

An excellent example of a fallacy in programming is represented by our Little League programs and their equivalents. What started out as a healthy, beneficial recreation activity, has, in some cases, turned out to be an overly competitive, nerve-wracking, tension-producing activity with much too much adult involvement. Some of the problems encountered in Little League activities include:

1. *Too much outside intervention.* Parents frequently get too involved and try to realize their own athletic goals through their children. They frequently manage teams to which their own children belong.

2. *Outside sponsorship that leads to adult competition.* Leagues are often sponsored by local businesses and the team members have the sponsor's name on their uniforms. This sometimes leads to adults aligning themselves with the teams represented by companies they may work for or do business with.

3. *Expecting too much from children involved.* Adult standards are frequently applied to a children's game. Practice time is too long and too frequent and many children complain of sore muscles and other game-related injuries.

Little League programs, like all programs, must concentrate on the group being served, and their interests and needs should be the primary consideration.

COMMUNITY-SCHOOL RECREATION PROGRAMS

The concept of schools and communities sharing recreation facilities and programs has already been generally discussed in Chapter 3. In this chapter, some specific community-school programs will be discussed, and their unique contribution to recreation will be examined.

Role of the School
in Community Recreation Programs

The community-school is a concept that has been in existence for a number of years. It was generally defined by the *52nd Yearbook of the National Society for the Study of Education* as: "an effective school, combining many desirable features of past educational emphasis with those of the present to form a concept of education that is sound and permanent, not a fad or passing fancy." It is a school that is closely related to the community and acts to meet the needs of the community by sharing its physical and human resources.

Some of the characteristics of a community-school concept include:

1. acts as a community center

Los Angeles has an outstanding community-school recreation program. Winners in the Boat Regatta. Photo courtesy of the Los Angeles City Schools, Youth Services Section.

2. uses community resources
3. provides activities for pre-school children, young persons who have left school, adults, and all community members having special needs or problems
4. maintains a comprehensive school curriculum
5. cooperates with community administrators
6. employs staff members who are active in community affairs

A community-school plan can only be successful when there is good communication between the school and community. Each has to be aware of what the other's goals are and what steps to take in meeting these goals. Some ways of insuring a successful community-school alliance are:

1. Presentation of an education program to explain the concept to community members
2. Provision for educational leadership that will stimulate the community to support programs by backing the school and involved community agencies
3. Careful evaluation of community education and recreation goals and needs
4. Cooperation of school boards and community organizations to improve school programs
5. Teacher involvement in program planning and administration, both in voluntary and paying positions

SAMPLE SUMMER PROGRAM

HOURS	MONDAY	TUESDAY	WEDNESDAY	THURSDAY	FRIDAY
12 to 1:30	**PHYSICAL RECREATION ACTIVITIES** (basketball, softball, touch football, volleyball, handball, track, bocce, badminton, table tennis, archery, bowling, gymnastics, tetherball)				
1:30 to 2:30	**MOVIES** (scheduled	**QUIET GAMES** (dominoes, checkers, chess, caroms, pool, labyrinth, other table games, quiz games)			**ROLLER SKATING** (scheduled on same day in alternate weeks)
2:30 to 4	at same time each week)	**ARTS AND CRAFTS** (wood, metal, plastic, leather, jewelry, model-making, mosaic, sewing, ceramics, and painting)			**WEEKLY SPECIAL EVENT**[2]
4 to 5	**DANCING AND MUSIC**[1] (social dancing, folk dancing, round dancing, square dancing, singing, listening to music)	**CLUBS**[1] (charm, music, travel, weight training, photography)	**TALENT**[1] (dramatics, modern dance, tap dance, vocal music, instrumental music)	**CLUBS**[1] (charm, weight training, stamps and coins, slot cars, homemaking)	(tours, arts and crafts exhibits, tournaments, bicycle rodeos, talent hunts and shows, watermelon feeds, picnic lunches, jamborees)
5 to 6	**BOYS' PHYSICAL FITNESS ACTIVITY** **GIRLS' PHYSICAL FITNESS ACTIVITY** (events involving strength, endurance, agility)				

1. If sufficient leadership is available, it is recommended that these activities be scheduled daily.

2. Certain special events require rearranging of the regular program on the dates concerned.

Reprinted by permission of the Los Angeles City Schools, Youth Services Section.

After-hours Use of School Buildings

One of the problems of using school buildings for community activities is reaching an understanding of who is responsible for maintenance of school facilities and property. Frequently, schools have "understandings" with certain groups but if damages result to school buildings, the "understanding" is forgotten. Schools must act in a legal manner to insure their rights in case of stolen or damaged property. Contracts should be drawn up that specifically designate time, place, rental cost, and responsibilities of the group that plans to use school space. Schedules must be carefully adhered to so that programs do not interfere with each other. In most cases, first preference for school building use should be given to students of that school. But students, too, must schedule their activities in advance so that conflicts with community activities may be avoided.

Another problem, common to urban areas, is outright vandalism of schools after school hours. If schools in these areas are open to public activities, then security guards are essential to insure the safety of the participants as well as the protection of school property. Cost of guards may be the responsibility of the group using the school or may be shared by the school and group or groups involved.

The Education Plaza Concept

This concept in community-education planning was suggested by the East Orange, N. J., Board of Education. In its booklet entitled *The East Orange Education Plaza*, it explains the concept as a step in coping with the increasingly congested urban area and its desire "to provide educational opportunity of the highest caliber ... and a cultural, recreational, and enrichment center for the entire community." This project, which would take about fifteen years to accomplish, will consist of a centrally located area of about fifteen acres. A building for all the school children of the community will be in the plaza and the children would be bused there. In addition, all recreational and park facilities would be located in and about this central "school" building that is in effect a school-community center. In addition to this center, neighborhood schools would continue to exist as neighborhood community centers with available recreation facilities. This type of program is valuable to a community like East Orange that is very urban, having about 80,000 residents in less than four square miles. Some persons object to this concept because they feel that neighborhood schools, especially in the lower grades, are essential to development of neighborhood spirit and close area relationships of residents.

Schools as Recreation Centers

It is desirable for many reasons that schools be used as centers for culture and recreation for the entire community. The most obvious reason for creating neighborhood recreation centers is economic. If schools are built to house educational, recreational, and park facilities, then separate facilities are not needed. Duplication of facilities is avoided. A neighborhood recreation-school area is usually within walking distance, and long car or public transportation trips are avoided. Land use is maximized, and new recreation land does not have to be obtained. All of these reasons point to why many communities have adopted this plan of sharing and improving existing school facilities. This concept can best be achieved by using existing school buildings and planning new schools to include enough land to house parks, playgrounds, ball fields, picnic areas, multiple use areas, swimming pools, and school buildings designed for educational, recreational, and cultural activities.

An example of how such a program works can be seen in Salem, the capital of Oregon. In 1917, school officials first decided to keep the schools' gymnasiums and activity rooms open for public use after school hours. The city's recreation program today is a completely joint city-school enterprise that meets the needs of all its citizens. Each contributes half of the needed recreation funds, and they pool all available properties suitable for recreation purposes. The properties include gyms, athletic fields, parks, libraries, auditoriums, and music rooms. Winter programs include basketball and volleyball games, dance classes, exercise classes, and adult programs; in the summer months there are baseball leagues, supervised playground activities, and numerous planned programs for adults and children alike. All members of the community, including clubs, special interest groups, and industrial leagues, use the school-park system.

Community-school Swimming Programs

Swimming pools in schools were once thought of as luxuries, but today when more and more inground pools are appearing in backyards, their value in schools should not be overlooked. A school swimming facility can serve the school and community and provide a beneficial activity that people of all ages can use and enjoy. If schools, especially secondary schools, house indoor and outdoor pools, they would greatly benefit the community. This concept would then take the place of the separate community pools that are being built in many areas of the country.

In order for a community-school pool program to be successful, it should fully use the pool on an afternoon, evening, weekend, and summer schedule. Swimming classes should be given during school hours, and related swimming activities should be planned. Some activities may include:

1. free swims
2. preschool swimming lessons
3. mother and toddler swims
4. swimming and diving classes
5. scuba classes

An example of where the county government provides swimming facilities for school children. Photo courtesy of the County of Westchester, New York, Department of Parks, Recreation, and Conservation.

6. American Red Cross lifesaving programs
7. water ballet
8. competitive swimming meets
9. water shows and carnivals
10. family-swim programs

Swimming pools offer such a great variety of activities that they can no longer be looked upon as a luxury. If properly used, they are well worth the initial investment.

One community that has had great success with a community-school swimming pool is Westside, Nebraska, a suburban school system within the city limits of Omaha. Several years ago, this community added an indoor pool to its high school and adopted the philosophy that a swimming program must be varied enough to meet the needs of the community and that there must be an opportunity for all residents to use the facility. It is estimated that the pool is used about 3,500 hours a year and serves approximately 40,000 people. Some of the programs offered include:

1. swimming classes (required and elective)
2. free swims

3. intramural water polo
4. competitive swimming
5. synchronized swimming and ballet
6. evening recreational swimming
7. summer classes for all age groups
8. Scout swims
9. scuba clubs
10. Red Cross courses
11. classes for mentally retarded and handicapped children and adults

SCHOOL RECREATION PROGRAMS

School recreation programs are widely diversified and include athletic, cultural, and special-interest groups or clubs. Photography, dance, glee clubs, stamp and coin collecting clubs, and numerous other extracurricular activities attract student interest. As discussed in Chapter 7, the school has a very special responsibility in educating students in the beneficial use of leisure time. In belonging to these extracurricular groups, students may find an activity that will develop into a life-time interest.

Unfortunately, many school systems require that a student have a certain grade average before he can join an extracurricular activity. This is especially true in subject-related clubs such as the math or science club. This type of thinking is very unfair to a student who might not be academically motivated but may get enjoyment and satisfaction from a special-interest club. A mediocre student may find classroom science boring but may be interested and successful in a science club that features nature programs and other outdoor recreation programs. All students should have an equal opportunity to explore extra-curricular activities regardless of grade averages.

The Discovery Program in Philadelphia

Philadelphia's Thomas A. Edison High School introduced what they called a "discovery" program a few years ago. This program was designed to interest disadvantaged youth in the cultural events around them. Some of the programs attended by the students included theater presentations, orchestral programs, opera, ballet, and numerous films. Students were prepared for the events by listening to the music, learning about the play, or by reading synopsis sheets of the operas. Credit for attendance was given if the students filled out an "Assay Journal" sheet on which they recorded their reactions to the performances. Concerts, live theater productions, and lectures of cultural interest were also brought to the school to try and reach as many students as possible. In addition, cultural events at nearby universities were frequently attended and a Great

Books Club was formed that involved a bimonthly discussion of assigned readings of classic works. Qualified volunteers led the group discussions. A city news company sponsored a bookmobile that stocked over 6,000 paperbacks and was brought into the school yard for the students to browse through.

OUTDOOR RECREATION

The term *outdoor recreation* seems to define itself; however, there are many different definitions, as a single broad concept of the term has never been developed. Outdoor recreation has encompassed camping activities, nature-study programs, water-oriented activities, conservation and ecology programs, and educational programs that relate to recreation. Outdoor education relates to those programs that use the out-of-doors as an extension of the classroom. Students may better understand text material when confronted with it on a first-hand basis, i.e., studying forest conservation by participating in outdoor programs sponsored by the local Forest Service Agency.

The Bureau of Outdoor Recreation was established on April 2, 1962, in the Department of Interior. Its primary purpose is to provide a focal point and leadership in the nationwide outdoor recreation movement. The functions of the Bureau are policy making, planning, assistance, coordination, and research. Its program concentrates on three main activities:

1. preparing a nationwide outdoor recreation plan
2. coordinating federal outdoor recreation programs
3. giving technical assistance to the states in preparation of their own state-wide outdoor recreation plans.

Types of Outdoor Recreation Programs

Nature-study programs of all types are popular outdoor recreation pursuits. These programs may include nature walks, bird watching, gardening, visits to zoological parks and museums, animal-care exercises, nature-collecting clubs (i.e., shells, rocks, butterflies, seeds, flowers, etc.), and trips to forests, ocean areas, farms, and different land formations.

Arts-and-crafts programs related to the out-of-doors may include use of natural material in art pursuits, such as the collecting and carving of driftwood or the painting of sea shells. In recent years, there has been a return to pioneer and Indian crafts, including basket weaving, loom-craft, and jewelry making, using natural materials such as shells, wood, and semiprecious stones.

Camping activities have become more and more popular in recent years. These activities may include backyard barbecuing as well as overnight camping trips to remote areas. With the advent of a wide variety of camping gear and recreational vehicles, camping is no longer as simple as it once was. Trailers, campers, and motor homes now can be seen on our roads throughout the year. Camping space is at a premium, so reservations must be made at major campsites well in advance, especially during the peak summer months.

Sports activities of all types flourish in the outdoors. In general, sports included in outdoor recreation programs are those that are not highly organized and are more individual in nature, such as water sports, cycling, jogging, and hunting and fishing. Many clubs have been formed to bring outdoor sports enthusiasts together. These groups include hiking, mountain climbing, alpine and youth hostel groups such as the American Youth Hostel, Inc., which provides low-cost accommodations to hiking or biking youth. Some outdoor groups such as the Sierra Club adhere to an outdoor recreation theme along with a strong program of conservation activities.

There are also a wide variety of clubs and organizations that have a special interest in some form of outdoor recreation. These clubs may be community-oriented and include bird-watchers, gardeners, ecologists, conservationists, and nature-study enthusiasts. Sometimes clubs become state- or nation-wide and hold conferences attended by community delegates.

Trends in Outdoor Recreation

The Bureau of Outdoor Recreation, in formulating its nation-wide plan, has discovered some interesting and startling patterns of recreation behavior. It has found that in 1960, outdoor recreation participation occurred on 4,280,000,000 occasions. They project that the number of occasions will rise to 16,846,000,000 in the year 2000. In other words, outdoor recreation activities will be four times greater in the year 2000 than they were in 1960. Even in the short span of years between 1960 and 1965 there was a fifty-one percent increase in outdoor recreation experiences. The greatest increase in activities, in order of participation, includes walking, swimming, driving for pleasure, outdoor games and sports, bicycling, sightseeing, picnicking, fishing, attendance at outdoor sporting events, boating, nature walks, camping, horseback riding, waterskiing, hiking, and attendance at outdoor concerts and plays. Swimming, for example, is becoming so popular that it is expected to be the number one outdoor activity in 1980 and remain in that position through the year 2000.

All of these present increases and proposed increases in outdoor activities sound encouraging – but is that really the case? As we all know, land for recreational use is not increasing; in fact, unprotected land is quickly becoming developed for nonrecreational use. The population is increasing and water-based recreation areas are rapidly becoming unusable or limited in use because of pollution problems. In addition, the areas where the greatest numbers of people live have the least amount of recreation land available. Therefore, recreation land areas near urban sprawls are becoming overcrowded with environmental damage occurring more and more frequently. With all of these problems, the question may be posed, "Why encourage greater use of outdoor recreational facilities?" This is not an easy question to answer, considering our available recreational land and water areas. The best solution may be in careful use of existing areas, protection of undeveloped land, education in ecology, conservation, and pollution problems, curtailing of some outdoor recreation publicity, and greater publicity given to those outdoor areas that are indeed "undercrowded," so that more people are encouraged to visit these areas instead of the well-known ones.

RECREATION PROGRAMS
FOR PEOPLE OF ALL AGES

Successful recreation programs should include activities and interest groups for the preschool child, school children, teen-agers, adults, and senior citizens. Handicapped and retarded persons should have special programs as well as being included in some activities of the other groups mentioned. As we discussed earlier, age, or segregation because of a handicap, should not exist as a major planning factor in the total recreation outlook. People of all ages and handicaps should be able to participate together in some activities. In fact, recent national programs such as VISTA and Foster Grandparents have involved different age groups in successful programs. For organization purposes only, activity programs have been grouped according to age groups and physical or mental disability — but keep in mind that some of the programs can be attended at the same time by all the groups discussed, except perhaps the preschool children.

It would be impossible in a book of this size to discuss all recreation programs for the groups mentioned, so a general overview of programs will be given with a few specific programs of special interest being noted.

Pre-school Children Offer a Challenge
to Recreation Programming

For many years pre-school children had been sorely overlooked in planning recreation programs. The two and a half to five year set is at a perfect age to begin some types of activities. Nursery schools that allow freedom and creativity are important in these early years. Experiences in group play, working with their hands, and nature programs are usually successful. In addition, many nursery schools go on field trips to zoos, farms, and local industry to get a first-hand look at the world around them. Other preschool activities include story telling, movies, story hours (when books are read and discussed), and swim and gym classes that are often combined, with one immediately following the other. Some communities have introduced mother-toddler swims and mother-toddler arts and crafts. These programs allow for the security of the small child and the involvement of the mother in the activity so that she can further carry over learned activities to the home. Communities should provide separate areas in playgrounds for the use of small children. Sand boxes, small slides, and wading pools are important features. All too frequently playground areas are shared with older children and the younger ones have a rough time asserting themselves. Day-care centers for the care of the children of working mothers is another important responsibility of good community recreation planning.

Programs for School-age Children

In most communities, the school-age group leads in recreation participation. This is true because of a strong desire to play. Even without organized activities, children of this age usually organize their own games, clubs, and leagues. Of course, organized supervision can make the most of the leisure time of this innately interested group. Many programs sponsored by Scouts, Boys and Girls Clubs, Y's, and other semipublic organizations have already been discussed. Community recreation programs usually include after-school, supervised playground recreation, baseball, basketball, and touch-football teams, supervised swim programs, and summer programs at local parks and recreation centers. Children of this age are also good candidates for field trips, camping trips, drama and dance presentations, and classes in arts and crafts, cooking, woodworking, and many other activities.

North Little Rock's Recreation Program provides a tumbling and gymnastic class for its school-age children. Community Center. Photo courtesy of North Little Rock, Arkansas, Recreation Department.

Camping has always been a major activity of the school-aged child. Children attend day camps, overnight camps, weekend camps, or have gone on camping trips with parents or relatives. However, the disadvantaged child rarely gets to have a camping experience of any type. This is what prompted a Saginaw County, Michigan, program that took ninety-seven children, aged nine to twelve years, on their first camping experience. The children, mostly third and fourth graders, were racially mixed, culturally and often physically deprived. A five-week program introduced them to camping, arts and crafts, swimming, sports, and playing and living together. There are many programs like this one including some that offer a two-week experience for inner-city children to visit with a family in the suburbs. The pros and cons of such programs come quickly to mind — but most programs like this one meet with great success, and more and more children and families seek to participate each year.

Another interesting program for children was introduced in Syracuse, N.Y., and is called a "Movie Bus." The Parks and Recreation Department purchased an old school bus and turned it into a mobile movie theater. The bus pulls into the city's playgrounds during the summer months and shows cartoons, movie features, tapes of "Sesame Street," and other films for children. This type of program is good in rainy weather as well as sunny weather and provides an educational and beneficial use of leisure time.

Reaching the Teen-ager
Through Recreation Programming

Recreation for the teen-age group is not quite as simple as for preschoolers and younger children. Teen-agers usually need to be challenged by creative recreation programs that are not repetitious of scouts, camps, or childhood club experiences. Many teen-agers have a communications gap with adults that prevents them from getting involved in organized recreation programs, other than some sports activities. Many of today's teen-agers are blasé about any type of organized recreation. They have been brought up, in many cases, in a very materialistic society where recreational activities are often watched rather than participated in. One study in Chicago on recreation and delinquency showed that twice as much time is spent in the movies as in established recreation programs.[2]

Recreation leaders should consider some of the following areas when planning programs for teen-agers:

1. Continuously evaluate the times that we live in and how they affect the standards and values of teen-agers generally.
2. Try to ascertain teen-agers' needs and act as a counselor as well as a recreation leader.

[2]*Recreation and Delinquency* (Chicago: Chicago Recreation Commission, 1942).

3. Recognize that teen-agers have a capacity for great dedication and are interested in volunteer projects related to recreation, i.e., working with youngsters, senior citizens, and the handicapped.
4. Give thoughtful consideration to challenging their energies in an interesting and beneficial manner.
5. Provide well-trained leaders that teen-agers can respect.
6. Involve teen-agers in the planning; activities that are of no interest to the group will not be well attended.

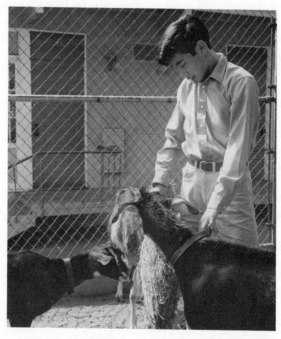

Teen-agers have a capacity for great dedication and are interested in pets and animals. Photo courtesy of the Los Angeles City Schools, Youth Services Section.

Ossining, New York, solved its teen-age recreation problems by creating a Teen Council that grew to a planning-group membership of over 100 teen-agers. One of their most successful programs is a teen-age night club called the "Cellar Discotheque." The teen-agers overhauled the basement of the recreation department building and created an unusual room with weird lighting effects, metallic paper, and "foot paintings" on the walls. Bands were auditioned and decided upon by a teen panel. Free membership cards were distributed to city teenagers and more than 800 have been issued to date. In addition to the discotheque, Teen Council meetings planned other recreation activities including bowling parties, ski trips, and other social events. The important lesson to be learned from Ossining is that activities planned by the teen-agers were well accepted as well as beneficial.

Teen-agers can be successfully involved in community programs, as witnessed by the 1967 National Youth Conference on Natural Beauty and Conservation. Young people from eleven national youth organizations, 500 teen-agers, met in Washington, D.C., in June, 1966, to plan community-improvement programs. Some of the programs' accomplishments included:

1. building new trails in a national forest near Seattle, Washington
2. construction of a courtesy rest stop and information booth in St. Johns, Arizona
3. planting trees in a burned-out area of San Bernadino, California
4. preservation of a wildlife refuge and "natural" area of a park in St. Paul, Minnesota

Teen-agers who are well challenged can contribute great energy to useful projects of all types.

Recreation for Adults

Adults are frequently overlooked in community recreation planning. Many recreation programs assume that adults would prefer to and do seek their own entertainment and recreation in a private manner. However, many adults have neither the financial means nor the exposure to leisure activities that would encourage them to seek out their own recreation experiences. The great popularity of adult-education programs points out the need for organized adult-recreation activities.

Some communities and urban areas have introduced the adult center as a way of serving the community on many levels: educational, social, recreational, and cultural. It is important to find out what the people need and want in the way of recreation programming. Surveys can be taken and delegates elected to attend planning meetings. Cultural programs of all types are usually well attended. In addition, guest lecturers can be brought in at a minimum cost to provide the impetus for discussion hours that might follow a lecture.

Frequently, adult programs should also be family-oriented programs. Programs that the entire family can appreciate bring the family closer together in a pleasant, enjoyable environment. One popular family event is a weekend of camping frequently sponsored by Y's or other organizations that have camp facilities. These groups open their camp grounds on specific weekends for families only. The camp staff is present to help in the supervision and use of facilities, and the entire family benefits personally and as a group.

Free art classes are popular as a recreation activity in Hempstead, New York. Photo courtesy of the Town of Hempstead Department of Recreation and Parks, Recreation Division.

Aging: a Creative Process

In recent years, recreation programs for senior citizens have been increasing in popularity throughout the country. More and more people, including senior citizens themselves, have realized the necessity of providing activities that are both interesting and creative. Some essentials of a good recreation program for this group include:

1. *Effective leadership that does not make the senior citizens feel that they are useless or unable to make decisions should be provided.* Any successful program for this group should encourage the planning of activities by the membership. Supervision should be present but not in a heavy-handed manner.

2. *A diverse and well-balanced program should be encouraged.* People of this age have a wide variety of interests and experiences that should not be overlooked. Programs may frequently be led by a member of the senior citizens group with particular expertise in some area. This will lend individuality to programs.

3. *Programs should include both formal and informal activities.* An entire program should not be devoted to just one type of activity. Time should be allowed for discussion groups and socializing.

4. *Spectator events are always popular.* Attendance at shows, concerts, benefits, and movies is usually high. It is important that costs be kept at

Golf for senior citizens, Maple Moor Golf Course. Photo courtesy of the County of Westchester, New York, Department of Parks, Recreation, and Conservation.

a minimum, which can usually be done by buying a large block of tickets and benefitting from senior-citizen discounts. Transportation at a small cost should be provided as many senior citizens do not have any transportation available to them.

5. *Senior citizens enjoy helping others and participating in community drives.* Volunteer services are always needed and are enjoyed by many senior citizens. They may also enjoy participating in election campaigns, hospital drives, and assisting in the location of other senior citizens in the community.

6. *Recreation of a physical nature is also important.* Spectator recreation may take precedence over physical activities, but many senior citizens do enjoy physical recreation too. Such activities as walking, jogging, table tennis, slimnastics, and even some more rigorous activities may be enjoyed by some group members.

An example of creative aging is shown by the programs of New York City's Serovich Day Center, which has sponsored its own symphony orchestra for more than twenty-five years. The orchestra, made up of members of the center, plays regularly for group members and charitable presentations. In 1965, it played on closed-circuit television at the New York World's Fair.

Another cultural activity for senior citizens is the Golden Age Art Exhibition conducted annually since 1965 by the New York City Department of Recreation and Parks, Recreation and Cultural Affairs Administration. This exhibition is limited to artists who are fifty-five years or older. The 1970 Exhibition was held at the Lincoln Center for Performing Arts, and artists from many states submitted entries. The exhibition is not limited to residents of the metropolitan area. The 1970 "United States Golden Age Painter of the Year" was an eighty-nine-year-old retired dentist, Dr. Nathan Gosen. The oldest painter exhibiting was ninety-four.

Programs for the Mentally Retarded

Volumes have been written concerning recreation programs for the retarded. There are many different degrees of retardation, and persons belonging to each of these groups need recreation programs suitable to their needs. Programs should cater to small groups and try to be individualized wherever possible. A one-to-one concept is ideal and should be used even if for only a short time each day.

In working with the retarded there are a few basic points to keep in mind:

1. Progress slowly, offering the familiar first, and permitting repetition in an activity program.
2. The supervisor must innovate, since retarded youngsters do not play spontaneously.
3. Activities should first be demonstrated.
4. Short attention spans and individual abilities should always be considered.
5. Participants should be given some choice in activities desired.
6. Kindness, firmness, and patience are essential to any program.

The Joseph P. Kennedy, Jr., Foundation has been very active in recreation planning for the retarded. In its studies, it has found that only about three percent of public recreation departments in this country are providing recreation services to the retarded. There is a definite need for establishment of community services for retarded adults as well as youngsters. Many of the adult retarded find it difficult to adjust to their leisure time after employment hours. They have never been taught how to use this time beneficially. The Kennedy Foundation has found day camps to be a very successful pursuit for many retarded youngsters. Day-camp programs include all types of athletics, music, arts and crafts, dance, dramatics, camping skills, and water sports. The program is much like that for other children, except that activities are taught more slowly and individually.

Mentally retarded adults must not be overlooked in recreation planning. Frequently, the older retarded people are forgotten, since many recreation programs are geared to children. Sheltered workshops where young and older adults can learn a trade and have recreation facilities available to them are very helpful. Some communities have adult centers for the retarded that sponsor social and cultural events. Some new programs have been established in which retarded adults are taken from institutions and placed in houses or apartments within the community. In these instances there is usually a married couple who act as house supervisors, and the retarded are taught to live as independently as possible. There is great improvement in self-confidence and outlook among the persons participating in this program.

Programs for the Handicapped

Generally speaking, the word *handicapped* describes persons with degrees of difference physically, psychologically, and socially. An inability to compete successfully in life labels a person as handicapped.[3] It is essential that any recreation program concentrate on the total person, not just his particular handicap. A physical handicap may result in profound emotional and social problems that must also be treated by activity programming.

An extensive study of hospital recreation programs was conducted in 1959 by the National Recreation Association. The report revealed that out of 3,500 responding hospitals, less than half (42.4 percent) indicated that they had an organized recreation program. However, ninety-eight percent of the Veteran's Administration hospitals reported active recreation programs.

Recreation programs for the handicapped may be offered at hospitals, training schools and centers, state institutions, public and semipublic organizations, camp facilities, and numerous other settings. Programs at hospitals, which are frequently passive, include reading, writing, watching television or movies, newspaper work, and hobby-related activities. There are some active games and sports, dancing, and also music and drama activities.

The park and recreation department of one large southwestern city decided to operate a day camp for one week during the summer for some of its handicapped children. Working with such community organizations as the Junior League and Boy Scouts, the camp program was initiated. Various agencies, dealing with the handicapped, suggested children that might be benefitted by such an experience. Persons from different organizations offered their voluntary services to make the camp a success. This type of program points out how recreation leaders can work with community groups to achieve a goal such as this.

The trend in treatment of the handicapped is toward their participation in the day-to-day activities of the family and community. This trend recognizes that segregation of the handicapped is unhealthy from an individual and social standpoint.

A working example of this trend can be seen in the annual patient-family weekend excursion sponsored by the Easter Seal Home Service in New York City. The Home Service sponsors weekend trips to the New Jersey shore at

[3]Valerie V. Hunt, *Recreation for the Handicapped* (Englewood Cliffs, N.J.: Prentice-Hall, Inc., 1955).

Beach Haven. Groups comprised of Home Service employees, volunteers, handicapped persons, and members of their families spend weekends in this seaside town enjoying the beach, shopping trips, deepsea fishing, boat rides, home movies, and musical programs. Many volunteers come from the town of Beach Haven itself. The patients find the trip an exhilarating and educational one in which their families are able to relax with their handicapped children and benefit from the experiences with other such children and their families.

QUESTIONS AND EXERCISES

1. Define the word *program*. Would your own definition differ from the one given by the text? If so, how would it differ?
2. What are some of the basic principles of program planning?
3. Give some major fallacies of program planning. What other fallacies can you think of?
4. What is meant by *busyness* in program planning? If you were a recreation supervisor, how would you go about curtailing busyness?
5. What is meant by *segregation* in program planning? What is your own opinion of this type of segregation? How can it be avoided?
6. What is a community-school? Does your community recreation department operate with this concept in mind? If so, report on how it works in your locality.
7. Why should schools also operate as community centers? Is this usually a feasible plan of operation?
8. What is a community-school swimming program? Does your community have such a program? If so, explain how it operates.
9. What is the discovery program and how does it operate? Is there anything like this in your community?
10. Define the term *outdoor recreation*. What types of programs are included under this term?
11. What are some recent trends in outdoor recreation? What others can you suggest?
12. Briefly identify the major recreation planning concepts in establishing programs for the preschooler, school-age child, teen-ager, adult, senior citizen, the mentally retarded, and the handicapped.

SELECTED REFERENCES

A Guide for Day Camps and Recreation Programs for the Retarded. Washington, D.C.: The Joseph P. Kennedy Foundation.

Bamberger, Gay, "A Symphony for New York's Elder Population," *Parks and Recreation,* Vol. II (May, 1967).

Batcheller, John, and Sally Monsour, *Music in Recreation and Leisure.* Dubuque, Iowa: Wm. C. Brown Co., 1972.

Caroson, R., et al, *Recreation in American Life.* Belmont, Calif.: Wadsworth Publishing Co., 1972.

Danford, Howard G., *Creative Leadership in Recreation.* Boston: Allyn and Bacon, 1964.

Dunn, Diana R., ed., *NRPA Recreation and Park Perspective Collection.* College Park, Md.: McGrath Publishing Co., 1971.

Gabrielson, M., and Charles Holtzer, *Camping and Outdoor Education.* New York: The Center for Applied Research in Education, Library of Education Series, 1965.

Gallivan, Patricia S., "Movie Bus," *Parks and Recreation,* Vol. VI (September, 1971).

Gold, Seymour M., *Urban Recreation Planning.* Philadelphia: Lea & Febiger, 1973.

Hjelte, George, and Jay S. Shivers, *Public Administration of Recreation Services.* Philadelphia: Lea & Febiger, 1972.

Kraus, Richard, and Joseph E. Curtis, *Creative Administration in Recreation and Parks.* St. Louis: The C. V. Mosby Co., 1973.

Lynch, Leslie, "The Role of Schools as Recreation Centers," *American School and University,* Vol. 38 (July, 1966).

McCarthy, J. J., "Little League Lunacy," *The National Elementary School Principal,* Vol. 43 (December, 1963).

Shipp, Robert E., "Expanding Program Services," *Parks and Recreation,* Vol. III (November, 1968).

Shivers, J. S., "Special Recreation Needs of Teen-agers," *Parks and Recreation,* Vol. II (August, 1967).

Staffo, Donald F., "A Community Recreation Program," *Journal of Health, Physical Education and Recreation,* Vol. 44 (May, 1973).

Stenek, Stanley, "Ossining Answers Teen Entertainment Turmoil," *Parks and Recreation,* Vol. II (August, 1967).

Stevens, Ardis, *Fun is Therapeutic: A Recreation Book to Help Therapeutic Recreation Leaders by People Who Are Leading Recreation.* Springfield, Ill.: Charles C Thomas, Publisher, 1972.

Waggoner, Bernice E., "Motivation in Physical Education and Recreation for Emotionally Handicapped Children," *Journal of Health, Physical Education and Recreation,* Vol. 44 (March, 1973).

9

ORGANIZATION AND ADMINISTRATION OF MUNICIPAL RECREATION PROGRAMS

Organized recreation programs differ widely in their services and settings. This is also true of the structure and administration of such programs. It has frequently been noted by experts in the field that a recreation program can only be as good as its administration. The types of administrations used by most recreation programs will be delineated in this chapter. No one type of administration is preferred over another, as successful recreation programs can be found that use entirely different methods of administration. A community should examine all the possibilities before deciding on a particular method of setting up its recreation program.

In this chapter you will learn about the organization and administration of organized recreation programs, how they are managed, financed, evaluated, and their legal responsibilities.

MANAGEMENT AUTHORITY IN MUNICIPAL ORGANIZED RECREATION PROGRAMS

There is no one acceptable plan of management of municipal recreation programs. Once a community has decided on the necessity of organized recreation programs, many avenues are open to it. However, before deciding on which way to administer a program, a community should consider some of the following factors:

1. *State legislation governing municipal powers.* Every state has different laws on the degree of self-determination which the community can have.

Some states may encourage school systems to administer recreation programs, whereas other states authorize municipal recreation departments.

2. *Community needs and special needs of the population to be served.* Persons from the community should have a say in the type of administration they desire. They should be represented on boards, committees, special service groups, and in volunteer capacities wherever possible. Community participation helps to accomplish program acceptance and promote community spirit.

3. *The authorization of funds.* The best way to raise and use funds is of primary importance in choice of management authority. Guidelines must be established that will preclude personal bias from having an effect on program funding.

4. *The ownership and control of land and facilities for recreational use.* All land assets should be examined and analyzed to try to achieve the best facilities, preferably those already established, with the least amount of new land expenditures. This can only be done by careful planning and cooperation among community agencies.

5. *Avoidance of political pressure.* This is an easy statement to write on paper but a very difficult concept to handle in reality. If political pressure exists in recreation administrations, it can involve the entire program in terms of who is hired, how money is spent, and where equipment is purchased. To protect any department from such intrusion, administrators should be nonpartisan and hire personnel on the basis of experience and qualifications, rather than political considerations.

6. *Strong leadership in all aspects of program planning.* This is essential to the success of any program, anywhere. Dynamic, innovative leadership can make or break a program. Management authority must keep this in mind at all times, especially in the inception of a program.

A 1970 Local Agency Survey conducted by the NRPA in cooperation with the U.S. Department of the Interior, Bureau of Outdoor Recreation, the U.S. Department of Housing and Urban Development, and the Office of Open Space and Urban Beautification reported on types of managing authorities for recreation programs. Of the 1119 reporting agencies, 856, or seventy-six percent, were municipal or community managing authorities. The remaining twenty-four percent was divided among other types of authority (not specifically explained), private schools, multiple jurisdiction (more than one community), special district, and county managing authorities.

It has been found that most community recreation programs are administered by one of the following ways:

1. departments of parks and recreation
2. separate recreation departments
3. park departments
4. school authorities

Each of these types of management authority will be discussed in the following sections of this chapter.

Department of Parks and Recreation

A combined department of parks and recreation is one method of program management. This type of management helps to coordinate programs that make use of park facilities in their recreation planning. Having these departments jointly operated eliminates the often excessive cost of duplication of equipment and manpower. In addition, most park and recreation departments use school, civic, and semipublic facilities in their programs.

Recreation Department

The recreation department usually consists of a separate committee, commission, or board that may be appointed by the mayor or the mayor and council, or may be elected by the public. Recreation as a department in the municipal government seems to be a very popular method of administering recreation programs because of its efficiency and ease of working with other departments within the community.

Many communities find a board or commission appointed by the mayor and approved by the council or appropriate body to be the most practical method of administering a recreation program. A system such as this, especially if it is bipartisan, allows for community representation on the board, a board membership that may include park and school representatives, and a recreation administrator who is directly responsible to the board.

The major advantages of having the recreation department as a separate function of municipal government are:

1. *As a separate department, recreation programs and facilities are its prime concern.* School and park agencies are often overburdened with their own primary responsibilities, and recreation takes a secondary role.
2. *Funding is separate and is used directly for recreation purposes instead of being combined with the budget of another department.*
3. *Recreation leaders hold full-time positions and have a greater opportunity to evaluate programs in terms of community needs and interest patterns.*

As in most situations, there are also disadvantages to a separate recreation department. Some of the disadvantages frequently given are:

1. *It is not necessary to encounter the problems and expenses of creating another community agency.* Many persons feel that school and park governing bodies are already well established, and it would be less difficult to add to these bodies than to create a new one.

PARK STATISTICS FOR THE DEPARTMENT OF PARKS AND RECREATION

Item	General Administration	1971	1972
1	Total Area in Square Miles	437	437
2	Estimated County Population	385,856	396,856
3	Number of County Parks	87	91
4	Number of Park Acres	2,744	3,001
5	Estimated Visits to Parks	4,462,726	5,235,459
6	Estimated Visits to Special Facilities	317,041	326,304
7	Supervised Recreation Attendance	636,379	816,480
8	Permanent Employee Positions	155	182
9	Seasonal Employee Positions	595	620
10	Total Number of Employee Positions	750	802
11	Administration Division Budget	$ 49,704	$ 58,510
12	Parks Division Budget	$ 845,324	$ 860,917
13	Planning Division Budget	$ 48,217	$ 38,204
14	Recreation Division Budget	$ 337,249	$ 481,028
15	Special Facilities Division Budget	$ 316,390	$ 340,675
16	Total Operating Budget	$1,596,884	$1,780,000
17	Land Acquisition Budget	$1,101,000	$2,250,000
18	Land Development Budget	$ 932,000	$1,095,000
19	Total Capital Improvement Budget	$2,033,000	$3,345,000
20	State Grants - In - Aid	$ 77,491	$ 98,402
21	Federal Grants - In - Aid	$ —	$ 200,000
22	Recreation Receipts	$ 9,965	$ 19,204
23	Special Facilities Receipts	$ 126,529	$ 207,694
24	Total Department Receipts	$ 213,985	$ 525,300

Item	Areas and Facilities	1971	1972
25	Baseball Fields - Regulation	8	8
26	Softball/Little League Fields	37	40
27	Football Fields	11	11
28	Soccer Fields	1	1
29	Basketball Courts	37	39
30	Tennis Courts	16	26
31	Boccie Courts	2	2
32	Playground Apparatus Areas	46	51
33	Public Beaches	1	1
34	Swimming Pools	4	4
35	Shuffleboard Courts	0	6
36	Field Hockey Area	1	1
37	Horseshoe Pits	24	24
38	Fishing Areas	3	3
39	Boating Area	1	1
40	Public Gardens	1	1
41	Public Statues/Shrines	7	7
42	Comfort Stations	6	8
43	Picnic Shelters	6	7
44	Picnic Sites	357	437
45	Stadium Complex	1	1
46	Golf Courses	2	2
47	Zoo	1	1
48	Horse Back Riding Stables	1	1

For Wilmington, Delaware. Reprinted by permission of the New Castle County Department of Parks and Recreation.

2. *Recreation departments may themselves control few properties or in some cases no property at all.* This is true in communities where most recreational property is owned and regulated by school and park authorities. Difficulty might arise in the supervision of property owned by another community agency.

3. *Recreation departments may find themselves in a position of competing with other departments for land and facility use.* When a recreation board exists, school and park department representatives may feel that their membership is just perfunctory, since the main purpose of the board is recreation.

Park Departments

Many cities administer recreation programs through a park department. This is a recognized method because most recreation areas are within the domain of this department. Since recreation is the basic function of this department, it seems logical to have them administer community recreation programs. Park departments are usually well established, with sufficient budgets to support recreation programming. However, there is also an opposing viewpoint concerning the desirability of park department control of recreation services and settings. Many park professionals are more concerned with park beautification than they are with recreation. Their training and qualifications are not in keeping with the modern-day recreation administrator. In addition, most parks do not have adequate indoor recreational facilities, and programs under park department auspices are usually devoted to outside or physical activities, rather than well-rounded recreation pursuits.

School Authority

In recent years, schools have been placed in an administrative position concerning recreation programs in many communities. Some of the reasons for this are readily apparent in that schools usually have the facilities to best sponsor recreation programs. School budgets are usually substantial enough to incorporate funds for recreation purposes. School authorities usually have the confidence of the community, and community involvement has already been established in meeting educational goals. In addition, schools frequently have the personnel available for supervision of recreation activities, and recreation programs, to some extent, may already be in existence as part of the school program.

There is much to say in favor of school authority; however, there are some adverse points worthy of consideration. Since the primary purpose of schools is education, can schools put recreation in the proper perspective? Although education is essential, recreation programs should not take a back seat. They should have a full-time staff, qualified leadership, and sufficient time to develop adequate programs. School authorities may view recreation as a program for

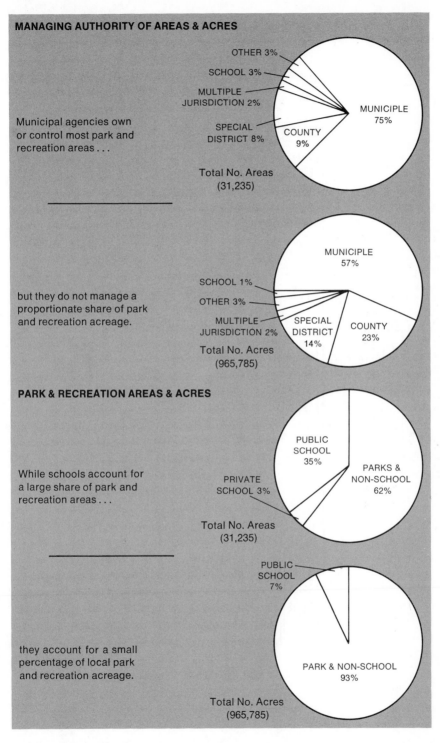

MANAGING AUTHORITY OF AREAS & ACRES

OTHER 3%
SCHOOL 3%
MULTIPLE JURISDICTION 2%
MUNICIPLE 75%
SPECIAL DISTRICT 8%
COUNTY 9%

Municipal agencies own or control most park and recreation areas . . .

Total No. Areas (31,235)

MUNICIPLE 57%
SCHOOL 1%
OTHER 3%
MULTIPLE JURISDICTION 2%
SPECIAL DISTRICT 14%
COUNTY 23%

but they do not manage a proportionate share of park and recreation acreage.

Total No. Acres (965,785)

PARK & RECREATION AREAS & ACRES

PUBLIC SCHOOL 35%
PARKS & NON-SCHOOL 62%
PRIVATE SCHOOL 3%

While schools account for a large share of park and recreation areas . . .

Total No. Areas (31,235)

PUBLIC SCHOOL 7%
PARK & NON-SCHOOL 93%

they account for a small percentage of local park and recreation acreage.

Total No. Acres (965,785)

Parks and Recreation, August, 1971. Reprinted by permission of the National Recreation and Park Association.

LOS ANGELES UNIFIED SCHOOL DISTRICT

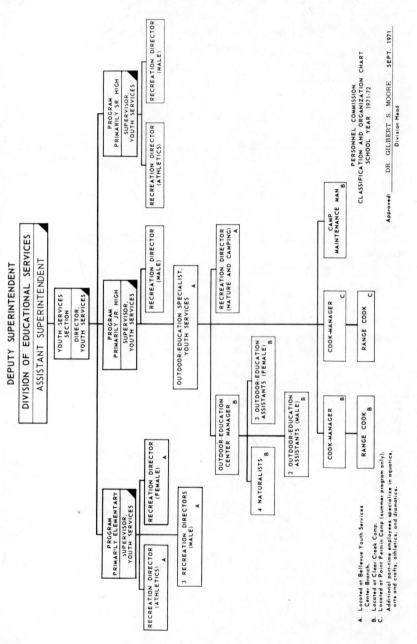

DEPUTY SUPERINTENDENT

DIVISION OF EDUCATIONAL SERVICES

ASSISTANT SUPERINTENDENT

YOUTH SERVICES SECTION

DIRECTOR, YOUTH SERVICES

PROGRAM PRIMARILY ELEMENTARY
SUPERVISOR, YOUTH SERVICES

RECREATION DIRECTOR (ATHLETICS) A

RECREATION DIRECTOR (FEMALE) A

3 RECREATION DIRECTORS (MALE) A

PROGRAM PRIMARILY JR HIGH
SUPERVISOR, YOUTH SERVICES

RECREATION DIRECTOR (MALE)

OUTDOOR-EDUCATION SPECIALIST, YOUTH SERVICES A

OUTDOOR-EDUCATION CENTER MANAGER B

4 NATURALISTS B

3 OUTDOOR-EDUCATION ASSISTANTS (FEMALE) B

2 OUTDOOR-EDUCATION ASSISTANTS (MALE) B

RECREATION DIRECTOR (NATURE AND CAMPING) A

COOK-MANAGER B

RANGE COOK B

COOK-MANAGER C

RANGE COOK C

CAMP MAINTENANCE MAN B

PROGRAM PRIMARILY SR HIGH
SUPERVISOR, YOUTH SERVICES

RECREATION DIRECTOR (ATHLETICS)

RECREATION DIRECTOR (MALE)

A. Located at Bellevue Youth Services Center Branch.
B. Located at Clear Creek Camp.
C. Located at Point Fermin Camp (summer program only).

Additional part-time employees specialize in aquatics, arts and crafts, athletics, and dramatics.

PERSONNEL COMMISSION
CLASSIFICATION AND ORGANIZATION CHART
SCHOOL YEAR 1971-72

Approved: _____ DR. GILBERT S. MOORE   SEPT. 1971
Division Head

170

Reprinted by permission of the National Recreation and Park Association.

children alone. Activities for different age groups and persons with special needs may be overlooked. School authorities may approach recreation as they would course work and be too authoritative in administration.

In addition, school budgets in many cities are not substantial, but, indeed, are hard pressed to the extent that many new budget proposals are defeated by the taxpayers. If recreation programs are under the school budget, they are defeated as well. Many people do not stop to think about what may be included in the school budget; they only think about keeping their property taxes down to a level they can afford.

As you can see, there are pros and cons concerning every method of municipal recreation authority. Any of the methods mentioned, however, might be successful if they include the following points in their management of recreation programs:

1. community representation to enhance confidence in programming and in finding out what the people want and need
2. effective, trained leadership in the person of a qualified full-time recreation professional who has authority over the recreation program
3. community agencies that cooperate in the sharing of facilities for recreation use by all members of the community
4. sound fiscal responsibility that is provided for in advance of instituting any recreation program
5. evaluation programs that continuously subject programs to careful study and introduce the best of what is current in recreation activities

If all of these points are considered and a strong effort is made to free recreation authorities from political influence, then any of the aforementioned authorities would have a chance of producing sound, diverse, and responsible programming.

ORGANIZATION OF RECREATION DEPARTMENTS

Once the type of management authority has been chosen, then the authority must be organized so that its purpose of serving the people in the best possible way can be realized. Organization varies, depending on the community and the type of management authority. The separate recreation department will be discussed here. A combination of the recreation and park departments usually offers a compromise in organization somewhere between the two. In this chapter, persons in leadership authority are mentioned, but their duties will be discussed in detail in Chapter 10, "Leadership in Recreation."

Most separate recreation departments have a board or commission as the managing authority. In some cases, a member of the school board, park board, and city council, as well as community representatives, make up the recreation board. Some of the major responsibilities of the board include:

1. Maintenance of a degree of excellence concerning leadership and programming
2. Communication with the municipal officials and the general public concerning aspects of the recreation program
3. Definition of powers of recreation leadership and appointment (sometimes with city council approval) of executive personnel
4. Determination of duties of personnel and appointment of all employees, usually upon recommendation from the recreation executive
5. Consideration and approval of all matters involving sources outside the recreation department and approval of departmental budget
6. Accounting to the city officials and public concerning use of funds and all program accomplishments and expenditures

If the recreation department is also responsible for the community parks, then these additional functions may be included:

1. Preservation of a degree of excellence in maintenance, development, and beautification of all park property
2. Studies to acquire additional properties and suggestion of plans for the best implementation of these lands
3. Plan, in cooperation with other agencies, for future development of recreation programs and properties

Major Divisions of a Recreation Department

As has been frequently stated, recreation departments and their divisions differ greatly. The general divisions that will be discussed here take into consideration the main concerns of every department responsible for recreation programs and properties. These divisions include:

1. recreation services
2. specialized facilities
3. finance and accountability
4. building and maintenance

In some departments, services and facilities are combined into one division. These divisions will be discussed separately, but one can readily see that they are all interdependent and must work together to provide high standards of recreation programming.

CHANNEL OF AUTHORITY

A. ORGANIZATIONAL STRUCTURE

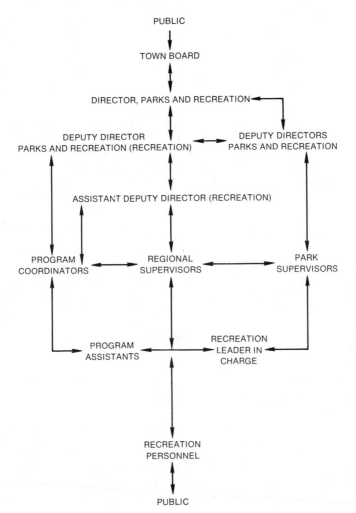

Reprinted by permission of the Town of Hempstead Department of Parks and Recreation.

1. *Division of recreation services.* This division usually has three major responsibilities that include: (a) playgrounds and indoor settings, (b) special-interest activities, and (c) special community services. There is usually a supervisor of each playground and indoor setting plus additional recreation workers. Some communities have playground supervision only during the summer months. However, recent trends

point toward year-round programs and supervision. This division is responsible for programming, equipment, community education and communication, and evaluation of activities for these settings. *Special-interest activities* include programs built around such pursuits as drama, nature study, music, art, athletic instruction, and various other activities requiring trained supervisors and workers. *Special community services* include responsibility for leadership and programming for the needs of senior citizens, the handicapped, and the retarded. In addition, responsibility includes liaison between other community agencies and industry.

2. *Division of specialized facilities.* This division is responsible for settings outside of the domain of the playgrounds and indoor centers. Such facilities may include beaches, swimming pools, golf courses, and day camps. This division is responsible for the leadership and programming of activities for use of these facilities.

3. *Division of finance and accountability.* The main functions of this division are keeping accurate financial statements and managing all business details for the other divisions of the recreation department. A record of fiscal accountability for all recreation expenditures must be carefully kept and presented, perhaps in the form of an annual report.

4. *Division of building and maintenance.* The size of this division will depend on the number of properties and facilities supervised by the recreation department. The responsibilities of this division include: (a) planning, engineering, and design of new facilities; (b) repair and maintenance of existing facilities; (c) groundskeeping, including cleanup and gardening; and (d) special maintenance involved in swimming pool complexes, tennis courts, ball fields, ice-skating rinks, and golf courses.

The persons employed in recreation positions in these divisions will be discussed in some detail in Chapter 10.

FINANCING OF RECREATION PROGRAMS

Community recreation programs cannot be run without adequate, well-planned financing. It is essential that members of the community are thoroughly acquainted with what programs are available and their cost. Frequently, the community is adamant about increased municipal budgets because they have not been made aware of the kinds of recreation programs available and how their families and other members of the community can avail themselves of these activities.

Communities have different ways to raise money for recreation services. The three most popular methods are:

1. municipal operating funds
2. recreation taxes
3. special fees and charges

In the case of obtaining funds for large purchases such as land, equipment, new buildings, and special improvements, revenue must be raised by the people (donations and philanthropic bequests), special assessments, bond issues, and federal funds. Each of these methods will be discussed in some detail in the sections that follow.

Municipal Operating Funds

Most communities have general funds derived from taxes, from which money is allocated for specific municipal agencies. In the case of a recreation department, a budget is submitted to the council or appropriate body for approval, and after careful review of proposed expenditures, funds are allocated. This system allows for review of all programs prior to allocation of any funds. In a system such as the one described, the recreation leadership of the community has the responsibility of demonstrating the value of their programs along with submitting the budget.

This method of fund allocation may sometimes result in budget cutbacks if the council places recreation in the position of being a secondary service. Fortunately, however, most councils are fair and the recreation department receives its fair share of the general fund. In some communities, especially in recent years, budgets have had to be cut because of insufficient funds. Inflation, resulting in higher prices and greater unemployment, frequently leads to general austerity programs. In such cases, recreation departments may suffer losses of personnel and programs. How can a city recreation department survive in a period of budget cuts? Some answers include:

1. involving more volunteers to aid in leadership of programs
2. using established buildings belonging to semipublic and other interested organizations
3. establishing fees for certain activities that would otherwise have to be dropped from the recreation program

A large city that recently underwent a severe austerity program is Boston, Massachusetts. How Boston resolved its funding problem is detailed in the following section.

Boston Gears Itself for Austerity. In the early part of 1971, Mayor White of Boston indicated that the budget for the city would have to undergo drastic reductions, and that the city's payroll would be reduced by over 500 employees. "Boston 71" was the name given to the austerity package that was aimed at insuring quality, quantity, and public involvement in the recreation activities and maintenance-work programs for 1971. Twelve specific steps were listed to help

Summary
HARTFORD MUNICIPAL RECREATION DEPARTMENT
PROPOSED 1972 BUDGET

Account #	Expense	1970 Budget	1971 Budget	1972 Proposed	Final
55113	Choir				$ 1,200
55104	Recreation Material	$14,113	$29,290	$ 8,540	8,040
52103	Recreation Outlay			1,950	1,950
55105	Recreation Contract Labor			11,760	10,660
55106	Washington School		8,309.95	9,825	5,395
51107	Salaries	29,909	33,594.50	35,172	37,825
55109	Vet's Pool Concess.	1,800	2,100.00	2,400	2,400
55107	Vet's Pool Materials & Supplies	(P. 10)	(P. 10)	3,100	3,100
55108	Vet's Pool Maint.	(P. 10)	(P. 10)	4,867	4,867
62104	Vet's Pool Outlay			1,863	1,863
21209	Sales Tax			300	–
55115	Union Pool			1,980	1,980
55116	Playground Maint.			7,040	440
62105	Playground Outlay			5,750	1,700
55110	Skating Rinks Maint.			1,200	–
		$56,337	$76,484.50	$95,747	$82,925

Account #	Revenue	1970 Budget	1971 Budget	1972 Proposed	Final
42709	Recreation	$ 2,995	$ 7,650	$ 6,940	$ 6,940
42710	Washington School		3,350	3,350	3,350
51107	Salaries	1,600	1,600	1,400	1,400
42801	Vet's Pool Passes	3,500	3,700	3,700	3,700
42802	Vet's Pool Lessons	2,000	2,000	2,700	2,700
42803	Vet's Pool Concess.	2,500	2,600	2,700	2,700
42804	Vet's Pool Admission	2,500	2,600	2,000	2,000
42805	Vet's Pool Rental	15			
21209	Sales Tax			300	–
42812	Union Pool Lessons			30	30
42814	Union Pool Admission			1,000	1,000
42815	Union Pool Rental			200	200
		$15,110	$23,800	$24,320	$24,020

		1970	1971	1972	Final
Cost Comparison		$56,337	$76,484.50	$95,747	$82,925
		15,110	23,800.00	24,320	24,020
Cost to City		$41,227	$52,684.50	$71,427	$58,905

Reprinted by permission of the Hartford Municipal Recreation Department, Hartford, Wisconsin.

Boston maintain its traditionally high level of parks and recreation services. The steps are as follows:

1. *Programming around neighborhood resources.* Such programming involves the use of local resources including church clubs, women's clubs, athletic clubs, veterans' halls, and art and dance studios. These resources are used to help citizen groups to expand their programs.

2. *Commercial recreation.* In almost every community, there are widespread commercial recreation facilities that are rarely utilized by recreation programs. By working with these interests, the recreation department can project a total community image as well as attracting visitors to the city. In addition, commercial recreation centers, such as bowling or amusement areas, can provide assistance to public recreation programs.

3. *Reallocation of funds and forces.* This will enable small, well-trained groups of people, assisted by volunteers, to carry on department functions. Busywork will be eliminated wherever possible, and only those efforts resulting in a maximum effect will be undertaken.

4. *Teamwork with universities.* Universities of all sizes have extensive facilities for recreational use. In addition, they have a great volunteer body to draw from. Facilities can be used whenever available, and summer programs, including camps and swimming instruction, can be conducted on college campuses.

5. *Volunteer teamwork.* Volunteers of all types are always needed for recreation programs. In the spring and summer of 1970, more than 25,000 volunteers completed major clean-up programs in Boston. Clubs and organizations near specific park areas were asked to aid in the maintenance of facilities and playground areas.

6. *Cooperation of religious organizations with recreation department.* Close cooperation between these two agencies can help both withstand strong financial pressure. Joint use of facilities, church-sponsored recreational and cultural activities, and church volunteers aiding in community programs is essential to improved recreational programs.

7. *Involvement of museums and other cultural institutions.* New programs are planned that will draw from the facilities and staffs of Boston's museums, cultural centers, and airports. Public relations with the community will be improved, and the recreation department can expand its programs without expanding its budget.

8. *Special events to encourage cooperation.* Such events as kite festivals, marathon races, holiday window painting, and similar activities will help to bring the community, industry, and commercial organizations together in recreation activities.

9. *Involvement of young adults.* A large percentage of our population is made up of people between the ages of eighteen and thirty-five years. The involvement of this age group in the planning and participation in recreation pursuits is helpful to the community and particularly needed by this age group.

10. *New approaches to funding.* Two steps were considered to help conserve finances. These steps included: (1) cooperation between all major

recreation-producing agencies in the city and (2) an appeal to several financial advisors and agencies in Boston to give time for analysis of the city's recreation and park administrative and financial practices.

11. *Navy and military liaison.* Establishment of close ties between the city and the military to share facilities and settings was planned.

12. *Liaison between all city departments.* All city agencies would cooperate by lending equipment, reassigning manpower, and, in general, in upholding a commitment to assist other departments in all projects.

The points mentioned above are an excellent framework for any community to follow in an austerity program and, in general, to help alleviate the possibility of enforced cutbacks in recreation programming.

Recreation Taxes

Some states have a special tax for the purpose of recreation. This money is placed in a fund that provides resources for parks, recreation, and schools. The practice of having a recreation tax was initiated because certain government officials felt that recreation would not get a fair share of its tax dollar unless special funds were set aside for this purpose alone. State recreation taxes are less frequently used today since communities have accepted the responsibility of providing recreation services.

Some communities have a property tax (sometimes called a "mill tax") to defray the cost of recreation. Frequently, this tax is voted for a number of years and then has to be renewed by referendum vote.

Special Fees and Charges

It is difficult for parks and recreation departments to derive all their income from the city and special state or community taxes. To meet the additional need for income, certain fees and charges are levied to aid facilities to be self-supporting. These fees may be charged at golf courses, swimming pools, tennis courts, and for special cultural events. Charges are usually minimal and insure a high quality of services rendered. Some communities limit their facilities to residents only, while other communities allow nonresident use, but at a higher fee charge than that established for residents.

There are many persons who oppose fees and charges for recreation purposes because it is thought that:

1. Certain people will be excluded from necessary services.
2. Fees tend to encourage more programs that are commercial in nature.
3. Any attempt to render facilities self-supporting detracts from tax support for recreation.

Those who favor charges and fees also have their own opinions, which include:

1. Services are frequently improved when fees are charged.
2. Programs can be expanded.
3. The public has more to say in programming when they are directly paying for it.

The opponents and proponents both have valid points to make. In general, fees and charges are helpful, especially to communities on limited budgets; however, a community must take great care in trying not to exclude persons from programs because of cost. Certain programs that have fees or charges attached to them should use some of this money for a subsidy fund for those who cannot afford to participate.

Bond Issues

As you recall, larger investments such as new buildings, land purchases, and quantity equipment purchases must often be financed separately from the methods previously discussed. Bond issues are frequently used to meet the costs of large expenditures. The *Park and Recreation Yearbook* reported issues of more than $272 million during a five-year period. Bond issues must be voted on by the public and paid for by future taxes.

Donations of Funds

Private and corporate donations are a valuable source of funds for large expenditures. It is important that recreation authorities be aware of this important resource.

Special Assessments to Property Owners

These assessments are usually made to pay for specific improvements in certain areas of the community. For example, if tennis courts in a neighborhood park need resurfacing and funds are unavailable for this, an assessment, with public approval, may be made on the property owners in that neighborhood. The problem of financing improvements in this manner lies in the fact that the poorer areas usually need the most improvements and can afford it least.

Federal Government's Role
in Supporting Parks and Recreation

The responsibilities of the government have already been mentioned in Chapters 2 and 3, but government expenditures in relation to community funding have not been specifically discussed.

The recent passage of revenue-sharing legislation will provide money directly to some communities for use in support of recreation programs. In addition, there are many federal grants available for different aspects of community programs. Federal grants are available for low-income neighborhoods, preservation of open-space areas, providing public access to open-space areas, and retaining community identity in certain neighborhoods.

There are matching assistance grants available under the Bureau of Outdoor Recreation's Land and Water Conservation Fund. Such projects must be outdoor-oriented to be eligible for grants. The Land and Water Conservation Fund program is designed with the state playing the central role. These funds are available under a statewide comprehensive outdoor recreation plan. Funds are given to basic facilities that have an outdoor orientation.

Many federal agencies have had, or presently have, federal grant programs that aid parks and recreation. These acts and programs include:

1. Older American Act
2. Education Act of Department of Health, Education, and Welfare
3. Housing Assistance, Neighborhood Facilities and Open Space Programs under Housing and Urban Development
4. Land and Water Conservation under the Department of the Interior
5. many programs under the Office of Economic Opportunity (OEO)

Most grants for cultural activities have been conceived and carried out by the OEO, which in recent years has suffered cutbacks and has had its very existence threatened.

LEGAL ASPECTS OF RECREATION

The different types of management authorities that were discussed are all subdivisions of the state and therefore must have legal authorization in order to execute recreation programs. Legal authority exists for every aspect of recreation, including land purchase, building construction, personnel functions, and levying and expenditure of taxes.

The first state laws passed that provided for recreation were mainly concerned with schools and provided for community use of school areas and facilities. These laws, however, did not allow communities to conduct separate recreation activities. New legislation was sought that would enable communities to provide recreation services. These laws were called "enabling acts" and the first such law was passed in 1915 in New Jersey.

What Are the Provisions of Enabling Acts? Prior to general enabling acts, each state had a multitude of laws pertaining to recreation. Frequently, these laws were repetitious, confusing, and were neither suitable nor acceptable to all

LIABILITY ACCIDENT NOTICE
(Not Automobile)

Name of Company	Name and Location of Agent

Policy No.	Policy Period	Nature of Business

Limits	Liab.	Med. Pay.	Elevator	Products	Contr.	Other (Specify)
B. I.						
P. D.						

Insured

Name
Town of Hempstead, Dept. of Parks & Recreation   Phone 489-5000

Address
Town Hall Plaza, Main Street, Hempstead, New York   11550

Location of Insured Premises
Coes Neck Park, Baldwin, New York

Time and Place

Date and Time of Accident
9-14-87   4 P.M.

Location
Football Field

Injured Person

Name
Ralph Jones   Age 62   Phone 222-1144

Address
168 Fred Street, Baldwin, New York

Occupation
Bus Driver

Employed by:
Ace Bus Company

What was injured doing when hurt?
Kicking Football

The Injury

Nature and extent of injury
Injured big toe on right foot.

Released to Emergency Squad - Baldwin Fire Department

Probable disability
unknown   Has injured resumed work?

Property Damage

Owner   Address   Phone
none

List damage   Estimated cost of repair $

Witnesses

Name   Address   Phone
Charles Smith   166 Fred Street, Baldwin, NY   222-4411

James Brown   82 South Street, So. Hempstead, NY 211-4221

Description of Accident

Injured was participating in football game,

kicked football and incurred injury.

Signature of reporting employee -

Date: _____   _____

Signature of Agent   Signature of Insured

I have read and I understand the information presented in the Recreation Staff Manual. I will comply with the Rules and Regulations set-forth in this Manual.

_____   _____

Signature   Date

communities within the state. There was a great need for a general state-initiated act that provided for adequate community recreation services. These acts differ from state to state but generally authorize local rule for recreation programs. The principal accomplishment of these acts is that they set forth:

1. the method of establishment of the managing authority for recreation programs (The choice of type of authority is left to the community, which has the power to choose leadership.)
2. the right to vote on bond issues for major expenditures involved in programming
3. authority to establish, equip, and maintain recreation areas and facilities
4. powers of financial responsibility for all aspects of programming
5. power to seek, accept, and reject grants from private, state, and federal sources
6. authorization for cooperative agreement among all community agencies
7. authority to hire personnel and fulfill salary requirements

These are the major provisions of state enabling laws, but some states have initiated laws that divide the state into districts for recreation purposes. These districts frequently include large cities and their surrounding suburbs. Such laws aid communities in the sharing of recreation facilities and settings.

When a community is prepared to establish a recreation program, it should first consult state enabling laws, if they exist, and carefully study the laws as they will pertain to its planned programs and facilities. The best way to accomplish this is to hire legal counsel to advise on municipal powers in relation to state laws.

After this has been accomplished and managing authority has been selected, the community itself should pass legislation that will govern the recreation authority. This legislation often takes the form of a charter amendment in states where there are home-rule powers, rather than state enabling laws. In cases where legal authority is based on state enabling laws, an ordinance or resolution is passed by the municipal government.

Are Communities Legally Liable for Injuries? In some states, community governments are not liable if the activity involved is considered a government function. Most recreational activities fall into this category. This immunity from liability, however, does not necessarily include the recreation workers who in cases of negligence can be personally sued. Many workers are provided with insurance coverage in case such a problem arises.

There is community liability for what is legally termed a "nuisance." A nuisance is cited when a recreation facility is not maintained or built properly and damage or injury can result. For example, boating allowed in waters that are hazardous on community-owned property can lead to injury that in turn may result in a nuisance case. Such a case might find the community negligent and therefore liable.

In order to protect the municipality and the recreation worker from the possibility of court action, recreation officials should: (1) briefly orient all personnel in the legal aspects of recreation, and (2) supply all employees with written information concerning legal responsibilities. This information should state the recreation laws of the state and any personal liability, if such exists. Court cases that may pertain to a recreation worker's job should also be given to clarify the state and community position in reference to personal liability. This educational approach involves little effort or money and will possibly aid the community in avoiding legal suits against them and their recreation personnel.

EVALUATION OF RECREATION PROGRAMS

Some general criteria for evaluation was previously discussed in Chapter 8. Any recreation department that fails to continuously evaluate its programs and personnel will probably suffer from loss of interest and sometimes loss of funding. Evaluation must be based on accurate records and a set of general standards for acceptability in areas of personnel, participation, programs, administration, and funding. When any part of the department is not meeting these standards, an investigation should take place.

Programs should be evaluated in relation to how they meet the needs of the community and the overall quality of the program. Just because a program is well attended does not necessarily mean that it is a good program. Opinions of participants should be surveyed and carefully considered in dropping or altering existing programs. In the same way, community members can be polled to find out the types of programs they would like to see introduced by the department. These surveys can save a community a great deal of time, effort, and money in planning new programs. When a program is going to involve a very large expenditure, public meetings should be held to educate and discover existence of public support. Frequently, recreation departments undertake programs such as swimming pool complexes, only to find out they cannot elicit enough initial support to start construction.

Research is a key word in any evaluation procedure. Adequate research may take the form of intensive studies undertaken by the recreation department itself or by an outside group under contract to the department. These studies may elicit information on where and what type of facilities are needed, programs that appeal to different segments of the population, impact of neighborhood changes on recreation needs, relationship between delinquency and recreation, prime age groups existing in the community, special needs and interests, community involvement, and many other related areas.

A recreation department that wants to serve the people must take evaluation procedures very seriously. Dynamic, interesting programs are the result of working closely with the community and the needs and interests of that population. Evaluation of leadership and personnel will be discussed in Chapter 10.

QUESTIONS AND EXERCISES

1. What are some of the major factors to be considered in choosing a recreation managing authority?
2. List and briefly explain the four most common types of managing authorities. What type is used in your community? Briefly explain its organization.
3. What are the major advantages of having the recreation department as a separate government function? Are there any additional advantages that you can think of? What are the disadvantages?
4. What are the major requirements for any recreation managing authority to be successful?
5. What are the major divisions of responsibility in most recreation departments? Briefly explain the responsibilities of each division.
6. What are the three general methods used to finance recreation departments? How is your community recreation department financed?
7. List and briefly explain ways in which communities can overcome austerity budgets. Has your community been affected by cutbacks in recreation programs? If so, how has it managed?
8. What are the reasons for use of bond issues in recreation programming? Have any bond issues for recreation purposes been passed in your community in recent years? Explain.
9. What is the role of the federal government in supporting parks and recreation? See if you can find some recent article that pertains to federal support of such programs.
10. Define and list the principal accomplishments of the state enabling laws pertaining to recreation.
11. Explain the legal liability of the community and recreation personnel in relation to injuries in recreation areas, injuries due to negligence, and nuisance suits.
12. What basic information is needed to evaluate the functions of any recreation department? Does your community recreation agency sponsor any type of public education programs or surveys to elicit public opinion and support?

SELECTED REFERENCES

American Association for Health, Physical Education and Recreation, *A Guide for Programs in Recreation and Physical Education for the Mentally Retarded.* Washington, D.C.: The Association, 1968.

Artz, Robert M., *School-Community Recreation and Park Cooperation.* Washington, D.C.: National Recreation and Park Association, 1970.

Brown, Roger K., "Sound Planning Stretches Capital Funds." *Parks and Recreation,* Vol. VI (July, 1971).

Butler, George, *Introduction to Community Recreation.* New York: McGraw-Hill Book Company, 1967.

Campbell, Charles, "Low-Cost Recreation Centers," *Parks and Recreation,* Vol. III (November, 1968).

Curtis, Joseph E., "A City Gears Itself for Austerity," *Parks and Recreation,* Vol. VI (March, 1971).

Duell, Charles E., *Elements of Park and Recreation Administration.* Minneapolis: Burgess Publishing Company, 1963.

Ford, H. T., "The Recreation Director Syndrome," *Journal of Health, Physical Education and Recreation,* Vol. 44 (May, 1973).

Frieswyk, S. H., "Federal Grants for Cultural Recreation." *Parks and Recreation,* Vol. II (February, 1967).

Gilbert, Douglas L., *Natural Resources and Public Relations.* Washington, D.C.: The Wildlife Society, 1971.

Gold, Seymour M., *Urban Recreation Planning.* Philadelphia: Lea & Febiger, 1973.

Hines, Thomas I., *Fees and Charges.* Washington, D.C.: National Recreation and Park Association, 1966.

Hjelte, George, and Jay S. Shivers, *Public Administration of Recreation Services.* Philadelphia: Lea & Febiger, 1972.

Kraus, Richard, and Joseph E. Curtis, *Creative Administration in Recreation and Parks.* St. Louis: The C. V. Mosby Co., 1973.

"Local Parks and Recreation Agencies," *Parks and Recreation,* Vol. VI (August, 1971).

Rodney, Lynn S., *Administration of Public Recreation.* New York: The Ronald Press, 1964.

Rutledge, Albert J., *Anatomy of a Park: The Essentials of Recreation Area Planning and Design.* New York: McGraw-Hill Book Company, 1971.

part IV
leadership
in recreation

Photo courtesy of the Los Angeles City Schools, Youth Services
Division.

10

THE RECREATION
PROFESSIONAL LEADER
AND VOLUNTEER

The terms *leader* and *leadership* have been used extensively in this text, usually in reference to the recreation field. A recreation leader may be defined as a person in a position of responsibility who guides and teaches others to learn about and derive enjoyment from participation in established interests and new activities. Leadership encompasses those traits of a leader that, in the area of recreation, might include: integrity, intelligence, devotion, responsibility, good health and humor, and enthusiasm. Some more specific qualities that are essential to a successful recreation leader will be discussed later in this chapter.

Recreation programs lacking strong leadership may in many cases be doomed to failure. The best facilities, settings, and financial support will not be sufficient if leadership is weak or unqualified. In this chapter, the history of recreation leadership will be discussed along with different types of leaders, their qualifications, training and certification, responsibilities, and other topics directly relating to leadership practices and problems.

CHANGE IN CONCEPT
OF RECREATION LEADERSHIP

The concept of leadership on a professional basis is still fairly recent to the field of recreation. Recreation leaders were once thought of as those persons who cared for equipment, organized a few games, and in some cases acted as coaches. The typical recreation leader today, however, is well prepared in a two- or four-year recreation curriculum in college, is well paid, and works in a variety of interesting and challenging positions that require management ability with both people and finances and an ability to react to people on a one-to-one basis as well as in groups. Counseling and determining the needs of people are essential to the recreator's leadership ability. The different types of recreation leaders will be discussed later in this chapter.

Recreation leadership is now considered by some persons to be a profession. The criteria that help to identify recreation leadership as a profession are given by Richard Kraus in his book, *Recreation Today,* as:

1. general acceptance in the field
2. a specific body of knowledge
3. the existence of basic research in the field
4. professional higher education
5. certification in the field
6. personnel standards
7. recruitment
8. professional organizations
9. a code of ethics[1]

Recreation fits all of these criteria to greater or lesser degrees.

Therefore, recreation may be considered a profession, and being considered as such is a definite asset for any field for the following reasons:

1. The professional worker is placed above the rank and file workers in terms of status and financial reward. He is recognized for his educational achievements and given appropriate responsibilities.
2. It defines the special qualifications needed for achievement in the area of specialty. It yields a feeling of self-respect and separates the fit from the unfit practitioners.
3. It brings public recognition to the field. A professional in most areas of endeavor is respected, and his skills and judgment are also highly thought of.

The number of recreation workers and professionals has grown as the field has received greater acceptance as a profession. The *1961 Recreation and Park Yearbook* compiled and published figures that showed more than 99,500 recreation personnel employed on a part- or full-time basis with an additional 277,000 volunteer recreation workers. In only nine years, the growth of workers in the field has been tremendous. A "1970 Local Agency Survey," conducted by the NRPA in cooperation with the Bureau of Outdoor Recreation and the Office of Open Space and Urban Beautification, showed more than 250,400 full- and part-time recreation personnel and approximately 87,700 full- and part-time recreation professionals.[2]

[1] Richard Kraus, *Recreation Today; Program Planning and Leadership* (New York: Appleton-Century-Crofts, 1966).

[2] Local Parks and Recreation," *Parks and Recreation,* 6 (August, 1971), 23.

The growth and changes in colleges offering degrees in recreation and the general quality of the curriculum in recreation courses also adds to our consideration of recreation as a profession. This will be discussed in detail in the section concerned with profession preparation later in this chapter.

The numbers of people employed, a high degree of specialized education on undergraduate and graduate levels, high salaries, professional personnel practices and standards, numerous professional organizations, and greater public appreciation and understanding have led the recreation field, indeed, to be accepted as a profession and its employees in leadership positions to be considered professionals.

The major changes in recreation leadership are the movement toward many different types of positions and the consideration that all people, regardless of age, physical handicaps, and socioeconomic level, need some type of organized recreation activity. Recreation is *not* just for children, and adults as well as children can and do benefit from trained recreation leaders. This is so because a leader is not someone who tells you what to do but works with you and teaches, counsels, and participates in helping you understand the activity being pursued.

QUALITIES
OF THE PROFESSIONAL RECREATOR

Some very general qualities were mentioned at the beginning of this chapter. Many qualities have been advanced as necessary for successful leadership in the field of recreation. Most leaders in this or any other area would be ideal persons for such positions if they possessed some of the following qualities to a greater rather than a lesser degree.

1. *A real interest in people.* Recreation is a person-to-person field, and a recreation leader must enjoy and understand people and be willing to get involved with them.
2. *Imagination and enthusiasm.* Imagination allows the recreation leader to evolve programs of interest and value and solve problems among his staff and program participants. The trait of enthusiasm or exuberance is frequently shifted from the leader to the participants and lends itself to thorough enjoyment of the activity. Of course, exuberance too must be tempered and altered to meet the needs of the particular groups being worked with.
3. *Sensitivity.* Sensitivity to the group and to the staff is vital if the leader wants to keep the channels of communication open. The leader must be sufficiently aware to sense problems, disagreements, and apathy that may exist among the people he has contact with.
4. *Honesty and fairness.* These qualities are necessary in any leader, for without them the trust of others is lost. Once this occurs, the position of leadership is a failing one.

The recreation leader must enjoy and understand people. Photo courtesy of the Town of Hempstead, New York, Department of Parks and Recreation, Recreation Division.

5. *Respect for one's self and others.* Self-respect and self-confidence are important traits for a recreation leader. If a person has a poor self-image, he will not come across well to his staff or the people he services. On the other hand, he must also respect others and not be overly authoritative.

6. *Patience and persistence.* A leader who discourages people too easily will certainly lose the interest of the group he is working with. In specialized groups, such as the retarded, for example, persistence is a prime requisite for any successful program.

In addition to the aforementioned qualities, there are many abilities that are desirable for a recreation leader to possess. These abilities indicate one's level of functioning in a leadership position. They include the following:

1. *Knowledge of one's limitations.* A leader should know himself very well and not try to take on something he knows nothing about or to "over-talk" an activity that he may know "everything" about. The old adage "know thyself" is quite appropriate here.

2. *Ability to act decisively.* The leader is the person who in most cases will make the final decision. Certainly, other persons' opinions must be considered, but when a decision has to be made, it should be accomplished quickly and efficiently.

3. *Ability to evaluate situations in their proper perspective.* The leader must thoroughly understand people and programs and analyze problems with scrutiny. He must see things in the light in which they exist, rather than in the light he wants them to exist.

4. *Ability to organize and plan.* When the responsibilities of leaders are discussed later in this chapter, it becomes apparent that administration, which includes organization and planning, is a prime function of the recreation leader.

PERSONALITY TYPES
IN RECREATION LEADERS

Leaders are generally categorized into one of three personality types: autocratic, laissez-faire, and democratic. Although it is recognized that many leaders will fit into one of these groups, it also is apparent that one may also show characteristics of another personality type in specific situations.

The Autocratic Leader

An autocratic leader can be defined as a person who wants unrestricted power. The word autocratic is derived from the Greek *autos* meaning self and *kratos* meaning power. Its definition becomes readily apparent from its derivation. The autocratic leader likes to set all policies, make all decisions, ignore group majority feeling, direct activities but not participate, and generally remains "above" a situation rather than becoming involved.

In a specific recreation program, the autocratic leader of a teen-age travel group might plan the program without ever eliciting the group's suggestions or approval. He might consider his position and education sufficiently superior to the group to warrant such action. He might hire a staff that he approved of, but one that would not necessarily relate to the group they were serving. Finances would be allocated, decisions made, and schedules arranged, without consulting the staff or group members. Only token consideration would be given to suggestions by the group or its officers. This type of leader might never accompany the group on trips, leaving that job to the staff while he or she was occupied with administrative functions.

It is highly doubtful that any recreation leader would be totally autocratic, but he might show enough of these tendencies to warrant being placed in this category.

The Laissez-faire Leader

This leader is frequently referred to as the "hands-off" type. In other words, he stays out of most situations and administers sparingly. He rarely makes suggestions, participates in activities, or helps in decision making. In many ways, he is the exact opposite of the authoritarian leader previously described. If he were involved in group leadership, he would delegate authority to others and let group members and assistants make all of the decisions. The theme behind a laissez-faire leader is one of complete uninvolvement and detachment.

The Democratic Leader

This type of leader operates according to the principles of a democracy, which include open discussions, votes, majority choices in most matters, and representation by the group being served. The democratic leader encourages his staff and group members, and he participates along with the others in group activities. He does not try to remain aloof from the group but takes an active interest in it.

RESPONSIBILITIES OF THE RECREATOR

The responsibilities of the professional recreation leader are both general and specific in nature. The general functions are applicable to most workers in the field. The specific duties will be discussed in accordance with the type of recreation position one holds.

Generally speaking, the overall main objective of a recreation worker is to help people to enjoy themselves while participating in all recreational activities. This ability to enjoy and derive satisfaction is aided by the qualities of a leader that were given in an earlier section (refer to page 191). Some of the functions of a recreation leader are given here:

1. *Teaching.* The leader must have the ability and desire to give instruction, interpret information, and generally broaden recreation horizons.
2. *Enthusiasm.* The leader creates an environment of enthusiasm as he inspires the group to do their best both individually and together.
3. *Planning.* Planning is of major importance, as a poorly planned program will be difficult to get started. Proper planning will insure adequate financial support, facilities, equipment, and any additional needs in increased staff members. The more initial planning that is accomplished, the better the ensuing program.
4. *Counseling.* The leader who guides also helps to identify goals and forsees problem areas. He is able to talk to the group and is sensitive to individual feelings.
5. *Evaluation.* This word is frequently used in this text as its importance cannot be overestimated. Society is constantly changing and so are people's needs. Programs must constantly be evaluated for their effect and overall contribution to the public. In addition, the recreation leader should constantly evaluate his own duties and how he is performing

them. Evaluation may also include the group member whose accomplishments should be recognized and given approval whenever such is earned.

HARTFORD MUNICIPAL RECREATION DEPARTMENT
EVALUATION REPORT

Name _____ Position _____
Employed from _____ to _____ Recommendation # _____

(1) Excellent   (2) Above Average   (3) Average   (4) Below Average   (5) Poor

Personal

	1	2	3	4	5
Enthusiastic					
Public Relations					
Mature					
Honesty					
Cheerful Disposition					
Well-groomed					

Supervisory

	1	2	3	4	5
Enforces Rules and Policies					
Responsible					
Dependability					
Understanding of People					
Tact and Diplomacy					
Common Sense					
Cooperative					

Professional

	1	2	3	4	5
Leadership Ability					
Adequate Planning					
Knowledge and Skills					
Keeps Records					
Teaching Ability					
Does Research					

EVALUATOR   TITLE   DATE

Reprinted by permission of the Hartford, Wisconsin, Municipal Recreation Department.

Other functions of a leader should include:

1. *Groups should be organized for the best possible level of accomplishment.* Poor group organization will result in lack of activity effectiveness. If widely different ages are represented, for example, in a music group, then most of the participants will be unhappy.

2. *Opportunities for participation should be open to all.* The good leader is the one who tries to get everyone into the act even when new activities are being tried.

3. *Furnish the best possible settings and equipment that are both pleasant and safe and also help to contribute to growth in character as well as ability.* A healthy environment both mentally and physically is very important. The mental attitude of the leader will dictate the attitude of the participants. Relaxation and enjoyment, not competitiveness, should be the goals of most recreation programs.

TYPES OF RECREATORS

The term *recreator* has been used throughout this book interchangeably with *recreation leader.* Both of these terms are generic and are used to describe a basic leadership position in the field of recreation. In this section, specific leadership positions and their general duties will be discussed.

1. *Recreation executive.* This person serves as the chief officer of a city or community recreation department, or he may be the head of an agency largely concerned with recreational activities. Some of the positions held by the recreation executive include: (a) superintendent of recreation and/or parks and recreation, and (b) assistant superintendent of either of these departments. The main duties of these people include: (a) planning and administration, (b) personnel hiring and management, and (c) promotion activities.

2. *Recreation supervisor.* The supervisor is usually in charge of a particular program area, such as dance or art, and in this capacity he is responsible for the administration, planning, publicity, and evaluation of the program. The general duties of a supervisor include: (a) to understand and communicate program policies and objectives, (b) to aid in communication between the executive and personnel, (c) to establish duties of personnel in this area and guide them in the best accomplishment of their work, (d) to assist in management and evaluation techniques, and (e) to work with personnel and participants to establish a situation with good rapport and respect. A recreation supervisor is sometimes in charge of district recreation programs comprising many recreation departments or centers. This is just a different use of the term compared to the usual definition of a person in charge of an activitiy area.

3. *Recreation center director.* This leader is responsible for a complete facility, whether it be a teen-center, playground, nursery, or camp

program. He has the responsibility of setting personnel standards, hiring and firing, planning, and aiding in management and program evaluation.

4. *Recreation leader.* This person is usually hired to work at a center, camp, playground, swimming facility or other indoor or outdoor recreation center. In this capacity, the recreation leader is usually in charge of an activity or may participate in many related activities as a group leader and assistant to the supervisor of the specific activity in question.

5. *Trainee positions.* These positions are to prepare young people for professional recreation leadership. These are not professional persons and should not substitute in leadership positions. Some of the specific trainee positions include: recreation intern, student recreation leader, and junior recreation assistant.

   a. The intern is usually a graduate with a degree in recreation and participates in various administrative and supervisory capacities. He frequently rotates to different departments as does the medical intern in different hospital services.

   b. The student recreation leader works under the close supervision of staff members and is given experience in promotion, administration, and leadership areas. This person is frequently enrolled in a college recreation curriculum.

   c. The junior recreation assistant is frequently a high school student or member of a service organization or club. He is constantly supervised and aids recreation leaders in their group activities. He is given some limited experience in leadership tasks.

6. *Auxiliary personnel.* These people include office workers, public relations people, consultants, buyers, budget specialists, and others who contribute to the smooth operation of a recreation department or agency that has a recreation division. Positions of leadership may include a recreation analyst, street worker, or a promotion director.

   a. The recreation analyst, frequently called an "administrative analyst," works on problems and management procedures concerned with department administration.

   b. The street worker, also called a "detached worker," under the leadership of the department executive, works mainly with youth groups with antisocial tendencies. He tries to speak with these groups and help them to reconstruct their lives. Many street workers have been involved with teen-age gangs, and some have been credited with controlling "warring" groups through meetings with them and direct counseling. Some workers have been injured and even killed while performing this function.

   c. A promotion director, often called an information or publicity director, has the very vital position of maintaining communications with the public concerning programs and public participation in them.

All of these leadership positions are very general in nature, and their titles and responsibilities may vary from department to department. For example, a large city may have many recreation leader positions with large staffs under each one. Frequently, assistant leadership positions are necessary for large indoor and outdoor recreation complexes. Some communities may be so small that one or two people can handle all of the recreation needs.

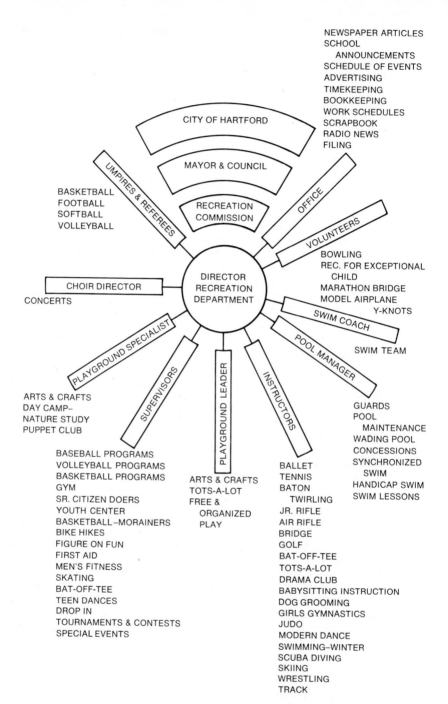

The City of Hartford, Wisconsin, utilizes many different types of recreators in its program as can be seen in this diagram. Reprinted by permission of the Hartford Municipal Recreation Department.

Volunteers were not mentioned in this section because their nonpaid status differs from the positions discussed. In addition, many volunteers are not in leadership positions. Volunteers will be discussed in the next section in some detail.

VOLUNTEER RECREATION WORKERS

The Recreation and Park Yearbook, 1966 Edition, reports that approximately 495,000 persons participated as volunteers in recreation programs in 1965. The same Local Agency Survey, previously cited, also reported on numbers of volunteers involved in recreation programs. Data submitted by 1,119 local park and recreation agencies showed a total of 314,840 volunteers, who contributed over twenty million hours of service in 1970. More than two-thirds of all volunteers were adults and eighty-six percent of them acted in leadership positions. These people were serving in all types of positions, which can be generally divided into four categories as follows:

1. *Administrative, promotional, or advisory.* This volunteer is frequently represented on boards or committees and meets with professionals in planning and management capacities. Frequently, volunteers are members of a special commission or task force assigned to investigate the possibilities of building new facilities, surveying community members concerning program interests, or working on promotional activities concerning established programs.
2. *Activity or group leadership.* This volunteer often organizes groups of people, under the direction of the department supervisor, in activities that he is familiar with. Many such volunteers bring their expertise in a hobby or other activity to the group. They assume the responsibility for organizing and instructing the group and are in an active leadership position.
3. *Aiding programs.* These volunteers aid the professional leader in a particular project or activity. They can act as chaperones, take small groups aside for special instruction, help with equipment, and generally just be available to the leader to help him with his activities.
4. *Junior volunteers.* These are young, usually school or college-age persons, who have an avid interest in people and recreation and volunteer their services in various capacities. They are usually assigned duties that match their interests and are very valuable in programs dealing with children.

What Are Some of the Contributions of Volunteers? The number of volunteers working in recreation programs shows an avid interest by these people. Many volunteers are parents interested in the welfare of their children.

However, older and retired persons frequently find volunteer service of this type extremely satisfying and helpful in keeping themselves constructively active. Some valuable contributions of volunteers are listed below:

1. They help to fill the gap left as a result of insufficient numbers of professional recreation leaders.
2. They frequently have special talents that they can offer in group instruction. A recreation leader may not have a talent in, for example, crewel or embroidery work. Here a volunteer leader can perfectly fill the bill. The department might not be able to afford to hire people with many different talents.
3. They foster good public relations and offer communication between the recreation department and the community. This is helpful when it comes time to approve budgets and vote on recreation-oriented referendums.
4. They frequently bring with them great enthusiasm and a different way of looking at things. Their enthusiasm is often contagious to leaders and participants alike.
5. Volunteers build morale in the department and create a feeling of oneness and work for common interests and goals.

Are There Any Difficulties in Using Volunteers? There are many problems involved in using individuals who are not holding their positions for income. These problems will be discussed later in this section. However, in most cases, volunteers contribute more to a program than they detract from it. A major difficulty arises when volunteers are not properly trained for their positions; this will be discussed in detail in the next section of this chapter.

Some of the problems encountered in using volunteers include:

1. Volunteers may look at their voluntary service as a secondary position. Their families, other organizations, and leisure time may interfere with their volunteer interests.
2. Problems may arise between the volunteers and paid workers. They may clash over who is to make decisions and participate in other phases of management.
3. There may be personality and status clashes between paid and nonpaid workers. Some very wealthy, status-seeking volunteers may think their social position dictates a position of leadership in the group. Other clashes may come about because volunteers may lack specific knowledge in dealing with people.
4. Sometimes volunteers have special interests that get in the way of their proper functioning. Such interests might include wanting to coach a team that their child is on or desiring to lead an activity that they have little ability in.
5. Frequently volunteers feel that they are working too hard. In some cases, this may be true, but in most cases they might feel this way because they are working as hard and long as the recreation leader and they aren't getting paid for their endeavors. Of course, the choice to be a volunteer is entirely their own.

6. Some volunteers overstep their positions and make decisions that should not be their responsibility.
7. Some volunteers may try to change department or agency policies. This is a very serious problem and must be handled decisively, but with tact.

Many of the problems discussed here rise directly from poor volunteer training. This will be discussed in the following section.

Establishing a Volunteer Program

Training and supervision of volunteers is essential if a volunteer program is to be successful. The volunteers must first be carefully selected. In a recreation program, which essentially deals with people, the type of volunteer is very vital. A careful screening process should first be set up to eliminate those people who show anti-social behavior, dislike of people, or other personality disorders that would obviously not benefit the agency or department. Interviewing should try to elicit whether the person shows such qualities as intelligence, specific knowledge, willingness to learn, enthusiasm, love of people, responsibility, dependability, and good humor. It is difficult to pinpoint all of these characteristics, but many become evident during interviews and open discussions. These interviews should also establish where in the department the chosen volunteer would be able to contribute the most.

Where Do You Find Volunteers? In some communities, volunteers are difficult to locate. Good places to look are church-related groups, senior citizen clubs, PTA members, organizations having a civic interest, retired people, and through surveys taken in neighborhoods, schools, and among business people. Younger volunteers can be found in schools, clubs, and service organizations.

Some communities have established volunteer service groups that are open to all people wishing to volunteer for all activities including those that are recreation-oriented. These "volunteer clearinghouses," as they are sometimes called, often sponsor surveys and promotional activities to make their presence known. Some of these volunteer agencies only serve retired people and others are oriented toward persons with specialized skills.

How Should Volunteers Be Trained? As previously mentioned, training is one of the most important factors in using volunteers. When volunteers do not know what is expected of them and how they are to function, problems are bound to arise. The volunteer, once selected, should meet with the recreation executive and supervisor for an overall orientation into the structure, services, facilities, and goals of the department. He should have a very good idea of how the department operates prior to beginning his work. He should be allowed to ask only questions concerning department operation, and it would be helpful if he were given printed material that outlined the department's functions. He should then meet with his immediate supervisor and learn about his assignment in detail. Duties, responsibilities, and schedule should be discussed, and any problems ironed out at this time. If problems arise after the volunteer has been working for a while, they should be immediately discussed on a one-to-one basis, with the supervisor and volunteer both trying to find solutions to the problem at hand.

Relationship of the Recreator with Volunteers

The recreator must take many things into consideration to have a good working relationship with volunteers. Some of these considerations are:

1. He must carefully select volunteers with his own method of operation in mind. Selection should be made on the basis of quality not quantity.
2. He should try not to be influenced by others in the selection of volunteers.
3. He should make sure that the volunteer understands his position as an aid to, not a replacement for, the supervisor.
4. Policies, methods of working, and organization matters should be thoroughly understood. Schedules should be established taking the volunteer into consideration.
5. The volunteer's accomplishments should be acknowledged. A pat on the back still goes a long way.
6. The volunteer should be assigned to the area where he will be happiest and contribute the most.
7. The volunteer should be involved in planning and organizing so that he feels he is indeed an important part of the operation.
8. Volunteers should have the opportunity to better themselves through greater responsibility and handling more people or activities. However, it is essential that a good volunteer is not taken advantage of by expecting too much work of him.

PREPARATION FOR THE RECREATION PROFESSION.

Professional education programs for park and recreation leaders are of recent origin. Over the years, the *National Recreation Association,* now part of the National Recreation and Park Association, has been the impetus behind bettering the profession through workshops, institutes, and a wealth of printed information. In 1926, this association founded the National Recreation School for Professional Graduate Training, which was conducted until 1935. This school was the first of its kind for the training of recreation leaders. Since then, there has been a rapid growth in college and university recreation training programs. According to the 1967 survey by the Society of Park and Recreation Educators (SPRE), there were 286 such educators teaching more than 6000 students. This represented a thirty-five percent increase over the 1966 study by the same organization.

NUMBER OF RECREATION & PARK CURRICULUMS
1930 TO DATE

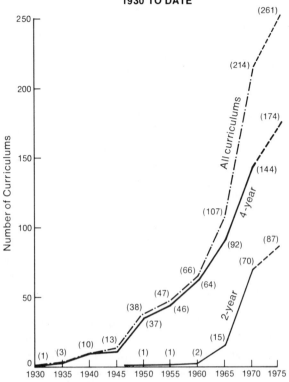

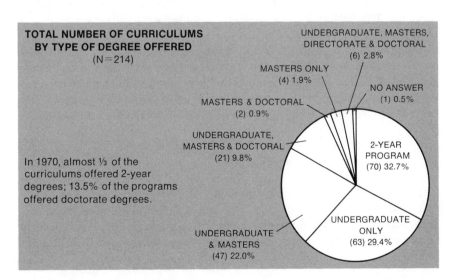

TOTAL NUMBER OF CURRICULUMS BY TYPE OF DEGREE OFFERED
(N=214)

In 1970, almost ⅓ of the curriculums offered 2-year degrees; 13.5% of the programs offered doctorate degrees.

UNDERGRADUATE, MASTERS, DIRECTORATE & DOCTORAL (6) 2.8%

MASTERS ONLY (4) 1.9%

MASTERS & DOCTORAL (2) 0.9%

NO ANSWER (1) 0.5%

UNDERGRADUATE, MASTERS & DOCTORAL (21) 9.8%

2-YEAR PROGRAM (70) 32.7%

UNDERGRADUATE ONLY (63) 29.4%

UNDERGRADUATE & MASTERS (47) 22.0%

The number of recreation and park curriculums is growing rapidly with different types of degrees being awarded. *Parks and Recreation,* August, 1971. Reprinted by permission of the National Recreation and Park Association.

A 1970 report by the SPRE Curriculum Study Committee showed 11,577 undergraduate majors in the recreation field, as opposed to 7,933 majors in 1969. This may not sound like a large number of programs, but one must consider that only ten programs were reported prior to 1940, twenty-three programs were reported in the 1940s, twenty more during the 1950s, and the greatest increase was recorded in the 1960s with seventy-seven programs. Recently thirty institutions indicated a parks and recreation program will be started by 1975. Another study taken by the National Recreation and Park Association's Educational Survey indicated that by 1980 there would be 343 colleges offering majors in parks and recreation management.

Undergraduate Requirements

Undergraduate programs in parks and recreation require a broad, general knowledge as well as specialized instruction in the major subject area. This is sometimes broken down by percentages to result in fifty percent general subject knowledge, thirty-three percent professional preparation, and seventeen percent in related subject areas. The following subject areas are frequently part of the requirements for recreation and parks programs: humanities, sciences, communications, administration involving business and government; public relations; health and safety; education courses; courses that deal with group behavior; history, philosophy, and theory of recreation; and actual field experience in a recreation setting. All of these courses will help in developing a well-rounded person with specific knowledge in handling people and administering recreation programs. The field experience enables the student to use his knowledge in a practical manner.

In general, the primary aim of an undergraduate program is a broad, general education. Specialized interests are usually pursued in the graduate and post-graduate programs. Graduate study is increasingly recommended for those persons desiring to serve in an executive leadership capacity in the area of parks and recreation. Graduate programs will be discussed in the next section.

Graduate Requirements
in Recreation and Park Programs

The 1970 SPRE study, cited previously, reported that there were 1,486 candidates for Master's degrees in 1971 and 257 Doctoral candidates in that same year. There was a thirty-nine percent increase in graduate enrollment in 1971 over 1969. The major objectives of the graduate program include the following:

1. Knowledge and managerial training in administration techniques
2. Opportunities for professional growth, research, independent study, and observation

3. Specialization offered in areas of interest pertaining to park and recreation management

4. Guidance and supervision in programs and future placement in field of predominant interest and training

The National Recreation and Park Association offers a *Directory of Professional Preparation Programs in Recreation, Parks, and Related Areas,* which is a joint publication of the American Association for Health, Physical Education, and Recreation (AAHPER) and the NRPA. It provides a comprehensive listing of colleges and universities offering programs in the park and recreation field. The listings indicate the institution, its address, and the degrees and options offered. It is a valuable tool to the person starting out in the field or looking for graduate study programs.

Junior Colleges and the Recreation Profession

There has been a phenomenal growth in junior colleges in recent years, especially in the latter part of the 1960s. This growth is continuing, and estimates are that by 1980 more than 100 such institutions will offer a two-year certificate in the field of parks and recreation. These associate degrees are offered by both private and community institutions.

The trend toward two-year recreation training will be a great aid in meeting the needs of employment in this field. In most cases, the two-year program prepares the student for a position as a program leader or activity-area specialist. Some persons take the two-year course and then transfer to a four-year school to complete their recreation degree. There are many job possibilities in this field, some that are not well known. The employment opportunities for two-year and four-year college graduates will be discussed in Chapter 12, "Employment Opportunities in Recreation."

Certification in Recreation

Certification means that a recreation leader has met certain standards of training and education. Just as teachers, lawyers, and persons belonging to other professions must meet certain standards before they are allowed to practice in a particular state, so will recreation leaders have to meet certain standards. Some states already require legal certification and others are in the process of adopting such laws.

Many recreation executives believe that certification is desirable, but that it should be administered by a group representing the recreation profession. This group would have the authority to establish classifications for recreation positions, set standards of requirements for these positions, fix fees, conduct examinations, and issue certificates in the area of specialty.

Several state recreation associations have already established a registry that allows for a voluntary listing of full-time recreation leaders. This listing promotes the professional nature of the field, is a first step toward certification in those states that do not require it as yet, and is helpful to the potential employer.

QUESTIONS AND EXERCISES

1. What are some of the important personality qualities of a recreation leader?

2. List the criteria that are important for any field to be considered a profession. Do you think that recreation is indeed a profession? Support your answer.

3. What are some of the necessary abilities for a person interested in recreation leadership to possess?

4. Discuss the different types of leader personalities. If you were presently a recreation leader, what category would you place yourself in? Explain your answer.

5. What are the major responsibilities of a recreation leader? Can you add to those listed in this text?

6. Discuss the major leadership positions open to professional recreators. Which of these positions appeal to you? Justify your choice.

7. In what ways can volunteers contribute to a recreation program? What difficulties can occur because of volunteer participation?

8. If you were a recreation leader and you encountered a volunteer who refused to go along with your program in terms of activity areas, schedules, and general policies, how would you go about dealing with the problem?

9. Discuss the growth of recreation curriculums in the United States. Discuss the undergraduate course of study for recreation and park majors.

10. Discuss the importance of graduate study and the trend toward junior colleges. Do you plan to attain a graduate degree in recreation?

11. Explain the term *certification*. Do you think that professional recreators should be certified? Explain your answer.

12. Who do you think should be in charge of setting up certification standards? Do some research to establish who in other professions set up these standards. Choose a profession and briefly report on its certification authority and standards.

SELECTED REFERENCES

Danford, Howard G., *Creative Leadership in Recreation*. Boston: Allyn and Bacon, Inc., 1964.

Ford, H. T., "The Recreation Director Syndrome," *Journal of Health, Physical Education and Recreation*, Vol. 44 (May, 1973).

Hawkins, Donald E., *Supply/Demand Study, Professional and Pre-Professional Recreation and Park Occupations.* Washington, D.C.: National Recreation and Park Association, 1968.

Hjelte, George, and Jay S. Shivers, *Public Administration of Recreation Services.* Philadelphia: Lea & Febiger, 1972.

Hormachea, Marion N., and R. Carroll, eds., *Recreation in Modern Society.* Boston: Holbrook Press, Inc., 1972.

"Local Parks and Recreation Agencies," *Parks and Recreation,* Vol. VI (August, 1971).

National Recreation Association, *Leadership Evaluation: A Checklist.* New York, n.d.

The National Recreation and Park Association, *Directory of Professional Preparation Programs in Recreation, Parks, and Related Areas.* Washington, D.C.: The Association, 1972.

Sessoms, H. Douglas, "Education for Recreation and Park Professionals," *Parks and Recreation,* Vol. II (December, 1967).

Stevens, Ardis, *Fun is Therapeutic: A Recreation Book to Help Therapeutic Recreation Leaders by People Who Are Leading Recreation.* Springfield, Ill.: Charles C Thomas, Publisher, 1972.

The National Recreation and Park Association, *Directory of Professional Preparation Programs in Recreation, Parks, and Related Areas.* Washington, D.C.: The Association, 1972.

part V
the profession

Photo courtesy of the Los Angeles City Schools, Youth Services Section.

11

PROFESSIONAL AND SERVICE

ORGANIZATIONS IN RECREATION

Organizations that speak for a profession and provide services to its members exist in all areas of professional employment. In addition, professional organizations establish codes of ethics, provide education and public relations programs, aid in curriculum guidance in their specialties, engage in research with the goal of improving the profession, and act as consultants in relevant areas.

Recreation, only recently accepted as a profession, has many organizations that represent and/or serve the profession in some way. Many of these groups are highly specialized and may serve only a limited membership. However, other organizations have large memberships and many affiliated groups representing specialized areas. A representative group of these organizations is discussed in this chapter.

Perhaps, the best known recreation organization is the National Recreation and Park Association, which was formed in 1966 by the merger of professional and nonprofessional organizations. This merger came about because of duplication and overlapping of activities, competition for membership, and conflicts of purpose. The formation of the National Recreation and Park Association united these organizations in a common goal of mutual cooperation and striving for accomplishments in the advancement and enhancement of the park and recreation movement.

The following organizations merged to form the NRPA in 1966.

1. *The American Institute of Park Executives.* This organization had its beginning in Boston in 1898. The membership was at first largely park executives, and its interests were primarily in the areas of zoos and zoo management, horticulture, and park development and maintenance. In later years, the Institute broadened its interests to include the recreation movement.

211

2. *The American Association of Zoological Parks and Aquariums.* The Association was formed in 1924 and its membership was primarily zoological park and aquarium executives and personnel.
This Association was part of the NRPA until 1971, when it again became an independent organization. It will be listed separately later in this chapter.

3. *The American Recreation Society.* This society, established in 1938, was originally called the Society of Recreation Workers of America. It served the recreation movement in activities involving the following areas: education, therapeutic recreation, industry, parks, state and federal agencies, private agencies, armed forces, religious groups, and public and rural recreation.

4. *The National Conference on State Parks.* This society was organized in 1921 and was primarily involved in improving public relations concerning state parks throughout the United States.

5. *The National Recreation Association.* This association was originally founded as the Playground Association of America in 1906. It was primarily a service-oriented group, having a membership comprised of all persons involved in the recreation movement. The NRA was well-financed and organized and created many committees that investigated areas of recreation education, curriculum standards, federal recreation and defense services, recreation programming, and administration. The NRA also sponsored many conferences and the National Recreation Congress.

**National Recreation
and Park Association (NRPA)**
1700 Pennsylvania Ave., N.W., Washington, D.C., 20006

ORIGIN. Founded in 1966.

PURPOSE. The National Recreation and Park Association is an independent, nonprofit service organization dedicated to the advancement and enhancement of the park and recreation movement and to the conservation of natural and human resources.

ORGANIZATION. The association is directed by a sixty-three-member board of trustees that meets several times each year to shape NRPA policies.

STAFF. A professional staff of specialists in parks, recreation, conservation and associated fields and additional professional representatives in eight district offices across the United States provide personal consultant service to park and recreation agencies at the municipal, county, state, and regional levels.

MEMBERSHIP. An active membership of 30,000 in the National Recreation and Park Association include: citizens interested in recreation, parks, zoos, and conservation of natural resources and wildlife; parks and recreation commissioners and board members; professional park and recreation leaders; government and private recreation and park agencies.

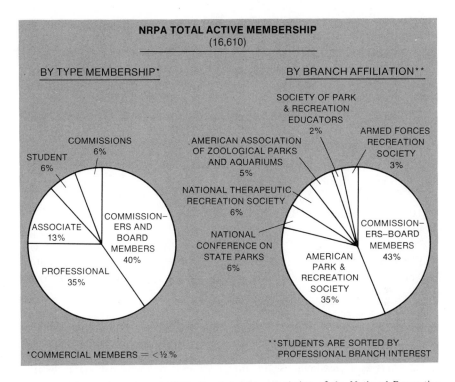

Parks and Recreation, August 1971. Reprinted by permission of the National Recreation and Park Association.

ASSOCIATED SOCIETIES. According to their specific interests, most NRPA members are also affiliated with one of six professional and volunteer branches: the American Park and Recreation Society, the National Conference on State Parks, the National Therapeutic Recreation Society, the Society of Park and Recreation Educators, and the commissioners and board members of park and recreation agencies.

SERVICES. As a service organization, NRPA works closely with public and private park and recreation agencies at the national, state, and local levels to foster the progressive development and wise administration of resources, facilities, programs, and personnel. Because of this close liaison, the association serves as a repository for a vast amount of factual information on a wide variety of recreation and park topics.

SUPPORT. The National Recreation and Park Association is financially supported entirely through public contributions, endowments, grants, and membership fees. Much of its income is raised annually through United Fund campaigns.

PUBLICATIONS. In addition to special publications, the following publications are issued at regular intervals:

1. *Parks and Recreation* magazine
2. *Recreation and Park Yearbook*
3. Management aids
4. *A Guide to Books on Recreation*
5. Newsletters
6. *Playground Summer Notebook*
7. Park Practice Program Series
8. *Journal of Leisure Research*
9. *Therapeutic Recreation Journal*
10. NRPA Membership Directory

SERVICES TO PUBLIC AND PRIVATE PARK AND RECREATION AGENCIES. NRPA serves the general public through cooperation with public and private park and recreation agencies. Among its many services to these agencies, NRPA:

1. Conducts nationwide efforts to acquaint all Americans with the benefits of physical fitness, conservation, beautification, and open spaces for recreation.
2. Acts as a clearinghouse for information among national, state, district, and local public and private agencies.
3. Conducts studies of specific agency problems and recommends solutions.
4. Serves as a consultant on legislation and policies.
5. Devises and suggests standards for facilities, programs, administration, and budget.
6. Gathers factual information on the present status of parks and recreation, and forecasts future trends.
7. Works with educational institutions to improve curricula.
8. Sponsors an annual fair of equipment and products.
9. Sponsors national promotional campaigns on behalf of recreation and parks.
10. Encourages public support for agency policies.

SERVICES TO INDIVIDUALS. NRPA also offers individual services to professionals and nonprofessionals interested in the park and recreation movement. NRPA:

1. Helps professionals keep abreast of new ideas and techniques.
2. Conducts schools, conferences, and seminars for professionals.
3. Sponsors national and regional congresses to provide forums for renowned experts.
4. Maintains a job placement service for professionals.
5. Sponsors an internship program for recent park and recreation graduates.

6. Conducts experiments with equipment and programs to evaluate effectiveness and insure safety.
7. Encourages improvement of recreation opportunities for special groups such as the handicapped, aged, and mentally retarded.
8. Provides information to all persons on specific park and recreation activities.
9. Promotes community recognition of outstanding volunteer efforts through an awards program.
10. Encourages individual participation in agency programs.

There are numerous organizations that relate to recreation in one way or another. Some well-recognized organizations active in this area are discussed in the following sections of this chapter.

American Association for Health Physical Education, and Recreation (AAHPER)
1201 16th Street, N.W., Washington, D.C., 20036.

ORIGIN. Founded in 1885.

MEMBERSHIP. Students in preparation for and educators in the field of physical education, dance, health, athletics, safety education, recreation, and outdoor recreation; 45,000 members.

OBJECTIVES. The improvement of health education, physical education, and recreation in the United States.

SERVICES RENDERED. Sponsors district conferences and a national convention every other year. Establishes and promotes personnel and program standards and supports legislation of interest to the profession. Helps recruit and place professional personnel in addition to providing technical and consultative exchange of information services.

PUBLICATIONS.

1. *The AAHPER Journal*
2. *Research Quarterly*
3. *School Health Review*
4. Bibliographies, conference reports, bulletins, rosters, surveys, and other material

American Camping Association (ACA)
Bradford Woods, Martinsville, Indiana, 46151.

ORIGIN. Founded in 1924.

MEMBERSHIP. Camp directors, camp staff members, educators, people concerned with the operation of camps and the camping movement; 7,800 members.

OBJECTIVES. To further the interests and welfare of children and adults through camping as a recreative and educative experience.

SERVICES RENDERED. Expresses the views of camping people at both the national and local levels, in addition to providing leadership in the development of new camping areas. Also, disseminates information on new camping trends, as well as developing standards and operating codes for the improvement of camping practices. Maintains library; conducts Campcraft Certification Program.

PUBLICATIONS.

1. *Camping Magazine,* which is published eight times a year
2. *National Directory of Accredited Camps*
3. Pamphlets, studies, reports, and other publications at various times during the year

Association of College Unions — International
Box 7286, Stanford, California, 94305.

MEMBERSHIP. College unions and college student associations designed to promote social and recreational opportunities and facilities for students; 840 members.

OBJECTIVES. To provide unions the opportunity to share interests and information and to assist in the development of college unions' programs and services.

SERVICES RENDERED. Conducts regional meetings and a national conference. Conducts research in union policies and practices, regional tournaments in union activities, and photograph-exhibition loan services. Also provides employment service in the student-union field, and protects the interests of members in entertainment bookings. Assists in development of new college unions; makes surveys on union practices; and provides architectural and program planning services to institutions undertaking new unions or additions.

PUBLICATIONS.

1. *Union Wire*
2. Bulletins
3. Paperbacks, monographs, pamphlets, and periodicals

The Athletic Institute
805 Merchandise Mart, Chicago, Illinois, 60654.

ORIGIN. Founded in 1934.

MEMBERSHIP. Manufacturers of athletic equipment and trophies and publishers of sports magazines.

OBJECTIVES. A service organization that encourages participation in sports activities.

SERVICES RENDERED. Active in development of visual aids, financing sports programs, and organizing and sponsoring workshops for people in the field. Has organized national conferences concerned with curriculum guidance in health, recreation, and physical education.

PUBLICATIONS.

1. *Sportscope*
2. Sports handbooks and pamphlets

It has also produced films that are valuable in understanding leadership in recreation.

International Council on Health, Physical Education, and Recreation (ICHPER)
1201 16th St., N. W., Washington, D.C., 20036.

ORIGIN. Founded in 1958.

MEMBERSHIP. Educational organizations and individuals concerned with health, physical education, sports, and recreation both in and out of school.

OBJECTIVES. International advancement of health, physical education, and recreation through education and communication.

SERVICES. Serves as a clearinghouse for exchange of information and ideas and as a spokesman for its membership internationally. Conducts study groups, prepares exhibits of educational materials, and conducts research in cooperation with national and international groups.

PUBLICATIONS.

1. *ICHPER Bulletin*
2. *Gymnasium: The ICHPER Review*
3. *Congress Report*
4. Other materials concerned with curriculum and teacher education

International Recreation Association (IRA)
345 East 46th Street, New York, N. Y., 10017.

ORIGIN. Established in Philadelphia, Pennsylvania, on October 3, 1956.

MEMBERSHIP. Citizens, professionals, and statesmen involved in the need for a world recreation movement.

OBJECTIVES. The primary objectives of the organization are as follows:

1. Serve as a central clearinghouse for the exchange of information and experience among recreation agencies of the world.

2. Aid countries to establish central recreation service agencies upon request.
3. Forward the development of a world recreation movement designed to enrich the human spirit through wholesome use of leisure.
4. Encourage the provision of land and facilities, training of leaders, development of varied programs, and public interpretation of the values of play for children, recreation for youth, and creative use of leisure for all ages.
5. Provide a medium through which the recreation authorities of the world may work in unity on common problems.

SERVICES. Services of the organization include:

1. Maintain a central office to service the world's recreation agencies.
2. Provide correspondence and consultation services on specific problems.
3. Provide field service to countries desiring help with central recreation agencies.
4. Provide field service on specific aspects of program.
5. Encourage the exchange of recreation leaders among nations.
6. Cooperate with the United Nations and its affiliated agencies.
7. Publish a bulletin for recreation agencies to exchange information.
8. Aid and encourage programs for leadership training in recreation.
9. Arrange for international and regional conferences.
10. Encourage the contribution of funds – public and private – to the development of recreation services for all mankind.

PUBLICATIONS. *IRA Bulletin* and other recreation material.

League of Federal Recreation Associations, Inc. (LFRA)
Tempo Building A, Washington, D.C., 20315.

ORIGIN. Established in June, 1958, following committee meetings, representing several employee associations, to draft a constitution and by-laws. Incorporated under the laws of the District of Columbia in 1960 as the League of Federal Employee Associations. The present name was adopted in 1963.

MEMBERSHIP. Members are limited to organized federal and Washington, D.C., employee associations whose primary purpose is promotion of the recreation and welfare of its members.

OBJECTIVES. It is a nonprofit organization composed of more than fifty federal and District of Columbia government employee associations. It acts as a sponsor for activities, a medium for exchange of ideas and experiences, and takes part in contributing to employee morale.

SERVICES. Provides special savings opportunities for employees; sponsors cultural activities and civic programs; and sponsors art, photographic, and hobby shows.

National Industrial Recreation Association (NIRA)
20 North Wacker Drive, Chicago, Illinois, 60606.

ORIGIN. Founded in 1941.

MEMBERSHIP. Athletic and recreation directors for commercial and industrial firms; 800 members.

OBJECTIVES. Advancement of profession and research in areas relating to industrial recreation.

SERVICES. Maintains library and placement service; operates regional workshops, gives annual awards for best industrial recreation programs.

PUBLICATIONS.

1. *Recreation Management*
2. President's bulletin
3. Manuals and research reports

National Therapeutic Recreation Society (NTRS)
1700 Pennsylvania Avenue, N.W., Washington, D.C., 20006.

ORIGIN. Formed by merger of the National Association of Recreation Therapists and the American Park and Recreation Society Hospital Section.

MEMBERSHIP. Founded in 1966, this organization has a present membership of 900. Membership is comprised of professional personnel whose full-time employment is directed to the therapeutic application of recreation in the treatment of the ill and handicapped.

OBJECTIVES. Enhancement of the profession and encouragement of professional growth through education, research, and communication.

SERVICES. Encourages professional growth through workshops, seminars, institutes, clinical conferences, and staff study; encourages research and advocates undergraduate and graduate curriculums toward national professional registration.

PUBLICATIONS.

1. *Therapeutic Recreation Journal*
2. *Therapeutic Recreation Annual*

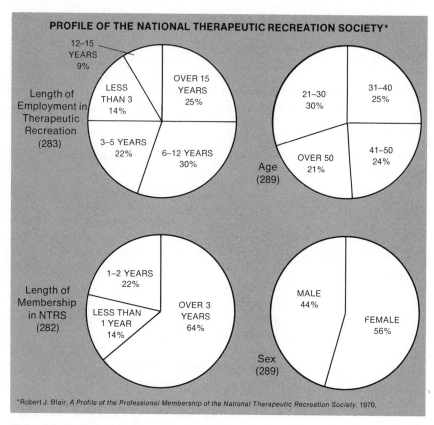

PROFILE OF THE NATIONAL THERAPEUTIC RECREATION SOCIETY*

*Robert J. Blair, *A Profile of the Professional Membership of the National Therapeutic Recreation Society.* 1970.

Parks and Recreation, August, 1971. Reprinted by permission of the National Recreation and Park Association.

Society of State Directors of Health, Physical Education, and Recreation (SSDHPER)
U.S. Office of Education, 400 Maryland Ave., S.W., Washington, D.C., 20202.

MEMBERSHIP. Present and past state directors of health, physical education, and recreation; 180 members.

OBJECTIVES. To promote sound programs in health, physical education, recreation, and athletics.

SERVICES RENDERED. Serves as a medium for exchanging information on results of studies on problems in these fields.

PUBLICATION. Newsletter

Other Organizations Concerned with Recreation

The following organizations are somewhat smaller and lesser known, but are still very active in the advancement of professionals in the area of recreation.

1. *American Association of Zoological Parks and Aquariums* (AAZPA). Oglebay Parks, Wheeling, W. Virginia, 26003. Zoological park and aquarium personnel interested in promoting zoos and aquariums for education, scientific research, interpretation of the natural sciences, and animal conservation.

2. *Bureau of Outdoor Recreation.* A division of the United States Department of Interior. Purpose is the development and coordination of effective programs of outdoor recreation. Activities are guided by the cabinet-level Federal Recreation Advisory Council.

3. *Cooperative Recreation Service.* Radnor Road, Delaware, Ohio, 43105. Collects and publishes folk songs, dances, and recreation materials from all countries.

4. *Federation of National Organizations for Recreation.* 1201 16th St., N.W., Washington, D.C., 20036. Federation of ten national organizations concerned with recreation, parks, camping, group work, physical education, and college unions.

5. *National Association for Physical Education of College Women* (NAPECW). Northeastern University, Boston, Mass., 02115. Professional society of women physical educators in colleges and universities.

6. *National College Physical Education Association for Men* (NCPEAM). University of Minnesota, 203 Cooke Hall, Minneapolis, Minn., 55145. Professional society of physical educators (men) employed in colleges and universities.

7. *Outdoor Recreation Institute* (ORI). 5003 Wapakoneta, Washington, D.C., 20016. To advance outdoor recreational interests at all levels — family, local, state, and national; to emphasize recreational objectives of natural resource conservation through technical research and educational activities.

QUESTIONS AND EXERCISES

1. What are the primary purposes of a professional organization? Do you think these are valid purposes? If not, explain your answer.

2. Give some of the history behind the formation of the NRPA. Briefly identify the organizations that merged to form the NRPA.

3. List some of the services to the public and private park and recreation agencies that are provided by the NRPA.

4. List some of the services that the NRPA provides to professional and nonprofessional persons interested in recreation.

5. Briefly discuss three major recreation organizations, including in the discussion their membership, objectives, and services.

6. List three of the lesser known organizations, including a brief discussion of their objectives.

7. Do you belong to any professional organization in any field at the present time? Discuss the organization, its objectives and services.

SELECTED REFERENCES

Carlson, Reynold, T. Deppe, and J. MacLean, *Recreation in American Life.* Belmont, Calif.: Wadsworth Publishing Co., 1972.

Gale Research Co., *Encyclopedia of Associations: National Organizations of the U.S.,* I (7th ed.) Detroit, Mich.: Book Tower, 1972.

Journal of Leisure Research. Washington, D.C.: National Recreation and Park Association.

Partners – Time for Reflection. Washington, D.C.: National Recreation and Park Association.

Shivers, Jay, *Leadership in Recreational Service.* New York: The Macmillan Company, 1963.

12

EMPLOYMENT OPPORTUNITIES

IN RECREATION

The job opportunities available to persons trained in recreation services are so numerous that any person seeking such a position will have a wide selection from which to choose. There are positions available on all government levels: federal, state, county, and local. In addition to these positions, there are industrial, school, hospital, nursing home, camp, agency, and armed forces positions available. The recreation worker must first decide the type of service he thinks he would be best at and the general age of people that he enjoys working with. His particular special interest may to some degree dictate his final choice. For example, a recreation leader with a profound interest in art would most likely lean toward a professional position which would capitalize on this interest.

Many positions in recreation have already been mentioned throughout this book and, of course, it would be an impossible task to list each and every possible recreation job opportunity in any text. This chapter will try to give the student an overview of some of the major areas of recreation employment, salary ranges, the role of civil service, and problems that may be encountered in seeking employment.

WHAT YOU SHOULD KNOW ABOUT RECREATION CAREERS

Recreation is a new, growing, and dynamic profession. It is, indeed, unfortunate that many young people graduating from high school have little or no conception of the career opportunities in this field. Many adults as well as young people think of recreation leaders as persons who enjoy playing games

223

and handling equipment. Their knowledge of the contemporary leader is practically nonexistent. In fact, if one were to ask graduating high school seniors about the possibility of majoring in recreation, they probably would not comprehend the question. Most persons have heard of physical education majors, but very few are aware that recreation and park programs do exist and people majoring in these programs are increasing in large numbers (as shown by the statistics given in Chapter 10, page 190).

How can more people be recruited by recreation programs? Recruitment is discussed here since, in many ways, it is a responsibility of persons in recreation leadership positions and is directly related to job opportunities. If people are aware that job opportunities exist in this field, they will be more interested in learning about the particulars involved. In a time when more and more young people are interested in people-oriented, ecological, and conservation concerns, recreation careers would certainly satisfy many of these needs. In addition, unemployment is always present in our society and though cutbacks have affected job opportunities in some areas, many areas, particularly those involved with therapeutic services, are in need of qualified recreation personnel.

The demand for qualified recreators has been estimated at about 3,000 new people per year. A 1971 estimate suggests that in 1980, 220,000 recreation specialists in the area of recreation and parks will be needed. This number must be compared with the present figure of approximately 169,000 full- and part-time workers currently employed.[1]

Many national, state, and local recreation agencies are conducting campaigns to stimulate recruitment. Some of the methods presently employed and suggested are:

1. Providing guidance counselors with information concerning recreation job opportunities, college and university program offerings, and literature and films that educate the public about the field of recreation.
2. Inviting representatives from the field to speak at career day programs, and having local and private agencies sponsor their own career-oriented talks, which aid discussions.
3. Introducing accredited high school courses in leadership training.
4. Making jobs in the field available to young people so that they may experience leadership in action.
5. Making more funds available for scholarships for students entering the field.
6. Making the public aware of the importance of having qualified, adequately paid recreation employees.
7. Inviting students to recreation board meetings and state recreation conferences. This first-hand experience allows the student to see how the profession operates and to have many of his questions answered.

[1] "Local Parks and Recreation," *Parks and Recreation,* August, 1971, p. 23.

An interesting approach to career recruitment in recreation is conducted by the Evanston, Illinois, Recreation Department as part of their "Careers in Recreation" training program. Its major purpose is to educate high-school-age youth about opportunities in recreation so that they can intelligently consider the field for advanced study and eventually a professional career.

The initial group of fifteen students was selected for an in-service training program for high school students. It was conducted by the supervisor of community centers and summer playgrounds. From the initial group, nine subsequently passed a written examination, served a practical five-week apprenticeship, and then accepted regular employment in the summer recreation program of the department. Six of the original nine returned for two more summers of recreational service. The positions held were salaried, and students received a certificate for completing the course. These students, and subsequent ones who qualified, received preferential consideration for part-time work during the school year. The program also introduced a scholarship competition for students wishing to major in recreation. The first scholarship winner was a four-year veteran of the program and had been on the recreation staff throughout his high school career.

The Evanston Department of Recreation did not limit its program to high school students but also endeavored to attract college students to the field of recreation. The department has cooperated with surrounding universities by offering an internship program for undergraduate credit.

Programs such as the ones offered by the Evanston department are essential in filling the gap of career education for those interested in recreation. Results, as in Evanston, are extremely gratifying, and program support is strengthened year after year.

How are recreation workers selected for employment? Generally speaking, recreation workers, like professionals in other fields, should be hired on the basis of merit. Most recreation departments and agencies identify positions by a classification plan, which "is a system of identifying and describing the different kinds of work in an organization and then grouping similar positions together under common titles..."[2] Job descriptions are given that indicate responsibilities, qualifications, and any specialized requirements. This system is a sound basis for recreation authorities to recruit new people, set salary scales and raises, indicate promotions, and evaluate job performance.

A person seeking employment should fit the job description given for the particular position available. Of course, one must be realistic and understand there may be some variance from the exact description as it has been prepared. Qualifying for the position, however, is only one step in the selection process.

The responsibility for selection of recreation personnel is usually authorized by state or local legislation and varies from area to area. Most frequently, the

[2]K. Byers, M. Montilla, and E. Williams, *Elements of Position Classification in Local Government* (Chicago: Civil Service Assembly, 1955).

responsibility is assigned to the managing authority itself, a personnel agency, a civil service commission, the city manager, or mayor. If a recreation department has a board, this board generally appoints employees upon the recommendation of the recreation executive. If there is no board, the executive is authorized to hire and fire recreation personnel.

In cases in which there is a civil service commission or personnel agency, it is their function to establish and administer a classification plan, which includes interviewing and testing of applicants. When such authorities exist, it is essential that they work in close cooperation with the recreation department.

If a person qualifies for a position according to the job description being used, he must frequently pass tests, go through interviews with key people, and finally be evaluated for the job. The position and level involved will frequently indicate the length and involvement of the hiring policy.

What about civil service positions? In order to insure the highest standards of hiring and promotion of recreation supervisors and administrators, certain screening policies have been established. Certification, discussed in Chapter 10 (page 205), is one of the methods utilized. Another method is through the federal state and county civil service commissions.

Civil service, once referred to as the "merit system," began in the United States as early as the 1870s. Congress enacted civil service legislature in the 1880s in order to alleviate the "spoils system," which involved favoritism, graft, and victimization of the taxpayer by government employees and people of their acquaintance.

Civil service positions at all levels of the government provide a job structure that states qualifications, experience, and examinations, if any, that are to be taken to qualify for a particular position. In many states, any college graduate who can do well on a civil service examination can be appointed to a recreation leadership position. Other qualifications may be substituted, and experience may not be thoroughly defined. Much too much weight is frequently given to the competitive examination; persons may be placed in highly responsible leadership positions and have neither the education nor management ability to handle these jobs successfully.

In general, civil service authorities prepare lists of qualified persons who have passed their civil service examination in the recreation and parks area. Appointments are made from these lists according to scores received on the test. However, there is usually a six-month probationary period when supervisors can observe the worker's attitudes, quality of work, and general accomplishment in the position. Some recreation supervisors would like to see this period increased from six months to two years to allow for thorough observation. During the probationary period, the supervisor should file reports at intervals to the civil service commission involved. At the end of the period, recommendations are made, either in support of or against the individual's employment.

When looking into employment opportunities in recreation, it is helpful to write to the federal government to find out about positions open in your field. In addition, one should also seek information from the county and state civil service commissions regarding possible employment. Much of this information is available at your public library.

What salary range can be expected? Salary standards are important in attracting and keeping good employees. There are variations in local salary rates, as living costs, working conditions, responsibility of position, and size of the municipality must be taken into consideration. Usually, the larger cities are able to offer larger salaries, particularly to their executives and supervisors.

Salaries recommended for recreation leaders, for example, were starting at about $4,000 in 1956-57. These salaries have, of course, risen, as recreation workers in the past did not receive adequate compensation for their work. Furthermore in many cases, persons in recreation leadership positions did not hold degrees, and advanced degrees were also uncommon.

Today's young person with a degree from an accredited university can expect to receive a starting salary in the area of about $8,000. This will vary, again, depending on the size of the community or agency involved. Supervisory salaries are in the area of $7,000 to $10,000, while higher administrative positions are often paid between $10,000 and $20,000. Many top executives make upwards of $25,000.

According to a 1970 *Classification and Compensation Schedule* for the City of New York, the following positions relating to recreation and their salaries were listed as follows:

Recreation Director:	$7,800-$11,000
Assistant Supervisor of Recreation:	$8,100-$12,700
Supervisor of Recreation:	$10,000-$15,100
Commissioner of Recreation:	$25,000
Recreation Director, Dept. of Social Services:	$4.10 per hour

This gives one some idea of how a large city pays some of its recreation personnel. The salaries are presently competitive and higher than some starting positions for new college graduates in other fields. This is definitely for the overall betterment of the profession, as more qualified people will be attracted to recreation employment.

Are there any fringe benefits attached to recreation positions? Many recreation positions include such benefits as sick days, vacation time, time off for professional study, conference expenses, overtime pay, medical and health services, retirement plans, and sometimes food and lodging. Different jobs will offer these benefits in varying degrees. They are certainly to be considered when applying for a job, for these benefits frequently compensate for a slightly higher salary offered in another position. Some workers in executive and supervisory positions are given the use of an automobile or are compensated for using their own car on the job. Full-time recreation workers are also usually entitled to social security provisions, workmen's compensation, and unemployment payments.

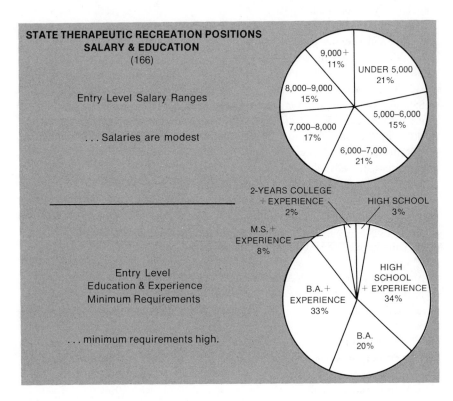

STATE THERAPEUTIC RECREATION POSITIONS SALARY & EDUCATION
(166)

Entry Level Salary Ranges

... Salaries are modest

9,000+ 11%
UNDER 5,000 21%
8,000–9,000 15%
5,000–6,000 15%
7,000–8,000 17%
6,000–7,000 21%

Entry Level
Education & Experience
Minimum Requirements

... minimum requirements high.

2-YEARS COLLEGE + EXPERIENCE 2%
HIGH SCHOOL 3%
M.S.+ EXPERIENCE 8%
HIGH SCHOOL + EXPERIENCE 34%
B.A.+ EXPERIENCE 33%
B.A. 20%

Parks and Recreation, August, 1971. Reprinted by permission of the National Recreation and Park Association.

Can one expect job advancement? In most cases job advancement or promotions are from within the department. This is a desirable policy as it is self-motivating, helps to attract quality applicants, and is a great morale booster. However, promotions should not be made only on the basis of length of service in the department. Merit must always be a major consideration. Sometimes this is difficult to accomplish in a very structured job classification or in a civil service position. Promotions in these cases are frequently through length of service, qualifications, and recommendations by persons in positions of higher authority. The morale of the department will be improved when the workers are awarded promotion and salary increases, based on their qualifications, further education, quality of performance, and examination scores.

CAREER OPPORTUNITIES AVAILABLE
FOR RECREATION GRADUATES

Even at a time when unemployment exists, career opportunities for recreation majors are greater than ever before. More positions are open than are able to be filled by qualified people in the field. Positions are available in many interest areas and leadership capacities. Persons desiring greater administrative duties can usually find supervisory or other direct leadership positions. Those persons desiring more direct, one-to-one contact can find jobs that meet this need. There are numerous jobs available working with different age groups, so one may be able to apply for a position with preschool, school-age, or teen-age groups. For those whose major interest is in adults or the aged, group work is available with these people. Special groups such as the retarded, emotionally disturbed, or handicapped offer very satisfying positions. Some of the generally available categories of recreation positions are given here for your consideration.

1. *Public recreation and parks.* Superintendent of recreation and parks; recreation supervisors (activity specialist and general area specialist); center director; special services, and numerous other job titles that vary from city to city. In general, people in this category provide leadership, supervision, and administration of programs conducted by city, county, or state departments, and school districts.
2. *Outdoor recreation.* The outdoor recreation specialist emphasizes management, conservation, interpretation, and utilization of forests, wilderness areas, waterways, and fish and wildlife preserves. Ecology and pollution are vital areas to the outdoor recreationist. Job opportunities are in both public and private sectors.
3. *Industrial recreation.* Positions in this field include program directors, program specialists, and directors of recreation for labor groups. Recreation leaders are expected to provide adequate recreation programs for industrial workers and their families. Recreation personnel are usually hired to supervise athletic programs, swimming pools, golf courses, and other facilities.
4. *Voluntary service agencies.* These agencies include Y's, Boys and Girls Clubs, Scouts, and other agencies receiving public support. Positions may include administrator, program director, program leader, field representative, and camp director.
5. *Park design and resource planning.* Positions are available in the identification and recommendation of park sites, preparation of master plans and site analyses, facility design, and project promotion for public support.
6. *Armed forces.* Many positions are available both in the United States and abroad. Some positions include service club directors, program directors, program specialists, Red Cross area directors, and youth activity leaders.
7. *Colleges and universities.* Faculty positions (usually requiring a postgraduate degree), recreation specialists, and program directors in charge

of student union activities. Supervisory, administrative, research, and field-work positions are also available.

8. *Institutional positions.* Opportunities for employment in recreation are numerous for those interested in working in hospitals, prisons, schools for the mentally and physically handicapped, homes for the aged, nursing homes, and specialized camping situations.

9. *State and federal recreation positions.* Such positions as naturalists, conservationists, program managers, recreation planners, park directors, and researchers are available.

10. *Camping positions.* These positions are found in both semipublic and private camp sites. Job opportunities include school and community camp directors, agency camp directors, private camp directors, program supervisors, and activity specialists.

11. *Rural recreation.* Rural, sparsely populated areas may have small or shared recreation departments. Job opportunities may include rural recreation specialists, district program supervisors, and 4-H Club directors.

12. *Church recreation.* Some churches may employ education and recreation specialists. If the church sponsors a community center, then center directors, program leaders, and activity specialists are also employed.

13. *Commercial recreation.* Recreation personnel are needed in managerial capacities for such facilities as golf courses, swimming pools, tennis courts, bowling alleys, and other resort activities. Private clubs, country clubs, and other private recreation establishments also hire recreation leaders in varying capacities.

Park and Recreation Occupations and Their Projections

The 1970 Local Agency Survey mentioned in Chapter 9, page 165, charted a number of major park and recreation occupations from over 1,000 reporting agencies; their present number of employees (1970) and 1973 employment projections were ascertained. The positions are listed below, with the first number indicating persons employed in the field in 1970, followed by the second number indicating 1973 employment projections. These figures give one a good concept of actual jobs and numbers of people in these positions.

Executive	900	700
Assistant Director	300	375
Division Head	650	625
Superintendent of Parks	375	385
Superintendent of Recreation	300	325
Administrative Support	1100	810
Clerical Worker	3375	3300
Related Park Professional	1100	1000
District Supervisor of Parks	420	440
Park Manager	980	990

Park Ranger and Police	1700	2250
Fireman	2830	2580
Skilled Park Personnel	90	82
Semi- and Non-skilled Personnel	235	215
District Supervisor of Recreation	390	430
Recreation Supervisor	1800	2050
Recreation Center Director	1900	2250
Recreation Facility Manager	1150	1420
Activity Specialist	3600	2900
Recreation Program Leader	70	78
Attendant and Aid	82	70

These figures are interesting, as in several cases the numbers projected for 1973 are down from the 1970 numbers. This is particularly apparent in the case of activity specialists. Projections show an approximate 700-person decrease in that three-year period. Possible causes for such decreases might be general cutbacks by federal and state governments, resulting in financial problems on the local levels. In addition, this was a period of high inflation, unemployment, and major cutbacks in all "special" programs, with the goal of trimming the federal budget.

However, these figures also present some healthy increases in job opportunities, as indicated by the small rises in many of the positions and the rather large increases in such jobs as recreation supervisors and recreation center directors. This may be accounted for by increases in recreational activities on the local level. Centers are often completely subsidized by local taxes and contributions, so federal cutbacks would not necessarily affect their programs.

A listing of this type is significant in that it gives job titles of existing positions in the field and also gives one some idea of the numbers of people presently employed and what to expect in the near future. Those jobs showing the greatest increase in numbers should be explored in depth for how they fit one's own career goals.

Position to Be Expected with an Associate Degree in Recreation

As mentioned in Chapter 10, associate degrees in recreation from two-year colleges are quite common now and definitely are increasing. The associate professional can help to meet the widening gap of trained recreation leaders needed to fill certain positions. This person can initially be expected to fill a role that requires minimal administrative and supervisory responsibilities and is more involved in planning, organizing, and conducting various recreation activities in different program areas.

There has been a five-fold increase in the number of junior colleges offering a recreation curriculum since 1960, and this number increases each year. In order

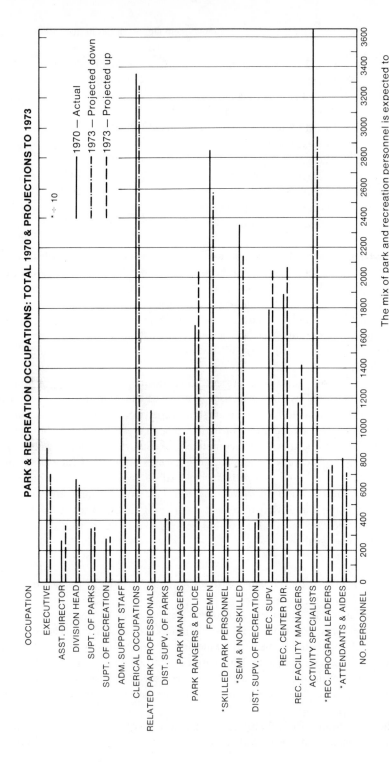

PARK & RECREATION OCCUPATIONS: TOTAL 1970 & PROJECTIONS TO 1973

* ÷ 10

——— 1970 — Actual

—·—·— 1973 — Projected down

— — — 1973 — Projected up

OCCUPATION	
EXECUTIVE	
ASST. DIRECTOR	
DIVISION HEAD	
SUPT. OF PARKS	
SUPT. OF RECREATION	
ADM. SUPPORT STAFF	
CLERICAL OCCUPATIONS	
RELATED PARK PROFESSIONALS	
DIST. SUPV. OF PARKS	
PARK MANAGERS	
PARK RANGERS & POLICE	
FOREMEN	
*SKILLED PARK PERSONNEL	
*SEMI & NON-SKILLED	
DIST. SUPV. OF RECREATION	
REC. SUPV.	
REC. CENTER DIR.	
REC. FACILITY MANAGERS	
ACTIVITY SPECIALISTS	
*REC. PROGRAM LEADERS	
*ATTENDANTS & AIDES	

NO. PERSONNEL 0   200   400   600   800   1000   1200   1400   1600   1800   2000   2200   2400   2600   2800   3000   3200   3400   3600

The mix of park and recreation personnel is expected to change in a number of significant areas by 1973.

Parks and Recreation, August, 1971. Reprinted by permission of the National Recreation and Park Association.

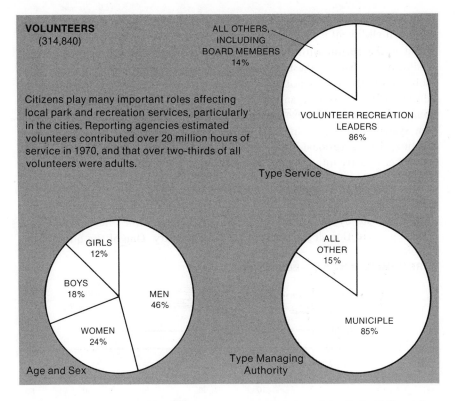

VOLUNTEERS
(314,840)

Citizens play many important roles affecting local park and recreation services, particularly in the cities. Reporting agencies estimated volunteers contributed over 20 million hours of service in 1970, and that over two-thirds of all volunteers were adults.

Parks and Recreation, August, 1971. Reprinted by permission of the National Recreation and Park Association.

to insure the best possible curriculum at these institutions, the National Recreation and Park Association, under the auspices of the U. S. Office of Education's Division of Manpower Development and Training,[3] completed a junior college curriculum study, which has been published. This study was developed for the purpose of providing minimal guidelines for two-year recreation programs.

Job opportunities for the two-year associate in recreation might involve one-to-one leadership of program participants. They could work in all settings, including hospitals, military bases, industry, and local agencies. Many of these jobs are currently being filled by recreational professionals who could then devote more of their time to administrative and organization tasks.

Promotions for persons holding associate degrees do involve merit, but, generally, higher education is the key to advancement. Once in a position, the student who wishes to reach higher levels could enter a part-time or full-time pro-

[3]*Recreation Program Leadership: A Suggested Two-year Post High-school Curriculum* (Washington, D.C.: U.S. Government Printing Office).

gram to achieve his four-year degree in recreation. That degree and proven on-the-job accomplishment is the surest way to promotion. We live in an age of specialists, and it is the person with demonstrated ability and accompanying educational qualifications that has the best chance of success in today's society. Of course, mobility on the job is not prevented if a person decides to discontinue his education. Responsibility and salary increases will, in most cases, be given to competent workers. However, if the organization has a structured job classification system, then it is difficult, sometimes impossible, to move up without meeting the educational qualifications. These are important factors for the job-seeker to delve into prior to accepting a position.

Survey of Employment Opportunities

A recent survey conducted by the authors elicited some interesting information from recreation departments around the country. One of the questions on

NTRS MEMBER PROFILE — EDUCATION

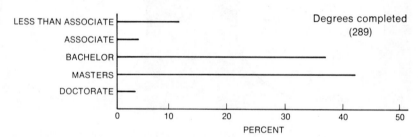

Nearly half of the professional members of NTRS have completed post graduate degrees, and . . .

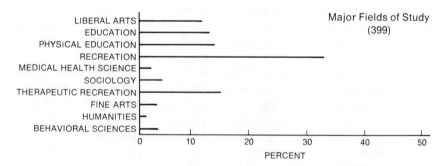

Nearly half of the members have received formal academic training in either recreation or therapeutic recreation.

Parks and Recreation, August, 1971. Reprinted by permission of the National Recreation and Park Association.

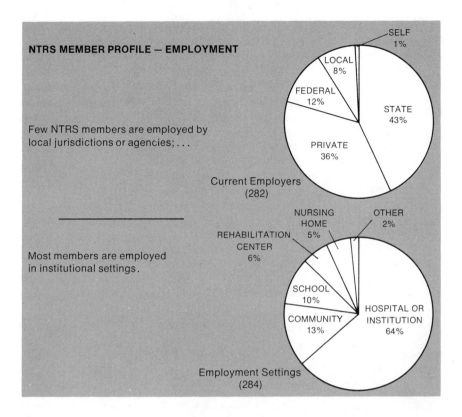

NTRS MEMBER PROFILE — EMPLOYMENT

Few NTRS members are employed by
local jurisdictions or agencies; . . .

Current Employers
(282)

SELF
1%

LOCAL
8%

FEDERAL
12%

STATE
43%

PRIVATE
36%

Most members are employed
in institutional settings.

NURSING
HOME
5%

OTHER
2%

REHABILITATION
CENTER
6%

SCHOOL
10%

COMMUNITY
13%

HOSPITAL OR
INSTITUTION
64%

Employment Settings
(284)

Parks and Recreation, August, 1971. Reprinted by permission of the National Recreation
and Park Association.

the survey was: Where do you feel the best employment opportunities are today
for a college graduate going into recreation? Some of the replies are given here
for your consideration:

1. handicapped, armed forces, government, and college departments
2. specialization in crafts, drama, sports, and administration
3. recreation planner, engineer, and landscape architect
4. governmental agencies (county, state, national)
5. therapeutic recreation, city, county, and federal agencies, outdoor
   recreation facilities
6. recreation supervision on the professional level including activity
   directors, center directors, program coordinators, and area supervisors
7. park planning, facility design, directors of recreation, and program
   specialists
8. private resort and industrial recreation management

In addition to the previous question, the survey also asked: What advice would you give the recent college graduate with regard to employment? Some of the answers to this question are given below.

1. Secure as much education as possible before entering the field. Graduate and postgraduate degrees are necessary in some administrative positions.
2. Understand the philosophy and policies of the agency you wish to work for.
3. Seek part-time or temporary (summer) employment in the field prior to committing yourself to the recreation field.
4. Develop a well-rounded philosophy and knowledge in all areas connected with people.
5. Look for employment early and thoroughly investigate job possibilities.
6. Establish short- and long-term career objectives, which should include remaining in an assignment for a long enough period of time to gain sound experience.
7. Do not be afraid of moving to any part of the country where a good position is available. Be flexible about your first job.
8. Expect to work odd hours, weekends, and evenings.

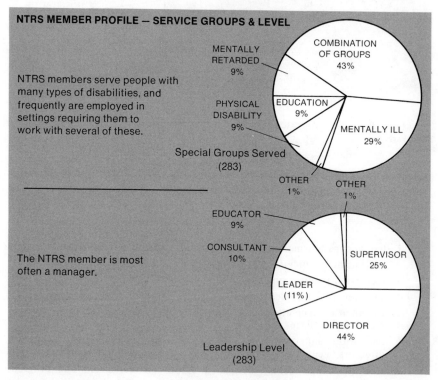

Parks and Recreation, August, 1971. Reprinted by permission of the National Recreation and Park Association.

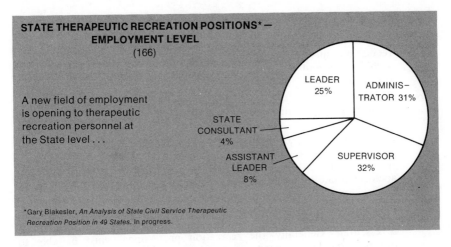

STATE THERAPEUTIC RECREATION POSITIONS*—
EMPLOYMENT LEVEL
(166)

A new field of employment
is opening to therapeutic
recreation personnel at
the State level . . .

LEADER
25%

ADMINIS-
TRATOR 31%

STATE
CONSULTANT
4%

ASSISTANT
LEADER
8%

SUPERVISOR
32%

*Gary Blakesler, *An Analysis of State Civil Service Therapeutic
Recreation Position in 49 States.* In progress.

Parks and Recreation, August, 1971. Reprinted by permission of the National Recreation
and Park Association.

The answers to both of these questions may be somewhat general in nature
but are valuable to consider when evaluating what you expect from a career in
recreation. All of the answers cited were given by currently employed
professionals in the field of recreation.

A Study of Existing Job Opportunities
in Industry

Much of the previous material in this chapter has been very general in nature.
It might be beneficial to conclude this chapter with a discussion of specific
recreation positions at a large American corporation, the Xerox Corporation. An
article published in *Recreation Management* outlines the recreation needs
of the Xerox Corporation in terms of available recreation postions, skills desired
for these jobs, necessary experience, and educational requirements.[4]

The Xerox Recreation Association recognizes a commitment to provide a
comprehensive recreation program for its employees and their families. The
requirements adopted by the Association reflect important qualifications for
persons applying for recreation staff positions. The basic requirements are given
here:

1. *Education.* A bachelor's degree in recreation from an accredited
   institution is a basic requirement. The practical application of principles
   and philosophy of recreation management should comprise much of the
   course work. In addition, courses in psychology, sociology, and the

[4]Frank W. Barnes, "Industrial Recreation, Professional Staff Standards," *Recreation
Management,* 1969, p. 12.

sciences are required. Staff members should also have a knowledge of cardiovascular fitness. Their additional course work should consist of current trends and practices in recreation, sports management, social recreation, sports management, social recreation techniques, landscape architecture, and maintenance of indoor and outdoor recreation facilities.

A master's degree in recreation or a closely related field (preference — business management) is required of all staff members above the rating of specialist.[5]

2. *Skills and abilities.* Xerox values the ability of person-to-person communication as a foremost requirement. A recreation staff member has to be able to effectively deal with people of all ages, interests, and socioeconomic levels. In addition, he must be able to get along with his co-workers, superiors, and subordinates. The ability of encouraging persons to actively participate in programs is another valued skill. The ability to grow with the job and be flexible in adapting to new situations is essential. Generally the recreation professional must be able to interpret the leisure needs of people into wholesome and interesting activities. His philosophy of recreation should be consistent with current trends and practices in municipal and industrial recreation.

3. *Experience.* Potential staff members should have considerable experience in working with people in recreation settings. The amount of experience is directly related to the job being applied for.

The Association gives as major factors in consideration of staff members the following: (a) people-oriented in career goals; (b) background indicates a desire to work with and for people; and (c) they should possess basic knowledge and skills for the competent performance of their job. Membership in the National Industrial Recreation Association shows a genuine interest in their chosen career area.

The levels of responsibility for a recreation position at Xerox are given in the following chart of minimum requirements.[6]

  I. Recreation Specialist
     A. Bachelor's degree in recreation
     B. Minimum of one year experience
 II. Senior Recreation Specialist
     A. Bachelor's degree in recreation
     B. Master's degree in recreation
     C. Minimum of two years experience in area of specialization.
III. Recreation Supervisor
     A. Bachelor's degree in recreation
     B. Master's degree in recreation or related field
     C. Two years experience in an industrial or municipal recreation operation, one year of which must be in a supervisory capacity

---

[5] *Rating* is explained under *levels of responsibility* given later in this discussion.

[6] Frank W. Barnes, "Industrial Recreation Professional Staff Standards," *Recreation Management,* 1969, p. 12.

IV. Manager of Recreation Program
   A. Bachelor's degree in recreation
   B. Master's degree in recreation or related field
   C. Five years experience in an industrial or municipal operation, two years of which must be in a managerial capacity
V. Manager of Corporate Recreation Services
   A. Bachelor's degree in recreation
   B. Master's degree in recreation or related field
   C. Eight years experience, five in a supervisory position, two of which must be in a managerial capacity in industry

QUESTIONS AND EXERCISES

1. In your high school, was recreation ever mentioned as a career possibility? If not, how did you become interested in this area of specialization?
2. List some ways that would be helpful in recruiting people into the field of parks and recreation.
3. How did the recreation department of Evanston, Illinois, go about recruiting young people into their recreation programs? Would you have any suggestions for improving their methods?
4. Give some of the ways in which recreation workers are selected for jobs.
5. Explain how the civil service works and how persons are selected for civil service positions.
6. Explain the general salary schedules for recreation workers. What fringe benefits frequently accompany postions in this field?
7. List the major career opportunities open to recreation graduates. Which area do you think you show a preference for at this time? Explain.
8. What are some of the reasons for downward employment projections in some types of recreation positions?
9. In what areas of recreation can a person holding an associate degree in the field expect to find placement? Is further education advised in terms of promotion and job security?
10. Briefly explain the basic requirements desired in order to apply for an industrial recreation position at Xerox Corporation.

SELECTED REFERENCES

Barnes, Frank W., "Industrial Recreation Professional Staff Standards," *Recreation Management*, 1969, page 12.

Bartholomew, Warren J., "Recreation Education in Selected Junior or Community Colleges," *Parks and Recreation,* Vol. II (January, 1967).

Careers in Recreation and Parks, Michigan Recreation and Park Association, Box 896, Lansing, Michigan, 48904.

Classification and Compensation Schedules. Department of Personnel, The City of New York, Municipal Building (December, 1970).

Cosgrove, Francis E., and Richard Kraus, "The Role of Civil Service," *Parks and Recreation,* Vol. VI (June, 1971).

Hawkins, Donald, and B. Tindall, *Recreation and Park Yearbook,* National Recreation and Park Association, 1966.

Leavitt, H. Douglas, "Certification," *Parks and Recreation,* Vol. VI (January, 1971).

"Leisure – A New Dawn in America," *Parks and Recreation,* Vol. VI [special issue] (August, 1971).

"Recreation Program Leadership – A Suggested Two-Year Post High-School Curriculum," Department of Health, Education, and Welfare, Office of Education.

Recreation As Your Career, American Association for Health, Physical Education, and Recreation, 1201 16th Street N.W., Washington, D.C., 20036.

"Research Briefs," National Parks and Recreation Association, Vol. VI (September, 1971).

Sarkisian, Sevan, "Career in Recreation," *Parks and Recreation,* Vol. VI (February, 1971).

Shivers, Jay, *Leadership in Recreational Service.* New York: The Macmillan Company, 1963.

Verhoven, Peter J., "Associate Professional Recreation Programs," *Parks and Recreation,* Vol. IV (April, 1969).

13

TRENDS AND CHALLENGES

IN RECREATION

Recreation and leisure time have become so much a part of our daily life that the media constantly exposes us to trends in these areas. Many magazines have weekly sections devoted to leisure, newspapers have daily leisure reports, and television and radio devote much of their air time to leisure-related activities. In fact, many people complain that too much television time is given over to sporting events, exercise programs, and programs with a leisure orientation.

There are many trends in the recreation profession that are both improving the preparation of persons entering the field and adding interest and diversity to recreation programming. In addition, there are social trends that bear a direct relationship to recreation. Some of these trends will be discussed in this chapter.

Recreation faces many challenges today and in the future. These challenges must be met by professional recreators so that more people can enjoy and be involved in a constructive use of their leisure time. There are also challenges to the recreation profession in the form of solving problems concerned with funding cutbacks, employment, certification requirements, and curriculum planning. Positive steps must be made to meet these challenges in order to strengthen the profession.

Many recreation trends have already been discussed in the chapters of this text where they were appropriate. No one text could hope to discuss every new trend; the ones reported here are important to the growth of the profession and the quality of our recreation programs.

PROFESSIONAL PREPARATION OF RECREATORS

Persons choosing a career in some area of recreation will find that a sound education is a major qualification for a leadership position. In past years, few recreation leaders had college degrees. If one did have a degree, it was frequently in the area of physical education. However, today more and more universities and colleges are adding curriculums in recreation that offer a student many interesting subject areas that one can major in and a greater selection of courses in areas relevant to a recreation major.

Trends in Curriculum

An interesting trend in recreation education is the type of courses being offered to majors. Such courses as sociology, psychology, group dynamics, and others related to the recreation leader as a person involved with people are essential to producing a well-rounded leader who understands human beings and their problems.

Along with a broadening of course content are active internship programs in which students are given the opportunity to work with agencies providing recreation services. This allows the student to put his education to actual use in working with the people. Internships in urban areas expose the students to the problems of the inner-city environment and how programs must be adapted to meet the special needs of these people.

Another curriculum trend is that of recreation breaking into many sub-disciplines, such as therapeutic recreation, industrial recreation, outdoor recreation, and park design. There are many varied employment opportunities now open to the person majoring in recreation. Recreation is an unlimited field in which recreation leaders can find satisfaction in working in an area that meets their special interests and goals.

Recent curriculum trends indicate that more and more frequently two-year colleges are offering recreation programs. Many communities now have two-year or junior colleges, and a major in the area of recreation will certainly aid in getting more persons into the field. Some students who graduate from a two-year school will continue on either a full- or part-time basis in a university that also offers a recreation major.

In addition to the trend toward two-year curriculums, there is the increasing trend toward graduate degrees in recreation. In an era when everything is becoming more specialized, many persons go on to receive master's degrees or doctorates in areas of recreation. More graduate programs are being added annually as the need for greater specialization increases.

CHANGING PROGRAMS IN RECREATION

Recreation programming has been gradually changing in recent years until today it has become well-diversified, dynamic, and thoroughly involved in

Erie Community College of Buffalo, New York, has a very active two-year program in recreation supervision. Photos showing arts and crafts and music are by courtesy of the Erie Community College Department of Recreation Supervision.

243

activities that meet the needs of people of all ages and interests. Activities are centered around physical and cultural interests. A well-rounded recreation program is as much oriented toward the arts as it is toward athletic pursuits. It is common to find community programs that sponsor art exhibits, concerts, dance programs, and dramatic and musical theater presentations.

In addition to the greater interest in cultural programs is the increased trend toward outdoor recreation activities. People are using the outdoor areas more and more for camping, swimming, boating, hiking, and recreation vehicles. Of course, this unprecedented use of outdoor recreation land and waterways has resulted in some very serious problems that serve as a real challenge to the recreation profession. This will be discussed later in this chapter in the section concerned with challenges to recreation.

Activity Trends

In recent years, there have been many new activities introduced to recreation programming, and many older activities have been given a new emphasis. In addition, there has been a trend toward more mobile recreation programs that bring recreation to the people, as in the case of mobile vans, and also programs that bring people to recreation through camping trips, biking and hiking club activities and other excursions.

Many activity trends seem to be significant in the recreation picture at this particular time. Some of the reasons for this may include:

1. increased media coverage
2. organized recreation program sponsorship
3. commercialization of the activity

Some of the activities that were very popular years ago and still have an active following today include baseball, bowling, and roller skating. However, in more recent years tennis, karate, chess, bicycling, and skiing have shown spiraling numbers of people engaged in these activities and seeking recreational outlets in the form of ski vacation properties, indoor and outdoor tennis clubs, and classes that teach the various arts of oriental defense. Some presently popular activity trends are discussed here.

1. *Tennis, the game of the 70s.* Tennis is not a new game, but it was always the sport of a select, relatively small number of players. Today, tennis is the fastest growing sport in the U.S. Today, approximately 13.5 million tennis enthusiasts are playing on more than 110,000 courts. The popularity of the game is evidenced by an abundance of tennis lessons, both public and private; indoor and outdoor tennis complexes; and the latest addition in the form of deluxe tennis camps or resorts.

   One of these resorts, Gardiner's Tennis Ranch in Scottsdale, Arizona, is an elegant ranch devoted entirely to teaching and improving one's tennis game. Instruction is aided by expert teachers, ball machines, and video-tape systems that record every move and then play them back. In case any reader may be interested, the average rate for a five-day week of extensive tennis is $350.

2. *The chess frenzy.* The summer of 1972 found everyone's minds and eyes focused on a championship chess game between Bobby Fischer of the U.S. and Boris Spassky of the Soviet Union. They were playing the World Chess Championship in Reykjavik, Iceland. Bobby Fischer won the championship and turned chess into a national trend with a great following. Once thought of as a game for the brilliant, elite, and powerful, now chess clubs are being formed across the country and fans are coming out by the thousands. Book stores have experienced a sudden run on chess books, and chess sets are reported to have risen in sales by 125 percent. Macy's reported that its sales, following the championship, quintupled. Plans are being made for televised United States chess games and organized chess teams.

3. *Bicycling – the activity for all ages.* Cycling has been building in popularity in recent years. The reasons are varied, including pollution control, health, exercise, the energy crisis, enjoyment, and the fact that it is an inexpensive mode of transportation. It is presently considered to be America's number one recreational pastime, and estimates reveal that a startling sixty-one million cyclists enjoy the activity. It has grown more than 105 percent since 1960. Bicyclists can be seen on country roads, on major highways, and amidst city traffic on their way to work. Many city office buildings provide bike racks, and some city streets and parks are closed on occasion for bike riding.

Communities have set aside bikeways for riders and introduced programs concerning bicycle accident prevention and how to care for and service one's bike. Organized bike races exist in many cities and smaller communities, and bike marathons are often held on holiday weekends. Marathon races can last a few days, in which riders stop for only short periods during the entire race.

Mobility of Recreation

Recreation activities have become increasingly mobile in recent years. The American population has also become very mobile, as indicated by frequent job changes, increased travel here and abroad, and greater use of all types of recreational vehicles, including campers, trailers, motorbikes, and snowmobiles.

The mobility of recreation activities is evident in the rapid growth of camping trips, trips to cultural events, touring programs, hosteling excursions, and such very new trends as mobile recreation vans and drive-in zoos. As examples of mobility, these last two trends are discussed here.

Mobile Recreation Van

A new and valuable asset to recreation departments around the country is the mobile recreation van. Recreation on wheels has already been mentioned in this text in reference to mobile movie vans and the New York City recreation vans that house swimming pools, gyms, trampolines, and other recreational equipment. This mobile approach to recreation is especially valuable in and around large cities that are unable to acquire additional land areas. One such district, the Niles Park District, located on the outskirts of Chicago, faced the land shortage problem by using mobile units wherever possible.

This is a new and revolutionary concept in reaching the people through recreational activities. Used in inner-city areas, mobile vans offer the equipment and leadership in recreation that is needed in these neglected areas of the city. Some youngsters, in certain cities, would not have any opportunities to swim or work with certain gym equipment without these vans. In addition, the vans are also valuable in communities with few financial resources. One swimming van can visit many park settings in just one day. Rural areas that do not have organized recreational activities can also benefit from a county- or state-sponsored mobile plan that would encourage all age groups to participate on a monthly, weekly, or biweekly program.

Drive-in Zoos

No, that is not a misprint. Zoos are now being introduced as drive-in facilities. People drive through the areas designated with windows up and doors locked, and the wild animals roam through the surrounding roads and woods. The first such endeavor, Lion Country Safari, opened in 1967, near West Palm Beach, Florida. Since then, more than a dozen such zoos have opened, and another dozen are on the drawing boards. The newest ones are Montreal's Park Safari African; Jungle Habitat in West Milford, N.J.; and Lion Country Safari in Atlanta, Georgia.

Most of these zoos are privately owned and very profitable. Admissions range from two to four dollars per person, and all are reporting good business. Some opponents of these commercial enterprises take a poor view of the conditions provided for the animals. Reports of overcrowding, unsanitary conditions, and contaminated water have been received by authorities. Some persons worry about what will happen to the animals once the current trend toward this type of establishment wanes. However, zoo spokesmen have repeatedly stated that the animals must always come first, and to further prove this point, the following sign exists at the Lion Country Park, near Dallas, Texas, "No trespassing! Violators will be eaten!"

A NEW LOOK IN SETTINGS AND FACILITIES

Recreation settings and facilities have taken on a new look in recent years. Park designs emphasize a total recreation concept that incorporates many facilities in one area. Some parks are designed for very small areas in large urban cities. Such parks are frequently called vest-pocket parks and tot-lots. The former may be a small green area in the midst of a busy city. The latter is a park designed for small children. Both of these innovations are very important to the community being served. Some of the new and interesting trends in settings and facilities will be discussed in the following sections.

Urban Redevelopment and Recreation Needs

A major trend in the redevelopment of urban areas through Model Cities' Programs and other reconstruction projects is the planning of recreation facilities for the inhabitants of these areas. As pointed out in Chapter 6, a lack of recreation facilities was listed as a major reason for riots and general unrest.

Recreation settings in these areas frequently include a community center with sufficient facilities for meeting rooms, indoor games, and a well-equipped gymnasium. In addition, space is allowed for park and playground areas. The community residents are often surveyed to find out their needs and interests in areas of recreation and activity programming.

Community participation is a very accepted phrase in today's society. Members of the community are a part of the decision-making process in operating a recreational facility. In addition, many programs have been established to train local people so that they can be employed in neighborhood recreational centers.

The Contemporary Playground

Have you ever seen a playground with a many-stepped pyramid, a minicastle, a treehouse, and fortress walls for children to play behind? All of these new concepts in playground design can be seen in an area of Central Park in New York City. This is just one park among many springing up around the country that emphasizes a child's sensory experiences and fantasy play. The traditional playground having swings, slides, and monkeybars allows little room for a child's imagination or need for choice of activities.

Traditional playgrounds become boring even to small children after a few visits. Some innovative ideas in new playground design include sculptured climbing and sliding forms, poles, ladders, bridges, rope and tire swings, and creative play areas with movable objects. These new playgrounds are also very flexible, designed with provisions in mind for community activities such as dances, art exhibits, concerts, and community fairs. Other desirable inclusions in playgrounds would be water areas for play activities, nature areas for plants and small animals, and even facilities for the children to prepare meals under proper supervision.

Trend Toward Housing and Recreation

Recent years have seen a definite trend toward the inclusion of recreational facilities in apartment houses, condominiums, and townhouse and single-dwelling residences. If you look in the real estate section of a newspaper, you are bound to find photographs of swimming pools, golf courses, and tennis courts. Sometimes it's difficult to believe that the advertisement is actually trying to sell homes instead of a membership in a local country club. Housing developers have come to realize that people want and need recreational facilities that they do not have to travel miles to reach. These facilities provide both a social and recreational outlet for residents.

In addition to permanent homes, many persons are also buying second homes or vacation homes primarily for the recreational advantages. Recent years have witnessed an explosion in vacation land sales of all types. Ski property, beach and lake property, and land developed primarily for recreation purposes have been selling at record rates. Land prices for such property have also been soaring. What sold for fifteen dollars an acre in the late 1950s is today going for over $1,000 an acre.

Some residents of these areas are complaining about the influx of people and poor planning and development of new recreation areas. One of the states whose residents are complaining most vehemently is Vermont. Vermonters are appalled by the increased numbers of vacation homes being built that are blotting out the landscape, adding to the air and water pollution, and commercializing areas with inexpensive housing and garish clubs and nightspots. Vermont has done something about the situation by instituting a tax that imposes a penalty on quick land turnovers with large profits. Some local communities have also changed zoning laws to limit lot sizes and slow down the building rate.

Retirement villages are also a trend of the middle-late sixties and continuing into the seventies. These retirement villages offer homes, condominiums, and apartments in a separate setting, usually near an urban area. The villages are completely independent of the areas around them, and they provide all types of services, recreational facilities, and organized entertainment programs. There are two readily apparent problems with this type of living: (1) they are only for the mid-upper-income people, and (2) it is not necessarily healthy for older persons to be completely segregated from the younger generations.

INCREASED MOBILITY OF AMERICANS

In past times, one often died in the same city that he grew up in. This is no longer true. Americans are moving constantly; their schooling and jobs take them to all parts of the country. They no longer stay with a job for the rest of their lives or even for a good number of years. Persons change jobs frequently and may own many homes before they retire.

They also travel to more places, more often than ever before. Vacations are frequently spent away from home, either visiting relatives and friends in different sections of the country, traveling abroad, or driving around the country. Camping has become a popular recreational activity, to the point where once-desolate camping sites are now overcrowded.

The contributions to water, air, and environmental pollution in general are enormous. In many cases, camping areas have had to put strict limitations into effect for purposes of environmental protection.

The mobile American family coming into a new city often feels displaced and very much alone. The recreation department of a community can be a great aid to this family by involving its members in activities in which they can relax and meet community members.

The Environment

Greater use of all facets of the environment by persons seeking recreation activities has produced a great burden of pollution and destruction. Pollution has already been discussed in Chapter 5, and let it suffice to say here that it is one of the greatest and most immediate problems that faces the United States and the world. Recreators and persons enjoying the environment for recreation purposes should always consider the land and water they are using, follow protective laws that have been established, and take an active role in groups devoted to environmental protection.

A recent example of how persons may abuse the environment can be seen in the desert areas of California, near Los Angeles, and in other areas of that state. Deserts have become the new recreation areas of this part of the country, and environmentalists are duly concerned about the increase in the number of persons visiting desert areas. The number of visitors to the desert areas of California rose from five million in 1968 to more than nine million in 1972. At stake are the more than 700 species of plants, some of which are found nowhere else in the world. The desert is also home to numerous species of endangered wildlife and the home of more than 1,000 archeological sites. To help in this area, the Sierra Club, an active environmental group, proposes that the desert be closed completely to off-the-road vehicles until further investigation can be made to determine which areas can sustain the increasing burden of people and vehicles.

The Energy Crisis

The energy crisis is a term that is very much in the thoughts of most people these days. Human beings feel the impact of such a crisis when gasoline is limited, brown-outs and black-outs are commonplace, heating oil is in short supply, thermostats are lowered, and the government finds it necessary to establish controls over energy supplies.

Recreation is affected by the energy crisis. One of the greatest impacts being felt by this field of endeavor is the limitation on fuels for recreational vehicles. This dilemma affects vacationers, motor-bike riders, boating enthusiasts, and other persons who use gasoline and oil in their activities.

It appears that the energy crisis will be with us for several years. During this period it will be necessary for recreation to take a hard look at how it can meet such a challenge. Among other things, it will mean less stress on recreational activities involving fuel-powered vehicles and a greater emphasis upon individual self-propulsion, whether it be by walking, bicycling, swimming, or some other way. Therefore, recreation programs will need to adapt their activities accordingly.

The energy crisis should result in many advantages for community recreation programs. Since people will not have the fuel to travel extensively it will mean that many persons will look to their own community for ways in which they can utilize their leisure hours. Community recreation programs, if they provide activities that meet the needs and interests of their residents, will be very popular and receive more support than has been the case in the past. In this way the energy crisis will act as a catalyst that will cause an explosive expansion in recreation programs throughout the country which will render a service to the nation and at the same time help this field of endeavor to achieve its destiny.

SURVEYING CURRENT TRENDS IN RECREATION

In Chapter 12, a survey that the authors originated was cited. This survey asked the following question of professional recreators throughout the country: What do you feel are some of the most important trends in recreation today? Some of the answers to this question are given here.

1. Recreation programming on a much broader scope trying to meet the needs of more people instead of the needs of a select few
2. The movement toward outdoor recreation with the introduction of area and regional parks rather than the traditional playgrounds in schools and neighborhoods
3. The community-school concept providing well-planned programs for all age groups
4. Natural recreation areas and a resurgence in activities such as hiking, bicycling, and walking that utilize such areas.
5. The year-round or forty-five to fifteen (forty-five days on, fifteen off) school year
6. The coordination of community recreation facilities and programs
7. The movement toward two-year recreation programs for a position as a recreation specialist

Exploring 18th Century medical artifacts.

Using a mortar and pestle to prepare a medical herb.

Recreating a page in medical history.

Photos courtesy of the New Castle County Department of Parks and Recreation, Wilmington, Delaware.

251

8. Development of neighborhood facilities and increased urbanization that require recreation to be brought to the people
9. The three-day weekend and a shorter work week
10. Combining of recreation and park divisions under one department
11. The fact that lack of recreation facilities is usually mentioned as a primary cause for social unrest, rioting, and militant revolution
12. The acceptance by the general public and support given to public recreation's role as an invaluable service to the community
13. Expansion of therapeutic recreation services and programs for the retarded and handicapped

MAJOR CHALLENGES FACING RECREATION

There are presently many challenges facing recreation as a whole and recreators as members of a profession. Two of these major challenges, which involve population trends and increased leisure time, are discussed here.

Population Trends

It is estimated that the United States will have more than 300 million people by the year 2000. The population of the world, if current rates of growth continue, may be double what it is today in less than fifty years. Longer lives and better health care have contributed to population growth. Population growth compounds already existing problems of land and food shortages, environmental destruction, energy supply, pollution of water and air, and poor housing and transportation facilities.

The problem of recreation is evident: with conditions of overcrowding in already overpopulated areas, less and less land will be available for recreational purposes. Local park and national parks are or will have to be sharply curtailed, as will leisure automobile drives, boating of all types, and commercial vehicle recreation trips. Financial resources once designated for recreation purposes may have to be used for the more pressing needs of food and housing.

The best approach to this problem is to think about it *before* it becomes a crisis. Well-planned communities that allow for recreation sites in initial growth stages will be very helpful. Attracting persons to less populated areas of the country by moving industry and other facilities to these areas will help to relieve the burden of the large cities.

Increased Leisure Time

This subject has been discussed in detail in the text but is mentioned here because it is a definite trend with a great impact on recreation and on our society. Predictions are heralding the coming of the four-day week, which has already arrived for some employees. In mid-1971, it was reported that some ninety small and medium-sized businesses with twenty to 500 workers had instituted the four-forty work-week (four days, forty hours); others were on a four-thirty-six work-week (four days, thirty-six hours).

In addition to the four-day week, one's leisure time is also increased by more vacation time, weekends and holidays, and year-round schools that provide greater free time at more frequent intervals. All of this points to increased leisure time, and the question that remains is, how to use it? The problem for recreation is twofold: education for leisure time and provision of programs and facilities to enhance leisure time without contributing to environmental destruction and pollution problems.

Additional Challenges

Many of the trends previously discussed in this chapter are also challenges for recreation personnel in that the problems they represent are still a long way from being solved. Most of the challenges given here may have been mentioned elsewhere in the text, but are presented in this comprehensive manner to tie together the major problems facing recreation today and in the future, or faced by society and which recreation can help to alleviate.

1. *The environment.* The challenge of the environment cannot be ignored. Pollution control and environmental equilibrium must be established if recreation activities are to continue and increase.

2. *Population control.* The control of population must be considered a primary challenge to all persons who value a good and healthy life for today's citizens and future generations. Recreation will become impossible on an overcrowded earth where all available land must be used for living space and for growing food supplies.

3. *Poverty.* Poverty must be erased so that all people can enjoy a life free from starvation, inadequate housing, and poor health. Recreators have an obligation to work toward this goal.

4. *Minority groups.* Minority groups live in all parts of the country but are primarily located in our large inner-city areas. These people have special problems of unfamiliarity, language difficulties, poverty, and lack of education. Their special needs can be met, in part, through adequate recreation programs and facilities.

5. *Social unrest.* Persons feeling neglected by the society around them often rebel to attract attention to their needs. Recreation, often lacking among these people, can be very helpful in preventing such uprisings.

6. *Crime.* The problem of increased crime is apparent in street crimes, gangs, drugs, and vandalism. The youth who participates in antisocial activities may be helped by organized programs that meet his needs on an individual basis. Counseling is an important part of the professional recreator's position as a leader.

7. *Specialized programming.* The days of one program for all are long since gone. Recreation must meet the needs of the individual through

community involvement in planning. In addition, the challenge of presenting programs for young people, the aged, the handicapped, and the retarded must be a primary consideration.

8. *Description of families.* The "trend" toward more single-parent homes is with us today. Children from these homes need stability and counseling in their recreation programs. Children should not represent just so many bodies that have to be occupied, but rather they must be treated as individuals with special needs, interests, and problems.

9. *Recreation funding.* Problems of funding recreation programs have been increasing in recent years. Communities may have problems in getting needed revenue; federal cutbacks in recreation areas are prevalent. Recreation should not have to take a back seat to other programs, as it has too great a contribution to make to the physical and mental health of the population.

10. *Recreation education.* This phrase encompasses two separate challenges, both involving recreation.

    a. Education of the people concerning the need for and value of good recreation programming.

    b. Provisions for excellence and increases in institutions providing degree programs in recreation. Recruitment and better leadership standards are all a part of improved education in this area.

11. *Research in recreation.* Research is greatly lacking in the area of recreation. Such research is needed to establish the best programming methods and treatment of specialized groups. In addition, research would be a great aid in facility and service improvements. Once established, research must be communicated to recreators efficiently.

12. *Quality recreation.* The challenge of the entire field of recreation is to provide quality recreation. This is recreation that is constructive, enjoyable, and educational, and one that generally contributes to a person's healthy outlook on life. Recreation must take the entire individual into consideration, providing for both cultural and physical outlets.

QUESTIONS AND EXERCISES

1. Discuss some of the recent trends in the professional preparation of recreators.
2. Explain what is meant by the term *activity trend?* What are some of the reasons for a particular activity being popular at certain times?
3. What is meant by the term *recreation mobility?* Discuss the advantages and disadvantages of mobile recreation programs.
4. Have you ever been to a drive-in zoo? Do you generally think that they are a good idea? Explain your answer.
5. Discuss some trends in recreational settings and facilities. Are there any contemporary playgrounds in your community? If so, describe them.
6. What is the significance of housing with planned recreation facilities?

7. How does the increased mobility of Americans affect recreation?
8. What is the *energy crisis?* How does it relate to recreation?
9. Discuss some of the challenges facing recreation today.
10. If you were a professional recreator, what would be your priority list of challenges that must be met?

SELECTED REFERENCES

"All the World's a Pawn," *Newsweek,* July 31, 1972, p. 42.

Bongartz, Roy, "The Great Outdoors—Cycling on the Enemy's Turf," *The New York Times,* April 16, 1972.

"Drive-In Zoos," *Newsweek,* July 31, 1972, p. 48.

"The Energy Crisis: Time for Action," *Time,* May 7, 1973, p. 41.

Gobar, Alfred, "Stadiums for Small Communities," *Parks and Recreation,* June, 1971, p. 31.

Grant, David, "With a Hop, Skip and Jump, Playgrounds Go Modern," *The New York Times,* June 17, 1973.

Graves, Charles M., "An All-electric Recreation Center," *Parks and Recreation,* May, 1969, p. 36.

McLean, M. T., Jr., "Keeping the Outdoors for the Future," *Parks and Recreation,* January, 1968, p. 3.

"Non-Yankee Stay Home," *Newsweek,* July 10, 1972, p. 86.

Samuels, Gertrude, "The Four-Day Week," *The New York Times Magazine,* May 16, 1971, p. 32.

"Tennis at Tiffany's," *Newsweek,* May 14, 1973, p. 103.

"Up the Sandbox," *Newsweek,* April 30, 1973, p. 73.

PARK AND RECREATION FACILITIES AND RESOURCES

FACILITY	*	MUNICIPAL	COUNTY	SPECIAL DISTRICT	MULTIPLE JURISDICTION	SCHOOL	PRIVATE	OTHER	TOTAL
AQUARIUMS	IND	10	1	3		1			15
	ODL	9		3					12
	ODN	6	2	1		1			10
ARBORETUMS	IND	134	11	15				5	165
	ODL	40	2	6	2				50
	ODN	236	26	11		1		6	280
ARCHERY RANGES-FIELD	IND	18			2				20
	ODL	8		1					9
	ODN	132	28	17	4	52		3	236
ARCHERY RANGES-TARGET	IND	70	1	6		1		2	80
	ODL	43	2	1	2			1	49
	ODN	270	35	23	13	6		6	353
ATHLETIC FIELDS	IND	29	17		2	36		18	102
	ODL	270	13	8	27	8	1	33	360
	ODN	400	25	34	16	98	1	24	598
BADMINTON COURTS	IND	782	58	146	11	212	3	21	1,233
	ODL	167	12	15	3	20	1	8	226
	ODN	968	249	35	19	13		3	1,287
90'-BASEBALL DIAMOND	ODL	922	84	194	37	9	1	80	1,327
	ODN	2468	176	179	46	114	1	175	3,159
75'-PONY LEAGUE DIAMOND	ODL	373	46	12	8	19	1	5	464
	ODN	741	61	76	12	78	1	48	1,017
60'-LITTLE LEAGUE DIAMOND	ODL	1000	67	241	35	6	1	48	1,398
	ODN	3086	207	426	73	123		186	4,101
60'-SOFTBALL DIAMOND	ODL	1801	175	63	62	10	1	88	2,200
	ODN	5466	530	396	164	293		260	7,109
BANDSTANDS	ODL	260	13	15	9	41		4	342
	ODN	218	19	10	1	6	2	45	301
BASKETBALL	IND	1482	89	257	50	303	1	193	2,375
	ODL	1697	73	498	23	66		237	2,594
	ODN	4450	400	412	225	1505	1	202	7,195
OCEAN BEACHES	ODL	13	3						16
	ODN	99	37	1	2			3	142
RIVER BEACHES	ODL	14							14
	ODN	67	36	10	2	1			116
LAKE BEACHES	ODL	63	5	30	4				102
	ODN	237	82	33	8	2		8	370
MARINAS	ODL	126	25	20	4			8	183
	ODN	239	80	32	13	1		10	375
BOCCE COURTS	ODL	9		4	6			6	25
	ODN	217	5	6		75		14	317
LAWN BOWLING	ODL	55	5	7					67
	ODN	79	7		1			11	98
DAY CAMPS	ODL	110	22	2	2			4	140
	ODN	353	186	43	5	14		57	659
OVERNIGHT ORG. CAMP	ODL	52	29	3	2	1		2	89
	ODN	94	122	50		1		7	274
TOURIST-TRAILER CAMP	ODL	71	118	15	4				208
	ODN	74	106	7	11				198
COMBATIVE AREA	IND	123	6	7	9	9		10	164
	ODL	46	12	1	2				61
	ODN	3	18						21
DANCE PAVILIONS	IND	167	4	5	5	1	1	2	185
	ODL	101	17	9	4			3	134
	ODN	33	13	2				2	50
EQUESTRIAN RINGS	IND	6	1	1				2	10
	ODL	21	2	5	1				29
	ODN	36	23	11				2	72
LAKE-RIVER FISHING	ODL	63	14	1	6				84
	ODN	707	307	113	72	2		14	1,215

*IND = INDOOR
 ODL = OUTDOOR LIGHTED
 ODN = OUTDOOR NOT LIGHTED

FACILITY	*	MUNICIPAL	COUNTY	SPECIAL DISTRICT	MULTIPLE JURISDICTION	SCHOOL	PRIVATE	OTHER	TOTAL
CASTING POOLS	IND	12			1	1			14
	ODL	51		11	1			1	64
	ODN	86	19	10	15	3		4	137
FISHING PIERS	ODL	56	14		2			1	73
	ODN	119	50		6	3		3	225
FOOTBALL FIELDS	ODL	867	51	222	32	47	1	57	1,277
	ODN	1827	140	189	30	139	1	133	2,459
MULTI-FUNCT. BLDG.	IND	1022	154	335	37	148	2	68	1,766
SCHOOL BUILDINGS	IND	4059	270	540	207	820	1	211	6,108
OTHER BUILDINGS	IND	1079	52	48	116	14		29	1,338
LARGE MULTI-USE REC. BLDG.	IND	841	71	220	30	9	1	84	1,256
OTHER MULTI-USE REC. BLDG.	IND	1288	182	159	38	39		162	1,868
ART-CRAFT CENTER	IND	237	17	5	11	10		8	288
NATURE CENTER	IND	74	19	10	2	4		5	114
MUSEUM	IND	118	24	10				3	155
OBSERVATORY-PLANT'IUM.	IND	27	5	9	5	3		2	51
TEEN CENTER	IND	402	18	17	27	12	1	19	496
SENIOR CITIZEN'S CENTER	IND	495	18	28	14	2	1	25	583
ARENAS-COLISEUMS	IND	55	3	3	4	1		8	74
PROSCENIUM THEATERS	IND	84	3	6	1	1		11	106
THEATER IN-THE-ROUND	IND	31		3					34
GOLF-MINIATURE	IND	20			2	1			23
	ODL	26	1	4					31
	ODN	4	1			1			6
GOLF-9 HOLE	ODL	33	5	1	2			2	43
	ODN	92	13	14	12	1		5	137
GOLF-18 HOLE	ODL	41		1					42
	ODN	206	54	25	5			6	296
GOLF-36 HOLE	ODL	2			1				3
	ODN	6		2	1				9
GOLF-PAR 3	ODL	23		3	1				27
	ODN	30	8	5					43
GOLF DRIVING RANGE	IND	32	5	2	10	1			50
	ODL	45	8	6	6			3	68
	ODN	55	18	9	3	1		2	88
HANDBALL COURTS	IND	171	23			2		8	204
	ODL	147	4	26		1		50	228
	ODN	354	27	14	3	926		21	1,345
HORSESHOE COURTS	IND	679	39	39	122	20		6	905
	ODL	1204	29	75	2	14		107	1,431
	ODN	2694	271	593	57	306		103	4,024
ICE SKATING-NATURAL	ODL	796	56	146	29	13		19	1,059
	ODN	653	70	63	22	12		38	858
ICE SKATING-ARTIFICIAL	IND	126	9	14	1	1	1	3	155
	ODL	170	5	3		22		4	204
	ODN	78	3	1	19	25		5	131
ICE CURLING RINK	IND	13	1	2	1				17
	ODL	7			1				8
PORTABLE PLAYGROUNDS	IND	124	13	26	1				164
	ODL	102	5	22	2			4	135
	ODN	820	91	17	57	45		53	1,083
PORTABLE POOLS	ODL	117	9	11	8	1		13	159
	ODN	150		4	1	9		5	169
PORT. PUPPET WAGONS	ODL	16							16
	ODN	21	4	1	1	1		8	36
PORTABLE STAGES	ODL	67	8	6	1			1	83
	ODN	42	4			1		3	50
PORTABLE HOBBY CENTER	ODL	1							1
	ODN	1	4						5
PORTABLE ZOO	ODL	12	4	4				1	21
	ODN	23	2	4				1	30

*IND = INDOOR
ODL = OUTDOOR LIGHTED
ODN = OUTDOOR NOT LIGHTED

FACILITY	*	MUNICIPAL	COUNTY	SPECIAL DISTRICT	MULTIPLE JURISDICTION	SCHOOL	PRIVATE	OTHER	TOTAL
PORTABLE-OTHER	ODL	9	2	1				1	13
	ODN	12	3	7		7		4	33
MODEL PLANE-ROCKET AREAS	IND	15		1					16
	ODL	16	1	1				1	19
	ODN	193	18	10	20	1		3	245
MOTOR REC. VEHICLE AREAS	ODL	58	1					1	60
	ODN	57	12	4	2			2	77
MUSIC SHELLS	ODL	137	5	15	7			2	166
	ODN	107	9	1		2		6	125
PICNIC AREAS	ODL	1650	307	54	70	13		29	2,123
	ODN	5790	1942	647	254	11		281	8,925
PLAYGROUNDS-YEAR-ROUND	ODL	964	3	23	2	31		30	1,053
	ODN	1774	89	133	18	553		72	2,639
PLAYGROUNDS-SUMMER ONLY	ODL	863	75	76	20	13		30	1,077
	ODN	5254	433	561	251	280	11	132	6,922
ROLLER SKATING RINKS	IND	49		10		1		3	63
	ODL	47	1			6		1	55
	ODN	142		3		9			154
SCENIC OVERLOOKS	ODL	32	5	1	1				39
	ODN	326	150	28	3	1		5	513
PISTOL RANGE	IND	54	1	7	3	1			66
	ODL	29	4	1				1	35
	ODN	45	12	5	1	1		1	65
RIFLE RANGE	IND	52	1	4	1	7			65
	ODL	20	2	1	2			1	26
	ODN	43	12	6	2			1	64
SKEET RANGE	IND	11							11
	ODL	28		3	1			1	33
	ODN	27	13	5	2			3	50
SHUFFLEBOARD COURTS	IND	400	24	16	5		1	15	461
	ODL	995	93	25	29	4		48	1,194
	ODN	2034	59	210	38	44		84	2,469
SKI CENTERS	IND	21		1					22
	ODL	25	12	2		1		2	42
	ODN	96	8	3	2	1			110
SOCCER FIELDS	ODL	134	12	10	2	6		7	171
	ODN	734	70	51	9	23		79	966
STADIUMS	ODL	273	9	7	9	47		13	358
	ODN	112	8	2	3	19		5	149
STREETS-PLAY	ODL	17	2						19
	ODN	61						12	73
STREETS-COASTING	ODL	71		5	10				86
	ODN	199	12		11			9	231
POOLS-SPRAY	IND	9		2				1	12
	ODL	75	14	7	1	11		9	117
	ODN	501	12	33	10	2		76	634
POOLS-WADING	IND	37	1	1				1	40
	ODL	322	15	33	8	9		6	393
	ODN	751	59	46	27	2	6	5	896
POOLS-SHALLOW	IND	15	1	1		11		2	30
	ODL	144	23	42	3	6		13	231
	ODN	303	13	4	2			15	337
POOLS-DEEP	IND	189	11	15	9	17	1	8	250
	ODL	810	85	123	23	7	1	42	1,091
	ODN	316	27	21	7	5	3	8	387
POOLS-INDOOR-OUTDOOR	IND	55		8		1		17	81
	ODL	63	2	25	1			15	106
	ODN	35	3	2				2	42
DIVING TANKS	IND	14		3		1		3	21
	ODL	79	11	17		1		4	112
	ODN	10	1	65	1				77

*IND = INDOOR
ODL = OUTDOOR LIGHTED
ODN = OUTDOOR NOT LIGHTED

FACILITY	*	MUNICIPAL	COUNTY	SPECIAL DISTRICT	MULTIPLE JURISDICTION	SCHOOL	PRIVATE	OTHER	TOTAL
ASPHALT TENNIS COURTS	IND	263	12	16	2	7			300
	ODL	1554	76	270	25	32		67	2,024
	ODN	3512	448	394	67	121		280	4,822
CLAY TENNIS COURTS	ODL	176		4					180
	ODN	601	36	13	4		1	3	658
CONCRETE TENNIS COURTS	IND	95		12		148			255
	ODL	1576	40	466	30	20		16	2,148
	ODN	1375	67	148	29	92		43	1,754
GRASS TENNIS COURTS	ODL	8							8
	ODN	11							11
SYNTHETIC TURF COURTS	IND	19							19
	ODL	69	15						84
	ODN	36	39		1	4			80
TOBOGGAN SLIDES	ODL	67	5	13				1	86
	ODN	159	25	33	10	7		3	237
TOT LOTS	ODL	188	2	33		33		49	305
	ODN	1771	267	219	37	76	1	145	2,516
VEST POCKET PARKS	ODL	154	17	8				1	180
	ODN	819	70	25	7			3	924
VOLLEYBALL COURTS	IND	807	63	69	16	152	2	105	1,214
	ODL	712	31	45	24	25		88	925
	ODN	2818	165	108	93	466	1	135	3,786
BICYCLE TRAILS**	ODL	9		2					11
	ODN	859	228	88	5			30	1,210
BRIDLE TRAILS**	ODL	1							1
	ODN	744	818	130	5			54	1,751
HIKING TRAILS**	ODL	31						2	33
	ODN	861	698	159	25	8		24	1,775
JOGGING TRAILS**	ODL	43							43
	ODN	566	188	79	4	6		13	856
NATURE TRAILS**	ODL	20	4						24
	ODN	479	222	51	6	48		23	829
MOTORCYCLE TRAILS**	ODL	5							5
	ODN	83	36	6	13				138
SNOWMOBILE TRAILS**	ODL	29							29
	ODN	249	223	7	20			1	500
NET TRAIL MILES	ODL	17		1					18
	ODN	1936	712	130	355			23	3,156
CHILDREN'S ZOO	IND	12	3	1				1	17
	ODL	21	3	4	1			1	30
	ODN	32	8	5	2				47
FAMILY ZOO	IND	18		1					19
	ODL	25	1	3	1			2	32
	ODN	35	7	3	1			1	47

*IND = INDOOR
ODL = OUTDOOR LIGHTED
ODN = OUTDOOR NOT LIGHTED
**TRAILS (IN MILES)

INDEX

r